D0592505

The Shakespeare Miscellany

The Shakespeare Miscellany

DAVID CRYSTAL
&
BEN CRYSTAL

THE OVERLOOK PRESS
WOODSTOCK & NEW YORK

First published in the United States in 2005 by
The Overlook Press, Peter Mayer Publishers, Inc.
Woodstock & New York

WOODSTOCK:
One Overlook Drive
Woodstock, NY 12498
www.overlookpress.com
[for individual orders, bulk and special sales, contact our Woodstock office]

NEW YORK:
141 Wooster Street
New York, NY 10012

Cataloging-in-Publication Data is available from the Library of Congress

Printed in the United States of America
ISBN 1-58567-716-7
1 3 5 7 8 8 6 4 2

CONTENTS

Acknowledgements

The authors and publishers would like to thank the following
for permission to reproduce illustrations on the pages shown:

Shakespeare Birthplace Trust: pp. 2, 91, 189

The College of Arms: p. 10

Public Record Office: (a), (d), (e), (f), p. 131

Guildhall Library, Corporation of London: (b), p. 131

British Library: (c), p. 131

Reproduced by permission of the Marquess of Bath,
Longleat House, Warminster, Wiltshire, Great Britain: p. 164

PREFACE

In 1565 the Bishop of Exeter, William Alley, published *The poore man's Librarie*. On his title page, we read: 'Here are adioyned at the ende of euery special treatise, certain fruitful annotacions called miscellanea, because they do entreate of diverse and sundry matters.'

This is the first recorded use of *miscellanea* in English. Exactly fifty years later, the year before Shakespeare died, a Puritan devotional book was published: *The Miscellanie, or Regestrie and Methodicall Directorie of Orizons*. This is the first use we know of *miscellany*.

Since then miscellanies have appeared on every conceivable topic, with entries ranging in length from several pages to the isolated quotation. The Victorian era was especially fond of them, and they are having a resurgence of interest today – hardly surprising, in an age which thrives on sound-bites, short encyclopedia entries and the thirty-word summary paragraphs that frequent the online news pages of the Internet.

The term has had a chequered history. Some have scorned the miscellany genre for the way it tempts authors to randomness and superficiality, and it is true that many have been written for no other purpose than – as John Norris, a seventeenth-century compiler, put it to a patron – 'for the entertainment of your leisure hours'. On the other hand, serious journals have used the term in their titles, as have major historical compilations. The Bible, indeed, has been called the greatest miscellany.

We believe a miscellany should, like the BBC, 'inform, educate and entertain', and in this compilation we have tried to combine these different goals. In the case of Shakespeare, we would have to add 'remind' to the list, for the essential biographical facts (and fictions) have been part of Shakespeariana for centuries. But we have aimed to include a great deal that will be unfamiliar to most general readers in relation to our chosen themes, and in some entries we have found ourselves exploring entirely new ground. We have been fortunate to have available, since May 2004, the advanced concordance search facility of our *Shakespeare's Words* website (www.shakespeareswords.com), and this has helped us provide a sharpness of focus where previously there was only general impression. The database we compiled for the book *Shakespeare's Words* includes the text of all the plays in the Penguin Shakespeare series, with the addition of *King Edward III*, and all the poems. Unless otherwise indicated, all statistics in this book derive from that database.

We have respected the tradition of including basic biographical information about Shakespeare, but we have not tried to be comprehensive about the great debates about his private life and social milieu that have preoccupied scholars and writers over the years. Because of our joint linguistic and theatrical interests, we have throughout kept our attention firmly on the texts of the plays and poems, and on the ways in which these would have been read or presented to an Elizabethan audience. Many of our entries, accordingly, are about the meaning and effect of Shakespeare's language and the methods and conventions of his stagecraft.

We are hugely grateful to Hilary Crystal for her help at all stages of this project, and especially for her work compiling the Timeline. Thanks are due too to Stanley Wells, Paul Edmondson, Will Sutton and Tim Klotz for their editorial comments, to Richard Marston for his design brilliance, and to Martin Toseland and Nigel Wilcockson for their production advice during the period of the book's preparation.

David Crystal and Ben Crystal

MISCELLANY

... my gentle verse,
Which eyes not yet created shall o'er-read,
And tongues to be, your being shall rehearse,
When all the breathers of this world are dead,
You still shall live (such virtue hath my pen)
Where breath most breathes, even in the mouths of men.

(Sonnet 81)

Understanding Shakespeare

He who desires to understand Shakespeare truly must understand the relations in which Shakespeare stood to the Renaissance and the Reformation, to the age of Elizabeth and the age of James; he must be familiar with the history of the struggle for supremacy between the old classical forms and the new spirit of romance, between the school of Sidney, and Daniel, and Johnson, and the school of Marlowe and Marlowe's greater son; he must know the materials that were at Shakespeare's disposal, and the method in which he used them, and the conditions of theatric presentation in the sixteenth and seventeenth century, their limitations and their opportunities for freedom, and the literary criticism of Shakespeare's day, its aims and modes and canons; he must study the English language in its progress, and blank or rhymed verse in its various developments; he must study the Greek drama, and the connection between the art of the creator of the Agamemnon and the art of the creator of Macbeth; in a word, he must be able to bind Elizabethan London to the Athens of Pericles, and to learn Shakespeare's true position in the history of European drama and the drama of the world. (Oscar Wilde, *The Critic as Artist*, 1891)

Career prospects

At Age 436, His Future Is Unlimited
(*New York Times* headline, 23 April 2000)

Birth day

The register of Holy Trinity Church in Stratford records the baptism of William, the first son of John Shakespeare, 'Gulielmus filius Johannes Shakspere' (see below). The date given is 26 April 1564. William's birthday is customarily celebrated on 23 April, but this is a tradition which began in the eighteenth century, not fact, fostered probably by a natural desire to see England's greatest dramatic poet associated with the feast-day of St George, England's patron saint. The baptismal practice of the time, as specified in the 1559 *Book of Common Prayer*, was this:

> *The Pastors and Curates shall oft admonish the people, that they deferre not the Baptisme of Infants any longer then the Sunday, or other Holy day, next after the Childe be borne vnlesse vpon a great and reasonable cause, declared to the Curate, and by him approoued.*

In 1564, the 23rd was a Sunday, and the main holy day in April, St Mark's Day, followed soon after, on the 25th. If the parents were following the usual practice, a child born on the 23rd would be baptized, at the latest, by that day. So why the 26th in the register? Maybe there was a 'great and reasonable cause' to delay things. Maybe the Shakespeares were influenced by the widespread superstition that St Mark's Day was unlucky. Or perhaps the baby was born on one of the adjacent days. Without any evidence, the tradition stands.

Ten days later?

April 23 in 1564 was not the same as April 23 today. By the mid-sixteenth century, the Julian calendar – so-called because it was devised by Julius Caesar – had fallen ten days behind the solar year, so in 1582 Pope Gregory XIII introduced a new system, the 'Gregorian calendar', which we follow today. Most European countries immediately made the change, but anti-papal England rejected the idea (and did not catch up until 1752, when 2 September was immediately followed by 14 September). This means that, in 1564, the date referred to then as 23 April corresponds to what we would today call 3 May.

Shakespeare's handwriting

Six definite examples survive: his signatures (p. 131), and the words 'by me' written before the signature at the end of his will. Three pages of the play *Sir Thomas More* are also thought to be in his hand.

And she as much in love?

The word *love* is used 154 times in *Romeo and Juliet* – over half the time (87 instances) by the two lovers. Which of them uses the word more? Juliet says it 35 times and Romeo 52 – but 16 of his usages have Rosaline, his first infatuation, in mind. When Juliet and Romeo actually meet, their opening scene together is appropriately balanced – each uses the word 11 times.

Even so suspicious

Be suspicious of people who want to play this part.
(W. H. Auden, *Essay on Hamlet*)

Good evening

Greetings in the sixteenth century sometimes differed from Modern English in their range of application. *Good even*, for example, might be said to someone any time after noon.

Anne Hathaway

It is not known when Anne Hathaway was born or baptized; but on her tombstone in Holy Trinity Church it is recorded that she was sixty-seven years old when she died on 6 August 1623. That would have put her birth in 1556 – seven or eight years older than William.

The changing canon

In 1955, the works thought to be wholly or largely by Shakespeare numbered thirty-seven, and the Royal Shakespeare Company had performed them all with the production of *Titus Andronicus* that year. Since then, support has grown for two further plays to be included in the canon: *The Two Noble Kinsmen* and *King Edward III*. These received productions at the RSC in 1986 and 2002, respectively.

Petty schools

Children in Elizabethan England would usually start attending school in their fifth year. They would go to a 'petty school' (from French *petit*, 'small') attached to a town's grammar school, and be taught there by a tutor known as an abecedarius, whose role, as the name suggests, was primarily to teach the boys to read. They would move on to the grammar school after two years, and stay there until age fourteen. It was a long day, beginning at six in the morning (in summer, seven in winter) and continuing until five in the afternoon, with breaks for meals and recreation. Sunday was the only day off.

School-teachers

Who were Shakespeare's teachers at Stratford grammar school? They were university graduates, some of whom went on to gain scholarly reputations in their own right. Students would receive a good education at their hands.

1569	Walter Roche	1575	Thomas Jenkins
1571	Simon Hunt	1579	John Cottom

Shakespeare was only seven in 1571, so Walter Roche had probably left by the time he moved up from petty school into Stratford grammar school. Nor is it likely that he received tuition from John Cottom. We do not know when Shakespeare left school, but after 1576 his father was in severe financial straits, so he may have had to leave early to help in the family business, as some scholars have suggested. Simon Hunt and Thomas Jenkins must have been his two teachers.

Studying Latin plays

Among the Latin texts Shakespeare would have studied in grammar school were those by the comic dramatists Terence and Plautus. In some schools, it is known that the students practised their Latin by acting scenes from their plays. Whether this happened in Stratford is a matter of conjecture, but there is no doubt that these authors would have provided Shakespeare with his first sense of a five-act play.

Reading the score

Shakespeare's text is a complex score that demands to be read as a piece of music, learned like the steps of a dance, or practised like the strokes of a duel.

(Peter Hall, *Shakespeare's Advice to the Players*, 2004, p. 18)

Hornbooks

Children would come to petty school with their hornbook – a wood-framed page covered with a transparent sheet made from a piece of cow's horn. They were of many different kinds, but typically at the top of the page would be the letters of the alphabet, large and small, and underneath would be listed some basic syllables (*ab, eb, ib, ba, be, bi*, etc.), often some numerals, and the Lord's Prayer. Hornbooks are referred to twice in the plays. In *Love's Labour's Lost*, Mote tells Don Armado that Holofernes 'teaches boys the horn-book' (V.1.45). And in *The Two Noble Kinsmen* one of the countrymen tells the others that the school-master will 'eat a hornbook ere he fail' (II.2.42).

The cross-row

In a hornbook, a cross was usually placed at the beginning of the top row of the alphabet, which accordingly came to be known as the 'cross-row'. In *Richard III* (I.1.55), George, Duke of Clarence, irritably comments on the way King Edward is ruled by superstition:

> He hearkens after prophecies and dreams,
> And from the cross-row plucks the letter G,
> And says a wizard told him that by G
> His issue disinherited should be …

Only very young children – or people acting like them – would be using a cross-row.

ABC books

After children had mastered their hornbook, they graduated to alphabetic readers ('ABC books') and the question-and-answer dialogues introducing them to formal Christianity (the Catechism) – the latter, along with some other prayers, taken from the 1559 *Book of Common Prayer*. We need to appreciate this context if we are to follow the allusion in *King John* (I.1.194), when Philip the Bastard, newly made a knight, imagines himself catechizing (asking questions of) the people he meets:

> Thus, leaning on mine elbow, I begin –
> 'I shall beseech you' – that is question now;
> And then comes answer like an Absey book:
> 'O sir', says answer, 'at your best command …'

Why an 'ABC book' should be part of a question-and-answer dialogue becomes clear when we see that it was originally linked with the Catechism.

Chronology of works

The earliest play?

Is *Titus Andronicus* Shakespeare's earliest play? A quarto edition is known only from 1594, but the date of composition might be up to a decade earlier, if we take a comment of Ben Jonson literally. In his Induction to *Bartholomew Fair* (1614), he talks of those who think that 'Andronicus' is one of the 'best playes' – a judgement, he says, which 'hath stood still, these five and twentie, or thirtie yeeres'. That would place it between 1584 and 1589. Most scholars, however, doubt that Jonson had a precise date in mind. On 11 April 1592 Philip Henslowe records a performance by Strange's Men of a play called 'tittus & vespacia'. If this is Shakespeare's, it suggests a composition date of 1591–2.

Love's Labour's Won

Francis Mere, in his book *Palladis Tamia* (see p. 143), refers to twelve Shakespeare plays, one of which is *Love's Labour's Won*. This play is either lost or, as some scholars have suggested, it is an alternative name for a different play (possibly *The Taming of the Shrew*).

Elizabeth's last play?

The Chamberlain's Men played before Queen Elizabeth on 2 February 1603 – probably *A Midsummer Night's Dream*. The Queen fell ill later that month and died on 24 March.

Cardenio

In 1653 the Stationer's Register records a play, 'The History of Cardenio, by Mr Fletcher and Shakespeare'. The name is known from Cervantes' *Don Quixote* (beginning in Part 1, Chapter 27), which recounts the love-story of Lucinda and Cardenio, 'The Ragged Knight of the Sorry Countenance'. *Don Quixote* was published in Madrid in 1605 and in London in 1612.* It was performed by the King's Men in 1613, but no copy has come down to us. Interestingly, 1612 is the only year missing a play in the chronology on p.6.

*Coincidentally, Cervantes' death is recorded as 23 April 1616 – though this would not have been the same death-day as Shakespeare in reality, due to calendar differences between England and Spain at the time (see p. 2).

To the point

*The play which, of all plays ever written, the world
could least do without.*
(Anthony Burgess, on *Hamlet*, Shakespeare, 1970, p. 175)

Family tree

Shakespeare's daughter Susanna had one child, Elizabeth, who had no children. His son, Hamnet, died in 1596 at the age of eleven. Judith, the youngest, married Thomas Quiney in 1616, two months before Shakespeare's death, but her three children all died young. His grand-daughter, Elizabeth, died in 1670, his last direct descendant.

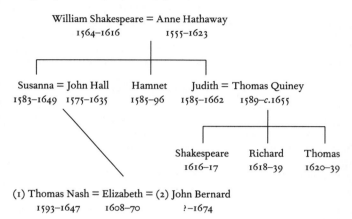

William Shakespeare = Anne Hathaway
1564–1616   1555–1623

Susanna = John Hall   Hamnet   Judith = Thomas Quiney
1583–1649 1575–1635   1585–96   1585–1662 1589–c.1655

Shakespeare   Richard   Thomas
1616–17   1618–39   1620–39

(1) Thomas Nash = Elizabeth = (2) John Bernard
1593–1647   1608–70   ?–1674

The missing play

Troilus and Cressida is included in the First Folio but it isn't mentioned in the Catalogue, or table of contents. Why?

It will be found between the Histories and Tragedies sections. The first page is the Prologue, set in a larger type than the other play texts, and this is followed by the opening of Act I Scene 1. The next two pages are numbered 79 and 80; and the remaining twenty-six pages of the text carry no numbers at all. What accounts for this curious pagination?

The evidence suggests that *Troilus* was originally placed at p. 80 in the Tragedies section, and four pages had already been printed before it was decided to withdraw it – perhaps because it was felt to be in the wrong place, or perhaps there were problems over permission to use the text. It was then replaced there by *Timon of Athens*. At a later stage, when the problems were resolved, a place had to be found for *Troilus*. Evidently the most convenient solution was to put the play between two of the major sections, but without revising the page numbers. By then, however, the Catalogue had been printed. As a result, the name of the play does not appear in the front of the book.

Mob control

A story is told of the Irish comic actor Henry Woodward, in *c.*1760, who was living opposite Parliament house in Dublin. One morning, an angry mob formed to protest against the passing of an unpopular bill, and Woodward's house was surrounded. They called for a bible to be thrown down to them, but Woodward's wife was unable to find one in the house. With great presence of mind, Woodward defused the situation by finding a different book to throw to the crowd, which was received with loud cheers. It was a volume of Shakespeare's plays.

The Shakespeare monument

The memorial sculpture in Holy Trinity Church, Stratford-upon-Avon, is located in the north wall of the chancel, above Shakespeare's grave. It was carved, mainly in white marble, by a London stonemason of Dutch background, Gheerart Janssen, also known as Gerard Johnson. It must have been erected before 1623, as its existence is referred to in Leonard Digges' memorial poem at the front of the First Folio. Shakespeare is portrayed with his hands resting on a cushion, a quill (originally a lead pen) in his right hand and a sheet of paper in his left. His lips are parted, as if in speech. The Shakespeare arms, helm and crest are carved above him, with a cherub on either side – one portraying work, holding a spade, the other portraying rest, holding a skull and inverted torch. A skull surmounts the whole. Underneath is a Latin motto (p. 163) and a six-line verse, ending with Shakespeare's death-date, 23 April 1616, and age.

STAY PASSENGER, WHY GOEST THOU BY SO FAST?
READ IF THOU CANST, WHOM ENVIOUS DEATH HATH PLAST,
WITH IN THIS MONUMENT SHAKESPEARE: WITH WHOME,
QUICK NATURE DIDE: WHOSE NAME DOTH DECK Y^S TOMBE,
FAR MORE THEN COST: SIEH ALL, Y^T HE HATH WRITT,
LEAVES LIVING ART, BUT PAGE, TO SERVE HIS WITT.

The abbreviated words in lines 4 and 5 are 'this' and 'that', respectively. The stonemason has made an error in line 5: 'SIEH' should have been 'SITH' ('since'). The authorship is unknown.

Story-telling

You need a good story in the Globe. If you're not wondering what's going to happen next, you become aware that you're standing, or sitting on a bench.
(Mark Rylance, *Sunday Mail*, 25 July 1999)

The Shakespeare coat of arms

Shakespeare's father, John, had tried to obtain a coat of arms when bailiff at Stratford in the 1570s, but the downturn in his fortunes made him unable to proceed with his application. He (or William) renewed it in 1596, and this time it was granted by the College of Arms. Rough drafts survive of the heraldic document granting the application, and they include a description of the proposed shield and a rough sketch:

> *Gould. on A Bend Sables. a Speare of the first steeled argent. And for his Creast or Cognizance a falcon. his winges displayed Argent. standing on a wrethe of his Coullors. supporting a Speare Gould. steeled as aforesaid sett upon a helmett with mantelles & tasselles as hathe ben accustomed and dothe more playnely appeare depicted on this margent.*

The motto at the top of the page reads: 'NON SANZ DROICT' – 'Not without right' – but there is no record of this ever being used.

gould: gold
bend: diagonal band
sables: black
steeled: of the point of a spear
argent: silver
cognizance: heraldic crest
wrethe: wreath
coullors: colours (of the Shakespeare family)
margent: margin

No commentary on Hamlet ... would be a more useful aid to a larger understanding of his character than a detailed record of the readings, gestures, the business employed in the successive performances of the part by Burbage, by Betterton, by Garrick, by Kemble, by Macready, by Forrest, by Booth and by Irving. They have been compelled by their professional training to acquire an insight into this character – an insight to be obtained only in the theatre itself and hopelessly unattainable in the library even by the most scholarly.

(Brander Matthews, quoted in Simon Callow,
Orson Welles, The Road to Xanadu, 1995, p. 178)

A handful of earlier Hamlets

Name	Dates	Notes
Richard Burbage	1568–1619	First ever Hamlet (at 235 pounds and thirty-seven years old)
William Davenant	1606–1668	Revived Hamlet in the Restoration, though heavily cut
Thomas Betterton	1635–1710	A member of Davenant's company; played Hamlet for forty years
David Garrick	1717–1779	Played Hamlet for forty-two years; made Shakespeare famous in Stratford in 1769
Sarah Siddons	1755–1831	Kemble's sister, who often played Ophelia to his Hamlet; one of the first women to play Hamlet in 1775
John Philip Kemble	1757–1823	Played Hamlet in 1783 to critical acclaim; revived in 1803
Edmund Kean	1787–1833	Considered the greatest Shakespearean actor of his day, but his Hamlet received mixed reviews; died two months after collapsing on-stage, playing Othello
William Henry West Betty	1791–1874	Inspired by a performance of Sarah Siddons, he played Hamlet at the age of twelve
Ira Aldridge	1807–1867	The first black actor to play major Shakespearian parts; famously replaced Kean as Othello in 1833
Edwin Booth	1833–1893	Rival to Kean; played Hamlet for 100 consecutive nights, 26 November 1864–22 March 1865; apparently fenced so furiously that his Laertes had to fight for his life; last stage appearance was Hamlet, in 1891, at fifty-eight
Henry Irving	1838–1905	First actor to be knighted; played Hamlet in his 1874 production at the Lyceum Theatre
Sarah Bernhardt	1844–1923	The first film Hamlet (1900); possibly the only Hamlet with a wooden leg
William Poel	1852–1934	Played Hamlet in 1881, using the First Quarto text, which at the time was unheard of
Johnston Forbes-Robertson	1853–1937	Played Hamlet for the first time at forty-four, after playing second leads to Irving; when Irving saw his Hamlet, he vowed never to play the part again; a silent film of Forbes-Robertson's Hamlet was made in 1913
Barry Jackson	1879–1961	Presented the first modern dress production of Hamlet (or any other Shakespeare play) in 1925
John Barrymore	1882–1942	Broke Booth's 100-night record of Hamlet with a 101-night run in 1922

Calling names

Shakespeare never lets the audience or the other characters forget the Jewish thing. You only have to look at the trial scene where he's called 'Shylock' only six times, but 'Jew' twenty-two.

(David Suchet on *The Merchant of Venice*,
in John Barton, *Playing Shakespeare*, 1984, p. 171)

Acoustic headaches

The position, so close to the river and with St Paul's Cathedral in the background, is very striking. I just hope the poor actors, sweating it out under a summer sky, aren't deafened by megaphones on the tourist boats informing the world, 'That's Shakespeare's Globe, his "Wooden O", burned down during a performance of Henry VIII on 29 June 1613.' By the time the guide gets that out his boat will have chugged under the bridge and another will have taken its place with the same information. Overhead aircraft will be droning their way to Heathrow.* Oh, I wish the actors good fortune but I wouldn't wish to be wearing their buskins or chopins and having to face such competition. It is the acoustics that will cause the headaches. I can't see any line being able to be said 'trippingly on the tongue' as Shakespeare requested.
(Alec Guinness, *My Name Escapes Me*, 1996, p. 52,
on visiting the building site of the reconstructed Globe)

*Guinness proved to be an accurate prophet. A helicopter exclusion zone around the Globe should be introduced by Act of Parliament!

Where did Shakespeare first live in London?

A William Shackspere, from the parish of St Helens in Bishopsgate, is recorded in 1597 as not having paid a local tax the previous year. In 1598 a further failure to pay a tax is ascribed to a William Shakespeare, the entry identifying him with reference to the adjacent counties of Surrey and Sussex. A further tax bill in 1600 also refers to a William Shakespeare living in an area south of the Thames (the Clink) belonging to the Bishop of Winchester. Evidently Shakespeare crossed to the South Bank around 1597 in order to stay close to the theatre where he worked.

The voice test

It is impossible to be a great Shakespearian actor without an idiosyncratic and extraordinary voice.
(Peter Hall, Theatre Royal Haymarket Masterclass, September 2002)

An actor's part would be written out on a long roll of parchment (a *scroll*) wrapped round a piece of wood. One line ran after the other, with around three cue words preceding each speech, so he would know when to enter or speak. For that reason, these rolls have become known as 'cue-scripts'. No actor would ever see the whole play.

====== Thou *or* you: *the general situation* ======

In Old English, *thou* was singular and *you* was plural; but during the thirteenth century, *you* started to be used as a polite form of the singular – probably because people copied the French way of talking, where *vous* was used in that way. English then became like French, which has *tu* and *vous* both possible for singulars. So in Early Modern English, when Shakespeare was writing, there was a choice:

Opener	*Situation*	*Normal reply*
you	upper classes talking to each other, even when closely related	you
thou	lower classes talking to each other	thou
thou	superiors to inferiors, such as:	
	• parents to children	you
	• masters to servants	you
thou	special intimacy, such as:	
	• talking to a lover	thou
	• addressing God or a god (e.g. Jupiter)	you
thou	character talks to someone absent	—

So, in a scene, when someone deviates from this normal pattern, it always means something – usually a change of attitude, or a new emotion or mood. It could be anything – for example, a sign of extra affection or of anger; an insult or a compliment; a piece of playfulness or an indication that the speaker is adopting a more business-like or professional attitude.

There are several examples in this book (see Index). The *thou*-forms are *thou*, *thee*, *thy*, *thine* and *thyself*. *You*-forms are *you*, *your*, *yours* and *yourself*/*yourselves*.

====== *Everyone loves the Macbeths* ======

Seeking an insight into his own character, Ian McKellen asked Trevor Nunn, 'He's Nixon isn't he, Macbeth?'

'No, no, he's not Nixon, he's Kennedy. It's the golden couple; everyone loves the Macbeths.' (Judi Dench, *With a Crack in her Voice*, p. 145, on the 1976 production of *Macbeth* at the Other Place)

Welsh English

Welsh pronunciation is the best represented of all the Celtic dialects in the plays. It is illustrated by some seventy-five words in the characters of Fluellen in *Henry V* and Evans in *The Merry Wives of Windsor*.

Welsh pronunciation	English equivalent	Welsh pronunciation	English equivalent
pattle	battle	falorous	valorous
pless	bless	Jeshu	Jesu
ploody	bloody	sall	shall
goot	good	'oman	woman

There are also a number of distinctive grammatical features – irregular plurals such as *disparagements* and *peradventures* – and words being assigned to the wrong part of speech, as in 'how melancholies I am' (*The Merry Wives of Windsor*, III.1.13). Fluellen also says *look you*, as Welshmen are imagined to do.

Irish English

There are just six words in the plays which represent an Irish way of speaking – all used by Captain McMorris in *Henry V*, III.2.85–109:

Irish pronunciation	English equivalent	Irish pronunciation	English equivalent
be	by	sa'	save
beseeched	besieged	'tish	'tis
ish	is	trompet	trumpet

Scottish English

These are the words in the plays which represent a Scottish way of speaking – all used by Captain Jamy in *Henry V*, III.2.80–115, and mainly affecting the vowels:

Scottish pronunciation	English equivalent	Scottish pronunciation	English equivalent
bath	both	mess	mass
breff	brief	slomber	slumber
capten	captain	suerly	surely
de	do	theise	these
feith	faith	vary	very
grund	ground	wad	would
level	leave	Chrish	Christ
lig	lie	sall	shall
gud-day	good-day	tway	two

Film versions of Shakespeare's plays

There have been 479 films based on, adapted (closely or loosely) from, or vaguely about Shakespeare's plays, according to Eddie Salmon's *Shakespeare: A Hundred Years on Film*, in the period up to 2000.

77	Romeo and Juliet	9	As You Like It
75	Hamlet	8	Twelfth Night
43	Othello	8	The Winter's Tale
42	The Taming of the Shrew	4	Henry V
32	Macbeth	3	Measure for Measure
24	Julius Caesar	3	King John
22	A Midsummer Night's Dream	3	Henry IV Part II
20	King Lear	2	The Two Gentlemen of Verona
18	The Merchant of Venice	2	Henry VIII
18	Antony and Cleopatra	1	Titus Andronicus
15	The Tempest	1	Richard II
15	Richard III	1	Henry IV Part I
11	The Comedy of Errors	1	Cymbeline
10	The Merry Wives of Windsor	1	Coriolanus
10	Much Ado About Nothing		

Plague

One of the consequences of the periodic epidemics of plague in London was the closure of the theatres. This is an extract from the order issued by the Privy Council on 28 January 1593:

> *all manner of concourse and publique meetings of the people at playes, beare-baitings, bowlinges and other like assemblyes for sportes be forbidden, and therefore doe hereby requier you and in her Majesty's name straightlie charge and commande you forthwith to inhibite within your jurisdiction all plaies …*

The plague raged from June 1592 to May 1594. The disease varied in its ferocity, so the theatres were allowed to open for some short periods, but for much of two years London saw no theatrical activity (see also p. 27).

Dramatis personae

In just seven cases, the First Folio gives a list of 'The Names of all the Actors' – really the characters in a play (the 'dramatis personae'): *The Tempest*, *The Two Gentlemen of Verona*, *Measure for Measure*, *The Winter's Tale*, *Henry IV Part II*, *Othello*, *Timon of Athens*. They are usually crammed into a small space on the page, at the very end of the play, but in the case of *Henry IV Part II* and *Timon* they are displayed in large type, taking up the whole of a folio page.

In David Garrick's 1748 rewrite of *Romeo and Juliet*, Romeo and Juliet are allowed to talk together in the tomb after V.3.114 – at 'righteous kiss'. (In the orthodox version, Romeo dies six lines later, before Juliet wakes up.)

> ... Arms, take your last embrace; and lips, do you
> The doors of breath seal with a righteous kiss;—
> Soft—she breathes, and stirs!　　　　　*[Juliet wakes.*
>
> *Jul.* Where am I? defend me!
>
> *Rom.* She speaks, she lives! and we shall still be bless'd!
> My kind propitious stars o'erpay me now
> For all my sorrows past—rise, rise, my Juliet,
> And from this cave of death, this house of horror,
> Quick let me snatch thee to thy Romeo's arms,
> There breathe a vital spirit in thy lips,
> And call thee back to life and love.　　　*[Takes her hand.*
>
> *Jul.* Bless me! how cold it is! whose's there!
>
> *Rom.* Thy husband,
> 'Tis thy Romeo, Juliet; rais'd from despair
> To joys unutt'rable! quit, quit this place,
> And let us fly together—　　　*[Brings her from the tomb.*
>
> *Jul.* Why do you force me so? I'll ne'er consent—
> My strength may fail me, but my will's unmov'd,—
> I'll not wed Paris,—Romeo is my husband—
>
> *Rom.* Her senses are unsettl'd—Heav'n restore 'em!
> Romeo is thy husband; I am that Romeo,
> Nor all th'opposing pow'rs of earth or man,
> Shall break our bonds, or tear thee from my heart.
>
> *Jul.* I know that voice—Its magic sweetness wakes
> My tranced soul—I now remember well
> Each circumstance—Oh my lord, my Husband—
> 　　　　　*[Going to embrace him.*
> Dost thou avoid me, Romeo? let me touch
> Thy hand, and taste the cordial of thy lips—
> You fright me—speak—O let me hear some voice
> Besides my own in this drear vault of death,
> Or I shall faint—support me—
>
> *Rom.* Oh I cannot,
> I have no strength, but want thy feeble aid,
> Cruel poison!
>
> *Jul.* Poison! what means my lord; thy trembling voice!
> Pale lips! and swimming eyes! death's in thy face!

Rom. It is indeed—I struggle with him now—
 The transports that I felt, to hear thee speak,
 And see thy op'ning eyes, stopt for a moment
 His impetuous course, and all my mind
 Was happiness and thee; but now the poison
 Rushes thro' my veins—I've not time to tell—
 Fate brought me to this place—to take a last,
 Last farewel of my love and with thee die.
Jul. Die? was the Friar false!
Rom. I know not that—
 I thought thee dead; distracted at the sight,
 (Fatal speed) drank poison, kiss'd thy cold lips,
 And found within thy arms a precious grave—
 But in that moment—Oh—
Jul. And did I wake for this!
Rom. My powers are blasted,
 'Twixt death and love I'm torn—I am distracted!
 But death's strongest—and must I leave thee, Juliet!
 Oh cruel cursed fate! in sight of heav'n—
Jul. Thou rav'st – lean on my breast—
Rom. Fathers have flinty hearts, no tears can melt 'em,
 Nature pleads in vain—Children must be wretched—
Jul. Oh my breaking heart—
Rom. She is my wife—our hearts are twin'd together—
 Capulet, forbear—Paris, loose your hold—
 Pull not our heart-strings thus—they crack—they break—
 Oh Juliet! Juliet!   [*Dies.*
Jul. Stay, stay, for me, Romeo—
 A moment stay; fate marries us in death,
 And we are one—no pow'r shall part us.
         [*Faints on Romeo's body.*

Heartbreaking

*The main purpose of his verse is to represent ordinary speech and tell
a story lucidly … That is why Shakespeare wrote in iambic pentameters; he didn't want to be 'poetic', he wanted to be understood. He
earns his poetry and his metaphors when the emotions become intense. He
can then move from plain speech to intricate images with ease. And
he is able to use the most banal things – Lear's button, or Cleopatra's
corset – to break our hearts.*

(Peter Hall, *Shakespeare's Advice to the Players*, 2004, p. 12)

The upstart crow

The first known public reference to Shakespeare is not a complimentary one. It occurs in 1592 in a pamphlet written by scholar-dramatist Robert Greene, called *Greene's Groatsworth of Wit*. Near death, and in a state of poverty, he reflects on his past life and bids a farewell to three of his fellow writers, warning them about an actor – an 'upstart crow' – who has achieved fame by playing parts from their works:

> *there is an upstart Crow, beautified with our feathers, that with his Tygers hart wrapt in a Players hyde, supposes he is as well able to bombast out a blanke verse as the best of you: and beeing an absolute Iohannes fac totum* [Jack of all trades], *is in his owne conceit the onely Shake-scene in a countrey*

Who is this man with a 'tiger's heart wrapped in a player's hide'? The phrase is a parody of a line in a speech from *Henry VI Part III* (1590-92), when the Duke of York accuses Queen Margaret of having a 'tiger's heart wrapped in a woman's hide' (I.4.138). The contemptuous 'Shake-scene' seems to confirm it. Why Greene was so antipathetic towards Shakespeare is another story . . .

Why 'upstart crow'?

Why was the Elizabethan writer Robert Greene so upset at Shakespeare? Various theories have been suggested. Greene, Marlowe and the other leading playwrights were all university men; Shakespeare was not. That the son of a rural glover, and a mere actor, might be setting his sights on becoming a member of the circle of well-educated authors would justify the description of an 'upstart crow'. But the reference to a 'tiger's heart' is quite fierce, especially remembering its origin in *Henry VI*, where the original speaker of the line, Queen Margaret, is being accused of extreme cruelty. Was Greene recalling some personal feud? Was he accusing Shakespeare of plagiarizing their work? We do not know. Perhaps he was simply bitterly envious of Shakespeare's growing success as a playwright.

Pragmatist

However great Shakespeare's genius is, it doesn't help to treat him as a sort of holy fool or a Messianic seer. He was a playwright, and an actor, and a theatre manager. He was utterly pragmatic; his plays wouldn't and couldn't have worked if they had been shrouded in obscurity and abstract conceits.

(Richard Eyre, *National Service*, 2004, p. 381)

A character-note

Henry Chettle published Robert Greene's pamphlet (p. 18) 'at his dying request', following his death in September 1592. Chettle seems to have been so embarrassed by the sneering reference to Shakespeare that in December of that year, in a preface to *Kind-Harts Dream*, he actually apologizes for not 'moderating' it, and adds a unique character-note:

> *I am as sory as if the originall fault had beene my fault, because my selfe haue seene his demeanor no less ciuill then he excelent in the qualitie he professes; Besides diuers of worship have reported his uprightness of dealing, which argues his honesty, and his facetious grace in writting, that approoves his Art.*

Early Modern English

The period in which Shakespeare wrote falls between two major linguistic stages in the history of English. The language spoken and written during the Middle Ages, most famously by Chaucer, is known as Middle English. Today we speak and write Modern English. By the end of the sixteenth century, the language had changed significantly from Middle English, and was in most respects very close to what we speak today. For that reason, the language of Shakespeare and his contemporaries is usually given the technical linguistic designation of *Early Modern English*, with *Elizabethan English* (but not *Jacobean English*) and *Shakespearian English* everyday alternatives.

Archaisms

Shakespeare's language often seems archaic to modern readers and play-goers, but he used archaisms too, usually taken from Chaucer and his contemporaries, or popularized by later writers with a historical consciousness, such as Spenser. The instances – such words as *clepe* 'call', *eke* 'also' and *wight* 'person' – occur in a variety of contexts:

- ❧ when characters are reading texts where an older style of language has been contrived, such as a love-letter, scroll or play script
- ❧ in certain types of character (such as school-masters) and in the speech of such bombastic personalities as Pistol (in *Henry V*) and Don Armado (in *Love's Labour's Lost*)
- ❧ in the poems, notably *Venus and Adonis* and *The Rape of Lucrece*
- ❧ in the Chorus monologues of the medieval poet Gower in *Pericles*.

Theatres of Stratford

In Stratford-upon-Avon, the options available to the theatre-going public have varied greatly during the past 125 years.

Theatre	Life	Type & Seating	Architect	Notes
The Memorial Theatre	23 April 1879–6 March 1926	Proscenium 711	William Frederick Unsworth, Edward John Dodgshun	Destroyed by fire
Stratford Picture House	As a theatre, March 1926–April 1931			Temporary site for the Shakespeare Festival, while the new Memorial Theatre was being built
The New Shakespeare Memorial Theatre	23 April 1932–20 March 1961	Proscenium 1000	Elisabeth Scott	Renamed The Royal Shakespeare Theatre
Open Air Theatre	1958–60	500		Riverside Gardens of the first Memorial Theatre; presented plays by visiting student companies
The Royal Shakespeare Theatre (RST)	20 March 1961–	Proscenium 1436	various	Several alterations carried out by different architects
The Swan Theatre	26 April 1986–	Thrust 465	Michael Reardon, Tim Furby	Designed inside the outer shell wall of the 1879 Memorial Theatre
The Studio Theatre	Summer/autumn 1973	Studio		Converted tin-roofed storage shed; renamed 'The Other Place'
The Other Place	1 June 1974–1989	Studio c.160		Performance licence withdrawn
The Other Place 2	1991–2001, 2005	Studio c.240–70	Michael Reardon	Will provide foyer for temporary theatre built on adjoining car park while RST is redesigned (2007–2009)

Visiting actors

Stratford became an independent township in the sixteenth century, and a busy market centre, known for its fairs. When the acting companies went on provincial tours, it was one of the calling points, with plays presented in the Guild-Hall. The Earl of Leicester's Men, for example, visited in 1569 and several times in the 1570s. Biographers have always felt it likely that the boy Shakespeare would have seen some of the performances, perhaps those of 1573 (when he was nine) or 1576. No one in a town with a population of only 2000 people could have missed knowing of such a visit. William, many think, might even have had a privileged seat at the front of the Hall, given that his father had held high civic offices. John Shakespeare was elected the town's chief citizen (High Bailiff) in 1568–9, and he had the position of High Alderman in 1571–2. Part of his duties as Bailiff was to pay visiting players.

Meeting Ros and Guil

Shakespeare might have met Rosencrantz and Guildenstern in the white streets of London, or seen the serving-men of rival houses bite their thumbs at each other in the open square; but Hamlet came out of his soul, and Romeo out of his passion.

(Oscar Wilde, *The Critic As Artist*, 1891)

False friends: baffle

MODERN SENSE: defeat efforts, frustrate plans

OBSOLETE SENSE: disgrace publicly

♣ Mowbray says to King Richard: 'I am disgraced, impeached, and baffled here' (*Richard II*, I.1.170).

SHAKESPEARE: expose someone or something to ridicule

♣ 'How have they baffled thee!' says Olivia to Malvolio, tricked by Sir Toby and his companions (*Twelfth Night*, V.1.367).

Appropriate names

All Shakespeare's late-play heroines are given innovative names which appropriately reflect their situations:

> Marina (*Pericles*) – born at sea
> Perdita (*The Winter's Tale*) – the lost one
> Miranda (*The Tempest*) – the admired one
> Innogen (*Cymbeline*) – the innocent one
> Fidele (Innogen's alias) – the faithful one

The contents page

As displayed at the front of the First Folio; apart from the distinctive spelling and capitalization, the Catalogue shows some interesting variations in the play titles.

A CATALOGVE
of the seuerall Comedies, Histories, and Tragedies contained in this Volume

COMEDIES.

The Tempest.
The two Gentlemen of Verona.
The Merry Wiues of Windsor.
Measure for Measure.
The Comedy of Errours.
Much adoo about Nothing.
Loues Labour lost.
A Midsommer Nights Dreame.
The Merchant of Venice.
As you Like it.
The Taming of the Shrew.
All is well, that Ends well.
Twelfe-Night, or what you will.
The Winters Tale.

HISTORIES.

The Life and Death of King John.
The Life & death of Richard the second.
The First part of King Henry the fourth.

The Second part of K.Henry the fourth.
The Life of Henry the Fift.
The First part of King Henry the Sixt.
The Second part of King Hen. the Sixt.
The Third part of King Henry the Sixt.
The Life & Death of Richard the Third.
The Life of King Henry the Eight.

TRAGEDIES.

The Tragedy of Coriolanus.
Titus Andronicus.
Romeo and Juliet.
Timon of Athens.
The Life and death of Julius Caesar.
The Tragedy of Macbeth.
The Tragedy of Hamlet.
King Lear.
Othello, the Moore of Venice.
Anthony and Cleopater.
Cymbeline King of Britaine.

Page numbers

The pages of the First Folio are not paginated throughout in a single sequence, as in a modern book. The three sections, Comedies, Histories, Tragedies, are numbered separately:

COMEDIES: numbered from 1 to 303.

HISTORIES: numbered from 1 to 232 – but the numbers from 69 to 100 are repeated.

TRAGEDIES: numbered from 1 to 399 (this last page actually misprinted as 993) – but there is another error, as page 156 is followed by 257, and no correction was made thereafter.

Makers

The first collection of Shakespeare's plays was published in 1623, collated and edited by two members of Shakespeare's company, John Heminge and Henry Condell. They were actors, not professional editors or publishers, and the First Folio was a huge volume, by any standards, so they needed a great deal of support. A consortium of publishers took on the work: the colophon at the end of the book lists W. Jaggard, Ed. Blount, I. Smithweeke and W. Aspley.

Contributors

In addition to the dedication and introduction penned by the editors, the preliminary matter to the First Folio contains several other items.

- ✤ Shakespeare's friend, playwright Ben Jonson, wrote a ten-line address to the reader as well as an eighty-line prefatory memorial poem.
- ✤ The scholar and poet Hugh Holland wrote a fourteen-line poem.
- ✤ The poet Leonard Digges wrote a twenty-two-line memorial poem.
- ✤ Digges' friend James Mabbe (signed only as I.M.) wrote an eight-line poem.
- ✤ The copper-engraved image on the title page was made by the young English engraver Martin Droeshout (born in 1601).

Publishers

The leading publisher William Jaggard, assisted by his eldest son Isaac, took the best part of two years to prepare the First Folio, and in view of the size and complexity of the work, it is not surprising that its appearance was delayed. The book was originally advertised to appear in 1622, but it was not ready until the following year, and copies of the edition were still being completed in 1624. William, already blind when the project began, died before it was finished. Isaac, along with Edward Blount, is named on the title page.

The 'first' folio

Partly due to the expense of paper, the folio format was only used for books of importance. Plays were not viewed as serious literature, and were printed only as quartos. Then in 1616, the year Shakespeare died, Ben Jonson published a folio collection of his own plays, the first Elizabethan dramatist to attempt a collected edition. It was a precedent for Heminge and Condell to do the same for Shakespeare in 1623.

Shakespeare Folios

As Shakespeare's fame grew, there was a regular demand for new editions of the First Folio of 1623.

* *The Second Folio, 1632* – a reprint with some modernized spellings and corrections of stage directions and proper names.
* *The Third Folio, 1663* – with some corrections and some new errors.
* *The Third Folio, second impression, 1664* – seven plays were added 'never before Printed in Folio, viz. Pericles, Prince of Tyre. The London Prodigall. The History of Thomas Ld. Cromwell. Sir John Oldcastle, Lord Cobham. The Puritan Widow. A Yorkshire Tragedy. The Tragedy of Locrine'.
* *The Fourth Folio, 1685* – a reprint of the Third Folio, with more corrections and errors, and including *Pericles* and the six other plays.

The Third Folio is extremely rare, because a large number of copies were destroyed in the great fire of London in 1666. It is, in fact, rarer than the First Folio.

They die, they live, they die

In *Roscius Anglicanus* (1708), John Downes records that *Romeo and Juliet* was given an early revival by Sir William Davenant's company (in 1661). It was evidently turned into a tragi-comedy by James Howard, 'preserving Romeo and Juliet alive; so that when the Tragedy was Reviv'd again, 'twas Play'd Alternately, Tragical one Day, and Tragicomical another; for several Days together'.

Operatic Shakespeare

The operatic genre is coincident with Shakespeare: the earliest opera with surviving music dates from 1600. Since then, there have been around 200 operas based on Shakespeare's plays. Henry Purcell's *The Fairy Queen* (1692) is usually considered the first, but its music relates to only a small part of *A Midsummer Night's Dream*. Among well-known later compositions are Rossini's *Otello* (1816), Wagner's *Das Liebesverbot* (1836, a setting of *Measure for Measure*), Verdi's *Macbeth* (1847), *Otello* (1887) and *Falstaff* (1893), and Berlioz's *Béatrice et Bénédict* (1862). Britten's *A Midsummer Night's Dream* (1960) is the only successful setting of Shakespeare's words. Famous musicals include Cole Porter's *Kiss Me, Kate* (1948), based on *The Taming of the Shrew*, and Leonard Bernstein's *West Side Story* (1957), based on *Romeo and Juliet*.

Not the house we thought it to be

The cottage near Stratford in which Mary Arden, Shakespeare's mother, grew up has attracted millions of Shakespeare tourists. It was originally identified by John Jordan in 1792. However, Jordan was one of the most famous Shakespearian forgers, allegedly attempting, amongst other things, a forgery of John Shakespeare's will. It transpires that the house has no connection whatsoever with Shakespeare. In spring 2002, Dr Nat Alcock wrote in the *Shakespeare Quarterly* that he had discovered deeds and church records which proved the house belonged to an Adam Palmer, who didn't build it until 1569 (long after Mary Arden had moved to Stratford). Glebe Farm, next door to Palmer's House, was built in 1514, and was the house that belonged to Agnes Arden, Mary Arden's stepmother. The Shakespeare Birthplace Trust – which owned both locations, having bought Palmer's Farm in the 1960s to avoid the site being developed – reversed the names. Mary Arden's House became known as Palmer's Farm, and Glebe Farm became known as Mary Arden's House.

Early genres

Chronologies of Shakespeare's plays are uncertain creatures (see p.6), but the following ten plays are widely thought to be the earliest, written in the five years or so after about 1589:

The Comedy of Errors	Love's Labour's Lost
Henry VI Part I	Richard III
Henry VI Part II	The Taming of the Shrew
Henry VI Part III	Titus Andronicus
King Edward III	The Two Gentlemen of Verona

Scholars disagree about the exact order, and the authorship, but there is no disputing one point: these plays represent all three of the major dramatic genres – comedy, history and tragedy – and indicate an emerging playwright of remarkable breadth.

European tours

Troupes of English players travelled around Europe in the 1580s and 1590s, performing plays in English. Members of Shakespeare's company, including the clown Will Kemp, are known to have taken part in these tours, but there is no evidence of Shakespeare himself being involved. In 1602 the first public theatre in Germany, the Ottoneum, was built at Kassel for one such company. It was used until 1613, and its outer walls still exist.

Sir Thomas More

The Booke of Sir Thomas Moore is a sixteenth-century play manuscript of twenty-two leaves, now lodged in the British Library. 'Booke' is not part of the title: the person who wrote it on the cover was simply using the word in its sense of 'script'. The play has never attracted much critical or theatrical interest (though the Royal Shakespeare Company had a production in 2005), but it is unique because of its manuscript character. Seven contributing hands can be distinguished, and one ('hand D'), writing 147 lines taking up three pages, is thought to be that of Shakespeare. The claim was first made in 1871 by Richard Simpson, a clergyman who became a writer and Shakespeare enthusiast. The case is based on a comparison of the hand with Shakespeare's known signatures, shared distinctive spellings (e.g. *scilence*) with known Shakespeare texts (*Scilence* in the Quarto text of *Henry IV Part II*), and certain points of similarity in the way themes are treated. The case is a strong one. If it is true, this is the nearest we are likely to get to seeing Shakespeare 'at his desk', because no diary, notes or personal manuscripts have ever been found.

The King's Men

King James' interest in the arts is illustrated by the speed with which he had a royal warrant prepared for Shakespeare's company. He gave the instruction only ten days after he arrived in London. The Royal Patent licenses and authorizes:

> *theise our servauntes lawrence Fletcher William Shakespeare Richard Burbage Augustyne Phillippes John heninges henrie Condell William Sly Robert Armyn Richard Cowly and the rest of theire Associates freely to use and exercise the Arte and faculty of playinge Comedies Tragedies histories Enterludes moralls pastoralls Stageplaies and Suche others like as theie have alreadie studied or hereafter shall use or studie aswell for the recreation of our lovinge Subjectes as for our Solace and pleasure when wee shall thincke good to see them duringe our pleasure …*

After the Patent was issued, 19 May 1603, Shakespeare's company became known as the King's Men.

Who says most?

Who has the most lines in *Twelfth Night*?
Viola? Malvolio? Olivia? Sir Toby? Feste? Someone else?
(See p. 63.)

Stationer's Register

The Stationers' Company of London governed the printing of all the books in England, apart from those printed by the University Presses. A publisher had to enter a play title into the Stationer's Register for a fee (four pence, later six pence) – a procedure which licensed the play, and gave the publisher the sole right to print or sell it. Shakespeare's First Folio was entered into the Register on 8 November 1623 (see p. 80).

Parentheses

The use of a pair of curved brackets to enclose parenthetical material, or to suggest a different tone of voice, was a late fourteenth-century invention. They were a frequent punctuation device in the First Folio, but practice is erratic. *The Winter's Tale*, in particular, has many examples, as in this speech of a Lord defending Hermione (II.1.129):

> For her (my Lord)
> I dare my life lay downe, and will do't (Sir)
> Please you t'accept it, that the Queene is spotlesse
> I'th'eyes of Heauen, and to you (I meane
> In this, which you accuse her.)

Modern editors would replace many of these by commas.

Plagues

Acting companies were seriously affected by the frequent epidemics of bubonic plague in London, for playhouses were closed to prevent the spread of infection when weekly deaths exceeded a certain number (often fifty, and sometimes less). During Shakespeare's playwriting lifetime, plague caused long periods of closure several times: during 1592–4, 1603–4 and 1609–10, with some minor closures between 1604 and 1608.

Waiting for Hamlet

In the theatre, someone playing Laertes will do twenty minutes at the beginning, wait two hours, then come back and do forty minutes at the end. Filming Branagh's Hamlet *(playing Laertes), I did one week at the beginning, waited eight weeks then did three weeks at the end of the shoot. You stand more of a chance doing the whole part well in the theatre, but you have an opportunity to be very specific, working on a few pages a day, when you work on film.* (Michael Maloney, Interview, Penguin UK website, March 2001)

Inverted commas

Opening and closing 'quotation marks', as we know them today, did not come into English until the eighteenth century. In the sixteenth century, the only comparable punctuation convention was the use of initial double inverted commas to draw attention to a quotation or a remark of special significance, and – from the last quarter of the century – to mark direct speech. However, usage remained sporadic and inconsistent, and examples are rare in Elizabethan manuscripts. An example is in the First Folio printing of *The Merry Wives of Windsor*, where we find Ford saying (II.2.198):

> ... I haue purchased at an infinite rate, and that hath taught mee to say this,
> "*Loue like a shadow flies, when substance Loue pursues,*
> "*Pursuing that that flies, and flying what pursues.*

False friends: table

MODERN SENSE: piece of furniture; arrangement of data
OBSOLETE SENSE: (writing-tablet), memo-pad, notebook

❧ The Archbishop says to Mowbray, of the King: 'therefore will he wipe his tables clean' (*Henry IV Part II*, IV.1.199).
❧ Sonnet 122 opens: 'Thy gift, thy tables, are within my brain'.
  It is most famously found in *Hamlet*, where the prince employs it three times:
❧ 'from the table of my memory / I'll wipe away all trivial fond records' (I.5.98).
❧ 'My tables – meet it is I set it down' (I.5.107).
❧ And in the First Quarto only, talking about a type of clown: 'gentlemen quote his jests down in their tables' (III.2.46).

Shakespeare as plaintiff

There are many myths and legends of what Shakespeare did when he lived in Stratford during the early 1600s. But among the facts are two records of his suing neighbours for their failure to pay money owed to him. In 1604 he takes Philip Rogers to court for owing him 35 shillings and 10 pence, plus damages;* the court judgement is not known. And in 1608–9 he took John Addenbrooke to court for a debt of £6, plus damages; the court ruled in his favour. We do not know whether Shakespeare ever got his money.

*In old British currency, there were 12 pence in the shilling and 20 shillings in the pound.

Who is Henry VI about?

Is *Henry VI* about Henry VI? Historically, of course. But dramatically, in terms of the way the lines are shared, others have the dominant roles. In *Part I*, Talbot takes the lead (406 lines), leaving Henry in fifth place. In *Part II* the King is in third place, but his part is smaller than York's. Only in *Part III* does Henry come more to the fore.

Part I
406 Talbot   254 Pucelle   184 Richard   183 Gloucester   179 King

Part II
379 York   316 Queen   314 King

Part III
435 Warwick   428 Edward   390 Richard   362 King

Replica Globes (and Roses)

Before the Sam Wanamaker-inspired reconstruction of Shakespeare's Globe in London in 1996, there had been a number of replicas built during the twentieth century. They include:

❧ 1912 London: A working Globe theatre was featured in an exhibition of 'Shakespeare's England' at Earl's Court.

❧ 1934 Chicago: At the World Fair, a small-scale Globe theatre was built by Thomas Wood Stevens in the English Village part of 'A Century of Progress'. It played twenty- to forty-minute productions of Shakespeare, with occasional longer shows. A fifteen-year-old Sam Wanamaker visited the fair, and saw some of the shows.

❧ 1936 Cleveland: The Great Lakes Festival included a mock Globe, in which a company led by Sam Wanamaker presented shortened versions of Shakespeare's plays.

In 1998 a full-sized replica of the Rose Theatre was built for the film *Shakespeare in Love*. When the filming was over, the production company, Miramax, gave the set to Judi Dench (who played Queen Elizabeth), who hoped to open it as a working theatre.

Staying strong

When you've the strength for it, you're too young,
when you've the age, you're too old. It's a bugger, isn't it?
(Laurence Olivier on *King Lear*, On Acting, 1986, p. 89)

School curriculum

There are no records of the curriculum or any of the students at Stratford grammar school, the King's New School in Church Street, in the time of Shakespeare. But educational practice was beginning to standardize under Elizabeth, so we can use what has survived about the curriculum in other schools as an indication of the formal education Shakespeare would have received once he left petty school (p. 4). The emphasis was entirely on the teaching of Latin. The main text was William Lily's *A Shorte Introduction of Grammar*, which gave an account of Latin grammatical structure written partly in English and partly in Latin. It had to be learned by heart. It was not just a written language: the children were expected to speak to each other in Latin, not English. Several Roman authors were studied. Although Ben Jonson said of Shakespeare, in a famous phrase, that he had 'small Latin and less Greek', the amount acquired after several hours a day, six days a week, for six or seven years must nonetheless have been substantial.

Always connect

One of the things I always liked was the thrill of hearing an audience respond at the end of a performance of a Shakespeare play. Everyone is always questioning Shakespeare's place in our lives – should he be on school syllabuses, is he any use, is he redundant, what's the point of him today? But in performance, suddenly there is a connection to a modern audience. They have gone on a journey. They won't have understood all the words but they will have understood the fundamental drama and characters will have come through. Shakespeare is contemporary – not always linguistically but in the things he addresses, and I do remember feeling the thrill that this great language was still connecting to audiences in a contemporary context.
(Ralph Fiennes, RSC *Brand* Interview, Summer 2003)

Publication

Shakespeare's plays begin to appear in print in 1598. Over half of them were published while he was still alive. The First Folio of 1623 is the first attempt to collect all the plays into one volume.

Coincidence

That Shakespeare was born (in the traditional account) and died on the same day, 23 April, is considered to be hugely interesting by some observers, and hugely uninteresting by others.

Born and died on 23 April

Some of the people who share the same birth and death dates
with Shakespeare.

BORN

1775   J. M. W. Turner, artist
1791   James Buchanan, fifteenth president of the USA
1804   Marie Taglioni, Italian ballet dancer
1858   Max Planck, Nobel prize-winning physicist
1891   Sergei Prokofiev, composer
1893   Billy Smart, circus proprietor
1895   James Seymour, screenwriter of *42nd Street*
1899   Vladimir Nabokov, writer
1928   Shirley Temple Black, actor
1930   Alan Oppenheimer, actor, the original voice of Mighty Mouse
1936   Roy Orbison, singer and songwriter
1940   Lee Majors, actor
1949   Paul Brickman, scriptwriter of the film *Uprising*
1950   Henry Goodman, actor

DIED

1616   Miguel de Cervantes, writer
1850   William Wordsworth, poet
1905   Joseph Jefferson, thought to be the earliest-born film-actor, who
        played Rip Van Winkle nine times
1915   Rupert Brooke, poet
1975   William Hartnell, a member of Sir Frank Benson's Shakespeare
        Company in the mid-1920s, who played the first Dr Who
1986   Otto Preminger, film director and producer
1998   James Earl Ray, the assassin of Martin Luther King

Birthday celebrations

Each year, on the Saturday closest to 23 April, Stratford-upon-Avon
hosts the Shakespeare birthday celebrations. There is a procession to lay
floral tributes on Shakespeare's grave, a civic reception, a special lecture,
a church service, and an evening play performance by the Royal
Shakespeare Company. At a birthday luncheon for some 600 local
people and guests, toasts are drunk to the Immortal Memory of William
Shakespeare and to The Theatre. During the procession, flags (including those of many nations) are unfurled in the main streets. The idea of
an annual celebration dates from the nineteenth century, but its origins
lie in the first Shakespearian Festival of 1769, organized by actor David
Garrick, which established Stratford as a place of literary pilgrimage.

Concordances

A concordance is an alphabetical listing of all the content words in a text (excluding such structural words as *the* and *of*). Several concordances have been compiled for Shakespeare, such as Alexander Schmidt's *Shakespeare-Lexicon* (1874) or John Bartlett's *Concordance to Shakespeare* (1927). Martin Spevack's *A Complete and Systematic Concordance to the Works of Shakespeare*, keyed to the Riverside edition of the works, was published in eight volumes (1968–70, 1975). A derivative work, the *Harvard Concordance to Shakespeare*, also edited by Spevack, appeared in 1973. An online concordance to the texts used in the present authors' *Shakespeare's Words*, including all of the New Penguin Shakespeare, has been added to the website at www.shakespeareswords.com.

Romeo and Juliet *on film*

Some of the films which have used the *Romeo and Juliet* story as a starting point:

Giulietta e Romeo (1910, Italy)
Roméo se fait Bandit (1910, France, 'Romeo Becomes a Bandit')
Indian Romeo and Juliet (1911, USA)
Romeo and Juliet in Our Town (1911, USA)
Romeo e Giulietta (1912, Italy)
Doubling for Romeo (1921, USA)
Villa Discordia (1938, Argentina)
Les Amants de Vérone (1948, France)
West Side Story (1961, USA)
The Teenage Lovers of Verona (1968, GB/Italy)
The Secret Sex Lives of Romeo and Juliet (1969, USA)
Romeo en Julie op de Bromfiets (1990, Netherlands, 'Romeo and Juliet on Motor-scooters')
Tromeo and Juliet (1996, USA)
William Shakespeare's Romeo and Juliet (1996, USA)

And not forgetting:
Romiet and Julio (1917, USA) a cartoon story of two cats (including a balcony scene).

No plays in Stratford

It is a sad irony that Shakespeare lived his later years in Stratford in a playless environment, for in 1603 the puritan-minded aldermen and burgesses had banned all performances of plays in the town. Even social visits by actors were viewed with suspicion.

William Poel

William Poel, born in 1852, began producing Shakespeare in 1881 with a First Quarto production of Hamlet. He campaigned for the restoration of Shakespeare's texts, and a simpler, fleeter staging of the plays. He was revolutionary for his desire to act the plays following what little was known about how Shakespeare's actors would have performed them. Peter Hall (*Shakespeare's Advice to the Players*, p. 195) explains why so little is known:

> *His rapid, witty speaking technique had been learned, he said, from Macready's actors in the mid-nineteenth century. They had been taught by Kean's actors, who had been taught in their turn by Garrick's, who had been taught by Betterton's. Then there had to be a stop because it is not possible to go further back. The traditions of Shakespeare's stage were destroyed by the Puritans when they closed the theatres in the Civil War. They stopped the greatest theatre culture since ancient Greece – arguably the greatest theatre culture ever.*

When the drawing of the interior of the Swan was discovered, Poel built 'The Old Fortune Theatre' (really a portable stage), based on it. What Sam Wanamaker actually later accomplished, Poel too tried in 1902, pushing the London Shakespeare Commemoration League to display a model for a proposed reconstruction of the original Globe Theatre. Since 1952 there has been a William Poel verse-speaking festival held for final-year drama students by the Society for Theatre Research, which since 2000 has been held at Wanamaker's reconstructed Globe.

Comedy, History, Tragedy

There are thirty-six plays in the First Folio of 1623. *Troilus and Cressida* is omitted from the Catalogue at the front of the book (see p. 8), but is included in the Folio along with the tragedies. Of the thirty-five listed :

fourteen are grouped as *comedies*
ten are grouped as *histories*
eleven are grouped as *tragedies*

Of the other plays considered to be partly by Shakespeare, *King Edward III* falls naturally within the histories; *The Two Noble Kinsmen* is often thought of as a comedy, despite its tragic ending; and *Pericles* is often called a tragedy, despite having a happy ending.

A line of poetry is often shared between more than one character, as in this example from *Othello* (III.3.103):

IAGO: My lord, for aught I know.
OTHELLO: What dost thou think?

Sometimes three or more people share a line. Such exchanges increase the tempo of the interaction, which in turn conveys an increased sense of dramatic moment. But the plays do not use shared lines equally, as is seen in the table opposite. In Shakespeare there is a noticeable trend to use them more frequently over time – an interesting index of his maturing control of the dramatic representation of a conversation. In the early plays, few characters swop part-lines in this way; but the proportion (column 3) steadily increases, with few exceptions. *Henry V* and *Pericles* have half the number we would expect, given their dates; and *The Two Gentlemen of Verona* and *The Taming of the Shrew* are ahead of their time.

======= *Famous forgeries* =======

As public fascination with Shakespeare grew, in the eighteenth and nineteenth centuries, the search for fresh biographical evidence motivated the compilation of forged documents purporting to be by or about the author or his connections. The most notorious forgers were William Henry Ireland (1777–1835) and John Payne Collier (1789–1883).

❧ Ireland, a lawyer's clerk, fabricated letters, contracts, and other legal documents, publishing them in 1796 as *Miscellaneous Papers and Legal Instruments under the Hand and Seal of William Shakespeare*. He also wrote a tragedy, *Vortigern and Rowena*. The deception was uncovered by Edmond Malone the same year, and Ireland wrote a *Confessions* in 1805.

❧ Collier, a journalist and lawyer, published from 1835 a series of works purporting to reveal new information about Shakespeare, culminating in his 'discovery' of a copy of the Second Folio with 'original' annotations. Published in 1852 as *Notes and Emendations to the Text of Shakespeare's Plays*, the findings were immediately questioned, and shown to be forgeries a few years later.

======= *Screen-writer* =======

At the end of 2004, the Internet Movie Database (www.imdb.com) listed 566 films with Shakespeare as the author, in part or wholly (see also p. 15). The first was *King John* in 1899, starring and directed by Sir Herbert Beerbohm Tree. Two plays have attracted far more film adaptations than any other: *Romeo and Juliet* (see p. 32) and *Hamlet* (p. 97).

A: No. of part lines	B: No. of lines of poetry	% (A/B × 100)	Play	Date
24	2892	0.8	Henry VI Part III	1591
28	2488	1.1	King Edward III	by 1595
37	2664	1.4	Henry VI Part I	1592
43	2580	1.7	Henry VI Part II	1592
70	2479	2.8	Titus Andronicus	1592
45	1543	2.9	The Comedy of Errors	1594
88	2752	3.2	Richard II	1595
134	3516	3.8	Richard III	1592–3
73	1943	3.8	Henry V	1598–9
78	1713	4.6	A Midsummer Night's Dream	1595
80	1613	5.0	The Two Gentlemen of Verona	1590–91
65	1276	5.1	As You Like It	1599–1600
143	2569	5.6	King John	1596
88	1547	5.7	Henry IV Part II	1597–8
122	2075	5.9	The Taming of the Shrew	1590–91
101	1665	6.1	Henry IV Part I	1596–7
24	338	6.2	The Merry Wives of Windsor	1597–8
186	2610	7.1	Romeo and Juliet	1595
170	2025	8.4	The Merchant of Venice	1596–7
158	1715	9.2	Love's Labour's Lost	1594–5
75	739	10.1	Much Ado About Nothing	1598
102	949	10.8	Twelfth Night	1600–1601
264	2250	11.7	Troilus and Cressida	1602
234	1903	12.3	Pericles	1607
281	2207	12.7	Julius Caesar	1599
424	2742	15.5	Hamlet	1600–1601
295	1707	17.3	Timon of Athens	1605
311	1634	19.0	Measure for Measure	1603
516	2345	22.0	King Lear	1605–6
324	1447	22.4	All's Well that Ends Well	1604–5
604	2599	23.2	Othello	1603–4
545	1948	28.0	Macbeth	1606
827	2808	29.5	Cymbeline	1610
464	1568	29.6	The Tempest	1611
820	2735	30.0	Henry VIII	1613
805	2570	31.3	Coriolanus	1608
699	2181	32.1	The Winter's Tale	1609
1004	3017	33.3	Antony and Cleopatra	1606
926	2641	35.1	The Two Noble Kinsmen	1613–14

Sword-and-buckler

Mentioned three times in the plays, the English sword-and-buckler was formerly the commonest fencing weapon combination, replaced in Shakespeare's time by the Italian rapier-and-dagger. The Italian styles of fencing were coming into fashion in London while Shakespeare was writing (the Italian masters teaching in the Blackfriars theatre). The sword was shorter than the rapier, and was used for cutting rather than thrusting. A carrier of sword-and-buckler would be using an older style of fighting which was rapidly becoming thought of as vulgar and dated (it is used as a term of contempt in *Henry IV Part I*, I.3.227). In *Romeo and Juliet*, Sampson and Gregory enter carrying them. However, Tybalt, as a 'courageous captain of compliments' (a fencing guard) and 'fashionmonger' would probably have carried a rapier. Bringing a quick weapon like a rapier to a sword-and-buckler fight would have been very unfair.

False friends: mean

MODERN SENSE: (adjective) spiteful, nasty; not generous, stingy; (American English) excellent

OBSOLETE SENSE: of low rank

♣ Lady Grey says to Edward 'I am too mean to be your queen' (*Henry VI Part III*, III.2.97).

OBSOLETE SENSE: lowly, humble

♣ Lucentio enters 'in the habit of a mean man' (*The Taming of the Shrew*, II.1.39, stage direction).

OBSOLETE SENSE: unworthy

♣ Helena refers to herself as someone 'too mean / To have her name repeated' (*All's Well that Ends Well*, III.5.59).

Finding your way about

The Norton Facsimile, published in 1968, was the first 'synthetic' version of the First Folio. The compilers scrutinized several surviving copies to select pages which were as legible as possible and which displayed the latest state of correction by the original typesetters. They also introduced a standard system of reference, called 'through line numbering', in which the lines of the 1623 edition are numbered in sequence throughout a play, disregarding the divisions into acts and scenes.

Weight watching

Get a Cordelia you can carry and watch your Fool!
(Donald Wolfit's oft-repeated advice on playing King Lear)

In Act III Scene 1 of *Hamlet*, Claudius and Polonius arrange for Ophelia to encounter Hamlet, as they watch, hidden near by. Ophelia uses *you* to Hamlet throughout, but Hamlet varies his pronouns. He begins with *you*, for it is a formal and distanced encounter, in which he is telling her he did not love her. Then he switches to *thou*, and the dialogue takes on a much greater emotional intensity.

HAMLET: I did love *you* once.

OPHELIA: Indeed, my lord, *you* made me believe so.

HAMLET: *You* should not have believed me, for virtue cannot so inoculate our old stock but we shall relish of it. I loved *you* not.

OPHELIA: I was the more deceived.

HAMLET: Get *thee* to a nunnery. Why wouldst *thou* be a breeder of sinners? …

Is it Ophelia's poignant reaction that makes him speak more intimately? Then, at the end of his haranguing speech he suddenly switches back to *you*:

… Go *thy* ways to a nunnery. Where's *your* father?

OPHELIA: At home, my lord.

The pronouns change the mood, from intimacy to serious inquiry, perhaps even suspicion – if, as happens in many productions, Hamlet becomes aware that he is under observation.

A thumbnail sketch

Orson Welles, in the book he wrote with Roger Hill, *Everybody's Shakespeare*:

Shakespeare said everything. Brain to belly; every mood and minute of a man's season. His language is starlight and fireflies and the sun and the moon. He wrote it with tears and blood and beer, and his words march like heartbeats. He speaks to everyone and we all claim him, but it's wise to remember, if we would really appreciate him, that he doesn't properly belong to us but to another world that smelled assertively of columbine and gun powder and printer's ink and was vigorously dominated by Elizabeth.

Thornton Wilder said of this paragraph:

The greatest thumbnail summation of Shakespeare's genius ever written. (Reported in Simon Callow, *Orson Welles, The Road to Xanadu*, 1995, p. 179)

Blank verse is probably the very centre of Elizabethan tradition and perhaps the most important thing in Shakespeare that an actor has to come to terms with. Or rather I should say that an actor needs to get help from. I stress that because many actors, particularly if they're not familiar with Shakespeare, very understandably look at the verse as some kind of threat. They know they will somehow come to grief if they ignore it or be chastised if they do it wrong. It becomes a mountain to be climbed or else an obstacle to be avoided. But no, it's there to help the actor. It's full of little hints from Shakespeare about how to act a given speech or scene. It's stage-direction in shorthand … Shakespeare was an actor, and I believe that his verse is above all a device to help the actor. (John Barton, *Playing Shakespeare*, 1984, p. 25)

======= *Cast-list* =======

Shakespeare and his fellow-actors are credited at the front of the First Folio.

The Names of the Principall Actors
in all these Playes

William Shakespeare.	Samuel Gilburne.
Richard Burbadge.	Robert Armin.
John Hemmings.	William Ostler.
Augustine Phillips.	Nathan Field.
William Kempt.	John Underwood.
Thomas Poope.	Nicholas Tooley.
George Bryan.	William Ecclestone.
Henry Condell.	Joseph Taylor.
William Slye.	Robert Benfield.
Richard Cowly.	Robert Goughe.
John Lowine.	Richard Robinson.
Samuell Crosse.	John Shancke.
Alexander Cooke.	John Rice.

======= *Inner rhythms* =======

The Elizabethans knew very well what iambic verse should be, and Shakespeare, in the interests of spontaneity, often comes near to destroying it. This produces a tension and therefore keeps the speech dramatic … he must have known, as his verse became freer and more irregular, that it was being spoken by actors who had an inner rhythm of the iambic line that they had lived and worked with for fifteen or twenty years. (Peter Hall, *Shakespeare's Advice to the Players*, 2004, pp. 22–4)

Making cuts

Long plays, such as *Hamlet* or *Richard III*, were routinely cut in Jacobethan performance. The cuts would have been made by the acting company, who owned the play, not the playwright. Title pages of published plays in the 1600s often included such remarks as 'more than hath been publicly spoken or acted'. The most explicit statement about the practice occurs in the Stationers' Address by Humphrey Moseley to the collected edition of the plays of Beaumont and Fletcher in 1647:

> *When these Comedies and Tragedies were presented on the stage, the actors omitted some scenes and passages (with the Authors' consent) as occasion led them; and when private friends desired a copy, they then (and justly too) transcribed what they acted.*

The Prologue to *Romeo and Juliet* suggests that a typical length was two hours or so – and presumably never more than three, given that the Chamberlain's Men were under a time constraint from Henry Carey their patron. On 8 October 1594 Carey wrote to the Lord Mayor, asking that the players be allowed to continue their work now that the plague was over, and adding:

> *they have undertaken to me that where heeretofore they began not their Plaies till towards fower a clock, they will now begin at two, & have don betwene fower and five …*

How many parts?

Excluding those lines which are given to several people speaking at once, and counting separately repeated roles in different plays (e.g. Falstaff appears in three plays), there are 1378 speaking parts in all the plays.

Starling growth

In 1890, Eugene Schieffelin released eighty starlings into New York's Central Park because they were mentioned in Shakespeare's plays. Hotspur says 'I shall have a starling shall be taught to speak' (*Henry IV Part I*, I.3.221). There are now over 200 million of them in America. Quite a return for a single line.

Who says most?

Who has the most lines in *A Midsummer Night's Dream*?
Puck? Oberon? Helena? Hermia? Bottom? Someone else?
(See p. 94.)

Sacrifices

For me, working on Shakespeare is a search for meaning, and that can be expressed in being utterly real, using an accent, not using an accent, putting it in modern dress, not putting it in modern dress, with an ongoing assessment of what the sacrifices you make are if you do any of those things. You normally sacrifice something. It's very hard to get everything out of a Shakespeare play. If you set Romeo and Juliet *in war-torn Belfast, it puts a terrific focus on the feuding – but Shakespeare's play is about a household feud, not a religious feud.*

(Kenneth Branagh, interview in *The Daily Telegiraffe*, 30 October 1995)

The lost years

Between 1585, when Shakespeare's twins were born, and 1592, when there is a first reference to him in London, there is no documentary evidence of his life. Traditional legends and anecdotes abound, but all is speculation. The period has been appropriately called the 'lost years'.

Acts and scenes

Shakespeare had encountered the division of a play into five acts in Latin dramatists (see p. 4), and his use of five Choruses in *Henry V* illustrates that he was well aware of the traditional structure. Eleven of the plays are printed in the First Folio divided into acts, and eighteen divided into both acts and scenes. However, six plays, though they open promisingly with 'Actus Primus – Scœna Prima', contain no further divisions: *Henry VI Part II*, *Henry VI Part III*, *Troilus and Cressida*, *Romeo and Juliet*, *Timon of Athens* and *Antony and Cleopatra*. In these plays, the only way we know a new scene begins is when the stage has been left empty. In *Hamlet*, the divisions stop after Act II Scene 2.

Modernizing

I don't really approve in my puritan soul of moving Shakespeare into a modern period in order to illuminate him. You merely illuminate some things and obscure others ... Shouldn't we now, if we want to do Shakespeare out of period, re-write it? It would be absurd, but at least it's logical. There is something pathetically stupid about Renaissance language in 1920s *Vienna.*   (Peter Hall, on a National Theatre production of *Measure for Measure*, Peter Hall's Diaries, 22 November 1973)

How many words did Shakespeare use?

It all depends what is meant by 'word'. If every instance of all words is counted, we get a total of 884,647 tokens for the whole canon, according to Martin Spevack's *Concordance*, based on the Riverside edition (excluding *King Edward III*, which would increase the total to 905,211). If we now group those tokens into types, we get 29,066 different words. But this total counts each variant form as a different word: so, for example, *take*, *takes*, *taking*, *took*, *taken*, *takest*, and so on would all be counted separately. When we ignore grammatical variations of this kind, the total is much lower, between 17,000 and 20,000 – the uncertainty depending on such factors as the edition used in the count, whether editorial emendations are included, whether proper names are counted, whether words are hyphenated or not, and whether 'phrasal verbs' such as *come in* and *go on* are tallied as one unit or two. Popular views abound that this was a huge vocabulary, and that Shakespeare used all the words in the language. In fact it was not exceptionally large, compared with that of other Jacobethan writers, and it was only about 12 per cent of the lexicon available in Elizabethan times. Shakespeare's enormously creative linguistic power resides not in the number of words he knew, but in how he used them. (See further, p. 169.)

Sixteenth-century theatres

There are only three extant theatre buildings in the world which were constructed in Shakespeare's lifetime:

- ❧ *c.*1581 Noh Theatre, Nishi-Honganji Temple, Kyoto, still in use
- ❧ 1585 Teatro Olympico, Vicenza, Italy, now used mainly as a concert hall
- ❧ 1590 Teatro all'Antica, Sabbioneta, now restored as a tourist venue

Two others were built soon after his death:

- ❧ 1618 Teatro Farnese, Parma, now reconstructed as a museum
- ❧ 1628 Corral de Comedias, Almagro, Spain, now a national monument

Shakespeare in comfort

It is nearly eleven and I have neither shaved nor dressed, just shuffled around in my old, frayed, blue towelling dressing-gown. It's comfortable and warm enough. Perhaps it is the right day to read a Shakespeare play with which I'm not familiar.

(Alec Guinness, *My Name Escapes Me*, 1996, p. 161)

Pirated editions

Pirated editions of plays were common in Shakespeare's time. One of the reasons Heminge and Condell give for compiling the First Folio was to set the literary record straight, as far as Shakespeare was concerned. They refer to the way readers have been 'abus'd with diuerse stolne, and surreptitious copies, maimed, and deformed by the frauds and stealthes of iniurious impostors, that expos'd them'. The maiming is reflected in the term now used to describe such texts: 'bad Quartos' – a term primarily used for the first quartos of *Romeo and Juliet* (1597), *Henry V* (1600), *The Merry Wives of Windsor* (1602) and *Hamlet* (1603).

The sources of bad quartos have been much debated. Some speeches are quite accurately reproduced; others are seriously distorted, heavily paraphrased, assigned to the wrong character, or omitted altogether. The usual explanation is that the texts were compiled from memory by hired actors who had performed in them, or from rival companies quickly scribbling in the audience.

Children

Shakespeare and Anne had three children, whose baptisms are recorded in the Stratford parish register:

> *Susanna, baptized 26 May 1583, died 1649*
> *Twins, Hamnet and Judith, baptized 2 February 1585: Hamnet died 1596, Judith died 1662*

They named the twins after their friends and neighbours, Hamnet and Judith Sadler – who reciprocated some years later, when they had a son, calling him William.

Sir John who?

In *Henry IV Part I* the character we now know as Sir John Falstaff was called Sir John Oldcastle. Oldcastle (Lord Cobham) was a fifteenth-century follower of John Wycliffe. He was put to death for his beliefs – a martyr, in Protestant tradition. As the Falstaffian portrait is not entirely flattering, a member of the Cobham family seems to have complained. The complaint was an effective one, for Shakespeare changed the name to Falstaff – a name he had previously used for a cowardly soldier in *Henry VI Part I*. It also moved him to write, in the epilogue to *Henry IV Part II*, that 'Oldcastle died a martyr, and this is not the man'.

Brave O'erhanging Firmament

The astronomer William Lassell discovered two Uranus satellites in 1851, and began the practice of naming the planet's satellites after characters in the work of Shakespeare or Alexander Pope. The nomenclature conventions set up by the International Astronomical Union in 1919 carried on the practice, which will continue as new satellites come to be discovered.

Name	Year discovered	Literary source
Titania	1787	A Midsummer Night's Dream
Oberon	1787	A Midsummer Night's Dream
Ariel	1851	The Rape of the Lock; also in The Tempest
Umbriel	1851	The Rape of the Lock
Miranda	1948	The Tempest
Puck	1985	A Midsummer Night's Dream
Cordelia	1986	King Lear
Ophelia	1986	Hamlet
Bianca	1986	The Taming of the Shrew
Cressida	1986	Troilus and Cressida
Desdemona	1986	Othello
Juliet	1986	Romeo and Juliet
Portia	1986	Julius Caesar; also in The Merchant of Venice
Rosalind	1986	As You Like It
Belinda	1986	The Rape of the Lock
Caliban	1997	The Tempest
Sycorax	1997	The Tempest
Prospero	1999	The Tempest
Setebos	1999	The Tempest
Stephano	1999	The Tempest
Trinculo	2001	The Tempest

One satellite originally photographed in 1986 (S/1986 U10), but whose existence was not confirmed until 2003, is as yet unnamed. Further satellites were discovered in 2003 using NASA's Hubble Space Telescope, bringing the total of known moons to twenty-seven. Expect more Shakespearian characters to appear in the firmament anon.

Sharing soliloquies

There are very few absolute rules with Shakespeare, but I personally believe that it's right ninety-nine times out of a hundred to share a soliloquy with the audience. I'm convinced it's a grave distortion of Shakespeare's intention to do it to oneself.

(John Barton, *Playing Shakespeare*, 1984, p. 94)

How much is a Folio worth?

The First Folio cost somewhere between 15 shillings (unbound) and £1 (bound in plain calf) – but how expensive was that, in 1623? In *The Shakespeare First Folio: The History of the Book*, Vol. 1 (2000), Anthony West makes it equivalent to forty-four loaves of bread. Using the same measure, we can see how the price goes up over the years. It had risen to 105 loaves in 1756, 900 in the 1790s, 5000 in the 1850s – and 96,000 by the beginning of the twentieth century. Today, the figures are astronomical. An edition sold at auction for over 6 million dollars in 2001. The cheapest loaf in our local superstore is 20 pence. That's (approximately) 17 million loaves. (And see p.189.)

A rare book dealer

Henry Stevens, one of the great nineteenth-century dealers in rare books, was heavily involved in buying and selling collections of Shakespeare Folios and Quartos for the bibliophile and philanthropist James Lenox. In one year, 1854–5, Stevens estimated spending more than $50,000 in making purchases for Lenox. In 1856 he secured the Baker copy for him for 156 guineas (the Baker folio is famous for bearing the printed date 1622, as well as containing two cancelled leaves from *As You Like It*). Stevens later sold Lenox thirty-nine quarto editions and the four earliest folios, in one transaction, for a total of £600. Wyman W. Parker's 1963 book *Henry Stevens of Vermont: American Rare Book Dealer in London 1845–1886* relates the sale details:

> Stevens invoiced the *Othello*, 1st edition, 1622, which he considered rare, at £75, while *The Merry Wives of Windsor*, 2nd edition, 1619, not being choice, was listed at 15 guineas.

False friends: mischief

MODERN SENSE: petty annoyance, vexatious behaviour
OBSOLETE SENSE: catastrophe, calamity
♣ Joan of Arc harangues her captors with 'mischief and despair / Drive you to break your necks' (*Henry VI Part I*, V.4.90).
OBSOLETE SENSE: wicked action, harmful scheme
♣ Romeo says 'O mischief, thou art swift / To enter in the thoughts of desperate men' (*Romeo and Juliet*, V.1.35).
OBSOLETE SENSE: disease, ailment
♣ Don John tells Conrade: 'thou ... goest about to apply a moral medicine to a mortifying mischief' (*Much Ado About Nothing*, I.3.12).

Soliloquies

Shakespeare did not know the word *soliloquy* – at least, not in the sense in which it is most often used today, as a dramatic stratagem which informs the audience of a character's thoughts or intentions. Famous examples include Hamlet's 'To be or not to be' speech and the opening speech in *Richard III* (the only example of a soliloquy beginning a play). Although the Latin word *soliloquium* had been known since the fourteenth century, the first recorded reference to it in English is in the first English dictionary, Robert Cawdrey's *Table Alphabeticall*. He did not include it in his first edition of 1604, but it is found in his third edition of 1613, where it is glossed as 'priuate talke'. This suggests that the word may have been coming into use in this general sense during Shakespeare's later years. But it did not have a literary application at that time: it would be another forty years before people began to use it in a literary context.

Globe 2

It cost £1400 to rebuild the Globe after the fire of 1613. And with what result? John Chamberlain wrote in a letter, 30 June 1614, 'the new Globe … is saide to be the fayrest that ever was in England'. It was pulled down on 15 April 1644 by the Puritans.

An early review

While studying at the Middle Temple, the lawyer and diarist John Manningham saw a performance of a Shakespeare play. There is no doubt which scenes stayed with him:

> At our feast we had a play called Twelfth Night, or What You Will, much like The Comedy of Errors, or Menaechmi in Plautus, but most like and near to that in Italian called Inganni. A good practice in it to make the steward believe his lady widow was in love with him, by counterfeiting a letter as from his lady in general terms, telling him what she liked best in him, and prescribing his gesture in smiling, his apparel, etc. And then when he came to practise making him believe they took him to be mad.

Modest thanks

> *Thank god for Philip Henslowe.*
> (Anthony Burgess, *Shakespeare*, 1994, p. 82)

Problem plays

In his book *Shakespeare and his Predecessors* (1896), the literary critic Frederick Boas described a group of four plays, written in the first few years of the 1600s, in which 'abnormal' conditions of mind arise and 'intricate cases of conscience' demand 'unprecedented methods of solution'. He was thinking of *All's Well That Ends Well*, *Hamlet*, *Measure for Measure* and *Troilus and Cressida*. They have also been described as a transitional group, falling between the earlier comedies and histories and the subsequent tragedies. In later discussion of these plays, the term 'problem comedies' was often used, thereby excluding *Hamlet* from the group. *Timon of Athens* is sometimes added to it. Some find such labels unpalatable. In the view of Levi Fox, director of the Shakespeare Birthplace Trust (1945–89), 'Shakespeare's plays are all problem plays.'

Murderers

There are only seven characters called 'Murderer' in the canon, although many more characters commit murder in the plays. An additional candidate is Demetrius, in *Titus Andronicus*, who dresses up as Murder along with his mother (as Revenge) and brother (as Rape).

Henry VI Part II	Murderer, First / Second
Macbeth	Murderer, First / Second / Third
Richard III	Murderer, First / Second

Unauthorized Sonnets?

Shakespeare's Sonnets appeared in 1609 in a quarto edition compiled by Thomas Thorpe. It is not known how long the poems had been in circulation. Some at least were known over a decade before, when sonnet cycles were fashionable. Francis Meres in 1598 talks of Shakespeare's 'sugred Sonnets among his private friends', and William Jaggard's poetic anthology *The Passionate Pilgrim* in 1599 contains versions of Sonnets 138 and 144. Thorpe's text was full of misprints, which led many people to think that Shakespeare had no hand in it. Whether the printed sequence reflects the author's intentions is a matter of speculation.

Surviving

There is such a lot of anal retention around Shakespeare. People are scared of sullying him. But he is better than that ... I think Shakespeare will survive, whatever I do.

(Jude Kelly, interview on her *Othello* production,
The Shakespeare Theatre, Washington, DC, 1997)

Before the RSC

The theatre in Stratford-upon-Avon now known as the Royal Shakespeare Theatre, managed by the Royal Shakespeare Company, has had a long and illustrious career. In the beginning, in 1879, it was known as the Shakespeare Memorial Theatre. From 1879 to 1885 short annual festivals were presented there by touring companies; from 1886 to 1918 the festival was presented by the Benson Company, led by the actor-manager Frank Benson; then from 1919 the annual programme developed into a longer season. Eight directors were involved before the RSC was established in 1960 under Peter Hall.

1919–34	William Bridges Adams
1934–42	Ben Iden-Payne
1943	Milton Rosmer
1944–6	Robert Atkins
1946–8	Barry Jackson
1948–52	Anthony Quayle
1952–7	Anthony Quayle and Glen Byam Shaw
1957–9	Glen Byam Shaw

Thou *or you*: *Beatrice to Benedick*

In *Much Ado About Nothing*, Benedick uses both *thou*-forms and *you*-forms to Beatrice, depending on the mood he is in. Beatrice, by contrast, always uses *you* to him – except in one speech. This is when she reflects on what she has overheard in the garden – the news that Benedick really loves her (III.1.111):

> … Benedick, love on; I will requite thee,
> Taming my wild heart to thy loving hand.
> If thou dost love, my kindness shall incite thee …

Thou is often used in speeches where characters talk to someone absent. But for Beatrice, perhaps, it is a rare moment where we see her letting her guard down.

Remembering Robeson

Paul Robeson was one of the first leading black actors to make a mark on British theatre when he played *Othello* at the Savoy Theatre in London in 1930. Peggy Ashcroft was his Desdemona. Robeson reprised the role in 1959 at the Shakespeare Memorial Theatre in Stratford-upon-Avon. Sam Wanamaker played Iago. It was the first Shakespeare play seen by the slightly older of the two authors of this Miscellany, who was studying the play for A-levels at the time.

Groundlings

In the Globe theatre, you could watch a play by standing in the yard that surrounded the thrust stage. It would only cost you a penny. In exchange for that penny you would get a close-up view of a whole play. But in addition to the actors and the atmosphere, you could get four other things.

- ♣ Wet, if it rained, because the yard was open to the heavens.
- ♣ A strong smell, because a lot of people were in a small space, a bath was a rarity, and calls of nature were answered using buckets, not lavatories.
- ♣ Fed, if you could afford it, because food and drink were on sale in the yard.
- ♣ Robbed, because pickpockets went to the theatre too.

If you want to be a groundling, you can have the experience at Shakespeare's Globe in London (or at other reconstructed Elizabethan theatres around the world). The smells and pickpockets are usually absent, but you can still buy food and drink, or – on those rare occasions when it rains in London – get wet (though plastic capes are on sale too).

Would cosseted modern theatre-goers stand for three hours to watch a play? At Globe performances, the yard is usually full. Mark Rylance's remark (p. 9) applies.

Palace of Varieties?

In the old days, the Globe Theatre was more like a Palace of Varieties. As you went in they gave you rotten fruit to throw at the actors, sort of audience participation, which they enjoyed.

That's why Shakespeare give 'em long speeches to do, so you could get yer eye in with yer fruit.

(From 'In Honour of Shakespeare', an oration given in 1974 in Southwark Cathedral by television star Alf Garnett – otherwise known as Warren Mitchell)

Short runs

During the early 1600s, plays began to be produced in short runs on consecutive days. The accident which caused the Globe to burn down in 1613 (p. 55) happened during the third performance of *All is True* (*Henry VIII*). One wonders what went wrong on that particular day.

Baseball groundlings

The groundlings are a new audience to the theatre. It's more like a baseball game now. You can drink beer and eat at the Globe. And if it's boring, you can come and go. It is not a lot different to a pub, where people stand and listen to stories — it is just that we're professional story-tellers. And there are lots of pretty girls and handsome boys, so even picking up is going on. When you're telling a love story on stage, you actually see people starting to kiss.

(Mark Rylance, *Sunday Mail*, 25 July 1999)

Personal scriptwriter

Mark Rylance plays Shakespeare like Shakespeare wrote it for him the night before.

(Widely quoted remark by Al Pacino)

Where to sit?

In the Globe, you had the choice of several places to watch and hear a play.

For a penny, you could stand in the yard around the stage, as a 'groundling'.

For twopence, you could sit on a wooden seat in a covered gallery set out in a semi-circle around the yard. There were three tiers of galleries.

For another penny, you could hire a cushion to make the seats a little more comfortable (despite the fleas).

For sixpence, you could sit in the Lords' Gallery at either side of the balcony at the back of the stage, which meant you were facing the audience, and looking down on the play from behind. Like the boxes of modern theatres, it was more for people who wanted to be seen rather than to see.

The options (but not the prices) are the same in the reconstructed Globe at Bankside in London.

Globes 1 and 2

How many people visited the first two Globes, between 1599 and 1644 (when the second Globe was pulled down)? Ten thousand? A hundred thousand? What kind of estimate would be given if it were known that the population of Britain in 1600 was only just over 4 million? Surprisingly, Barry Day, in his *This Wooden 'O'*, the story of Globe 3, estimates that some 15 *million* people probably saw a play during that forty-five-year period.

Rhythm Our auditory perception of regularity in the stream of speech: a pattern of recurring units of prominence.

English rhythm In English, the phonetic basis of rhythm is an alternating contrast between syllables which are perceived to be strong and syllables which are perceived to be weak. The former are called *accented* (or *stressed*) syllables; the latter are called *unaccented* (or *unstressed*) syllables.

Metre or *Meter* The rhythmical organization of lines of poetry, defined with reference to the number of rhythmical units allowed in a line and by the combinations of strong and weak syllables allowed within those units.

Verse Any text written in lines which have a metrical structure. The term contrasts with *prose*, where the lines have no predictable rhythmical length or structure, simply reflecting the rhythm of everyday speech.

Blank verse Verse which has a metrical structure but does not rhyme.

Foot A unit of rhythm within a metrical line. Lines can consist of any number of feet, but rarely more than six:

monometer	a line consisting of a single foot
dimeter	a line consisting of two feet
trimeter	a line consisting of three feet
tetrameter	a line consisting of four feet
pentameter	a line consisting of five feet
hexameter	a line consisting of six feet

In Shakespeare, most lines are pentameters.

Types of foot There are only so many ways in which strong and weak syllables can be combined to make a foot. Five types are most widely recognized in English verse, but it is not always easy to identify these units in a Shakespearian line, because of the many rhythmical variations found there.

Weak + Strong – the IAMB (an IAMBIC foot) – the commonest type in English, and the usual one in Shakespeare:

> Once <u>more</u> / un<u>to</u> / the <u>breach</u>, / dear <u>friends</u>, / once <u>more</u>, /

Strong + Weak – the TROCHEE (a TROCHAIC foot):

> <u>Where</u>fore / <u>art</u> thou / <u>Ro</u>meo?

Two Weak + one Strong – the ANAPAEST (an ANAPAESTIC foot), spelled ANAPEST in American English:

> *I am <u>dead</u>,* / Horatio …

One Strong + two Weak – the DACTYL (a DACTYLIC foot):

> <u>*See*</u> *what a* / grace was seated on this brow …

Two Strong – the SPONDEE (a SPONDAIC foot):

> <u>*On*</u>, <u>*on*</u>, / you noblest English …

Feminine ending Extra unaccented syllables at the end of an iambic or anapaestic line of poetry, often used in blank verse:

> My lord, as I was sewing in my clos<u>et</u>,

Caesura A rhythmical break in a line of verse, often in the middle:

> To be, or not to be – that is the question …
> Love? His affections do not that way tend …

End-stopped line A line of verse in which there is a natural pause, suggested by the meaning, at the end, usually indicated by punctuation:

> He took me by the wrist and held me hard.

Run-on lines A line of verse in which it would be unnatural to pause at the end of a line because the thought continues into the next line:

> Whether 'tis nobler in the mind to suffer
> The slings and arrows of outrageous fortune …

Stanza A division of a poem consisting of a series of lines separated from the rest of the poem by lines of white space above and below. In the Shakespearian narrative poems, the stanzas all have the same number of lines and a recurrent pattern of metre and rhyme. In *Venus and Adonis*, for example, each stanza consists of six lines, each in iambic pentameter, with rhymes linking lines 1 / 3, 2 / 4 and 5 / 6. Repeated letters are commonly used to show the rhyming pattern – in this case, *ababcc*. In everyday usage, the term *verse* is loosely used instead of stanza, but this conflicts with the more general meaning of *verse* given above.

Stanza lengths Stanzas typically run from two to eight lines:

couplet	2 lines	quintet	5 lines	septet	7 lines
tercet	3 lines	sestet	6 lines	octave	8 lines
quatrain	4 lines				

Sonnet A verse form consisting of fourteen lines of iambic pentameter. In the sonnet form that developed in England, the lines are grouped in three quatrains with six alternating rhymes, followed by a final rhymed couplet: *abab cdcd efef gg*.

Jargon

Everybody says, all the time, iambic pentameter, Shakespeare, iambic pentameter – what is that supposed to mean?

(Al Pacino, *Looking for Richard*, 1996)

Mentioning 'blank verse'

Shakespeare uses the term *blank verse* three times:

* ♣ Jaques says to Orlando, 'God buy you, an you talk in blank verse' (*As You Like It*, IV.1.28).
* ♣ Hamlet says, 'the lady shall say her mind freely, or the blank verse shall halt for't' (*Hamlet*, II.2.325).
* ♣ Benedick reflects on some classical names that 'run smoothly in the even road of a blank verse' (*Much Ado About Nothing*, V.2.34).

Iambic pentameters

This technical term for describing blank verse (see more on p. 50) emerged in English in the 1580s. Shakespeare and other authors introduced many variations into this basic pattern, which can be heard in the opening lines spoken by Henry before Agincourt (*Henry V*, III.1.1):

> Once more unto the breach, dear friends, once more,
> Or close the wall up with our English dead!

Blank verse

Blank verse was first used by Henry Howard, Earl of Surrey (1517–47), who was translating Virgil's *Aeneid* and, wanting to find a verse-form which would correspond to the Latin metre, looked to Italian sources for a model. The word *blank* was used because, in the late sixteenth century, one of its meanings was 'simple, unadorned'. 'Blank' verse thus meant the use of metrical verse without the adornment of rhyme. Surrey's publisher drew attention to this novelty on the title page, calling it a 'straunge metre', but within fifty years it was the usual measure of English dramatic and epic poetry, and it is Shakespeare's normal style.

Improv

You can't improvise this shit!

(Dustin Hoffman, on iambic pentameter, in rehearsals for *The Merchant of Venice*, directed by Peter Hall)

On Othello

*In many Shakespearian heroes there exists a companion fault, that of
self-deception. Macbeth does not suffer from this weakness, Othello
most certainly does. It is almost impossible to believe seriously that
any human being on entirely uncorroborated evidence, as flimsy as a
handkerchief embroidered with strawberries, could that same night
strangle his wife in her bed and afterwards in all sincerity, describe
himself as '... one not easily jealous'.*

(Laurence Olivier, *On Acting*, 1986, p. 210)

Propriety

*I met a Moor and asked him, when Othello comes off and says 'Oh my
fair warrior,' and kisses Desdemona three times in front of his army
and the Cypriots, where would he kiss her? And he said, 'On the fore-
head. It's symbolic, because he is kissing away all the lines that will
appear when she gets old. And when he kills her, he would kiss her on
the neck.' And he also said that Othello, as indicated, would never
take Iago by the throat; a Moorish person would never lose dignity in
that way.* (Robert Stephens, *Knight Errant*, 1996, p. 152)

An appropriate name?

Several names of Shakespearian characters seem to have been carefully
chosen (see p. 21). For example, Iago, in *Othello*, is the Spanish equivalent of James. Saint James (*Santiago*) was the Slayer of Moors. Iago is
never addressed by name in the tale by Giraldi Cinthio (1565) which
Shakespeare used as a source.

Keeping going

*I'm pretty sure I can get through the killing of Desdemona eight times
a week. Yes, I think we can do that ... But then, you see, I have
another 25 minutes of stage time after she's dead. All Desdemona has
to do at that point is lie in bed. There are stories of Desdemonas who
have actually fallen asleep and come to with a great start, wondering
where they were. But Othello goes on. I've got to keep the play going
for 25 more minutes!* (Patrick Stewart, *The Washington Post*,
12 November 1997)

This table shows the number of scenes in each play (excluding Prologues and Epilogues), according to modern editorial practice. Texts do occasionally differ in the number of scenes they recognize. History plays tend to be towards the top of the list, partly because several of their battles take place on stage.

42	Antony and Cleopatra	20	Henry IV Part II
29	Coriolanus	19	Richard II
28	Cymbeline	19	Henry IV Part I
28	Henry VI Part III	18	Twelfth Night
27	Henry VI Part I	18	Julius Caesar
26	Macbeth	17	Timon of Athens
26	King Lear	17	Measure for Measure
25	Richard III	17	Much Ado About Nothing
24	Troilus and Cressida	17	Henry VIII
24	Romeo and Juliet	16	King John
24	Henry VI Part II	16	King Edward III
23	The Two Noble Kinsmen	15	The Winter's Tale
23	The Merry Wives of Windsor	15	Othello
23	Henry V	14	Titus Andronicus
23	All's Well that Ends Well	12	The Taming of the Shrew
22	Pericles	11	The Comedy of Errors
22	Hamlet	9	The Tempest
22	As You Like It	9	A Midsummer Night's Dream
20	The Two Gentlemen of Verona	9	Love's Labour's Lost
20	The Merchant of Venice		

Balancing act

Speaking Shakespeare is like riding a bicycle or skating at the local ice rink – it suddenly happens.
(Peter Hall, *Shakespeare's Advice to the Players*, 2004, p. 13)

Junius Booth

Junius Booth (father of the great Shakespearian tragedian Edwin Booth and the presidential assassin John Wilkes Booth) was also a great actor of his time. He is said to have had a particularly eccentric nature, not to mention being something of an alcoholic. While playing the lead role in *Othello* one night, he prolonged his character's death scene for as long as he possibly could, before eventually jumping to his feet, and asking the audience 'Well, how did you like that?'

The Globe burns down

The first Globe burned down on 29 June 1613, during a performance of *Henry VIII*. This is how Sir Henry Wotton reported the event in a letter to his nephew, Sir Edmund Bacon (E. K.Chambers' transcription):

I will entertain you at the present with what has happened this week at the Bank's side. The King's players had a new play, called All is True, representing some principal pieces of the reign of Henry VIII, which was set forth with many extraordinary circumstances of pomp and majesty, even to the matting of the stage; the Knights of the Order with their Georges and garters, the Guards with their embroidered coats, and the like: sufficient in truth within a while to make greatness very familiar, if not ridiculous. Now, King Henry making a masque at the Cardinal Wolsey's house, and certain chambers [pieces of ordnance] *being shot off at his entry, some of the paper, or other stuff, wherewith one of them was stopped, did light on the thatch, where being thought at first but an idle smoke, and their eyes more attentive to the show, it kindled inwardly, and ran round like a train, consuming within less than a hour the whole house to the very grounds. This was the fatal period of that virtuous fabric, wherein yet nothing did perish but wood and straw, and a few forsaken cloaks; only one man had his breeches set on fire, that would perhaps have broiled him, if he had not by the benefit of a provident wit put it out with bottle ale.*

A new Globe was built within the year – with a tiled roof.

False friends: security

MODERN SENSE: safety; pledge

OBSOLETE SENSE: over-confidence, carelessness

♣ Scroop cautions Henry V against forgiving the drunken man who had been abusive about the king: 'That's mercy, but too much security' (*Henry V*, II.2.44).

♣ Artemidorus warns Caesar that 'security gives way to conspiracy' (*Julius Caesar*, II.3.6).

♣ Hecat advises her witches that 'you all know security / Is mortals' chiefest enemy' (*Macbeth*, III.5.32).

♣ Aumerle says to Richard, 'we are too remiss, / Whilst Bolingbroke through our security / Grows strong' (*Richard II*, III.2.34).

Saying 'I do'

Until the Marriage Act of 1753, people could enter into a binding marriage contract simply by exchanging words (or even gestures) of consent. But there was one constraint: the verb had to be in the present tense (in legal jargon, *verba de praesenti*), such as 'I take' or 'I do'. A future tense ('I will') wasn't enough. And this is why disguised Rosalind quibbles, when entering into a mock marriage with Orlando, in *As You Like It* (IV.1.112). Celia asks him: 'Will you, Orlando, have to wife this Rosalind?' and he replies 'I will.' 'Ay, but when?' intervenes Rosalind, perhaps anxious that such a marriage would not be binding. 'Why, now, as fast as she can marry us,' he replies. And Rosalind concludes: 'Then you must say "I take thee, Rosalind, for wife."' This he dutifully does, and she affirms the match – using the same tense.

False friends: quick

MODERN SENSE: rapid, swift

OBSOLETE SENSE: living, full of life

* Anne rejects the thought of marrying Dr Caius by saying 'I had rather be set quick i'th'earth, / And bowled to death with turnips' (*The Merry Wives of Windsor*, III.4.84).
* Laertes tells everyone to 'pile your dust upon the quick and dead', and Hamlet picks up the word when he compares his love of Ophelia to that of Laertes: 'Be buried quick with her, and so will I' (*Hamlet*, V.1.247, 275).

OBSOLETE SENSE: lively, animated, vivacious (often of someone's character)

* The Constable refers to the 'quick blood' of the French (*Henry V*, III.5.21).
* Brutus talks about Antony's 'quick spirit' (*Julius Caesar*, I.2.29) and Casca's 'quick mettle' (I.2.293); Nestor describes Cressida as 'a woman of quick sense' (*Troilus and Cressida*, IV.5.54).
* Emilia describes Arcite as having a 'quick sweetness' (*The Two Noble Kinsmen*, IV.2.13).

Heavy rep

The diary of theatre manager Philip Henslowe illustrates the heavy workload of the Elizabethan acting companies. In a 31-month period to January 1597, the Admiral's Men performed 63 different plays in 568 performances, 44 of them new productions. A new production was put on roughly once every three weeks.

Hill and Welles

In 1934 Orson Welles (aged nineteen and performing Romeo) together with his mentor Roger Hill (head of Todd School, Woodstock, Illinois), produced the book *Everybody's Shakespeare*. It included 'Three plays edited for reading and arranged for staging': *Twelfth Night, Julius Caesar* and *The Merchant of Venice*. In his introduction, Roger Hill wrote:

> *On Studying Shakespeare's Plays*
> *Don't!*
> *Read them. Enjoy them. Act them.*

Orson Welles explained later in the book why the best way to study Shakespeare's plays is by acting them:

> *This is because I think the theatre the pleasantest, speediest and safest way to that zealous and jealous love which most intelligent people, once exposed to him, must inevitably feel for Shakespeare.*

The demand for plays

Touring companies in Elizabethan England, then as now, needed only a very small repertoire of plays, because there would be a fresh audience at each port of call. But as soon as companies settled into permanent theatres, the situation changed. To maintain an audience day after day, there had to be variety. We know from the records of theatre manager Philip Henslowe that a play was rarely performed twice in one week, and that at one point twenty-three plays were being performed in repertory. This put huge pressure on the dramatists to write new plays, either alone or in groups. Collaboration was the norm: as many as five authors might cooperate in writing a play. Shakespeare is unusual in writing so many works alone; but even he collaborated (see p. 174).

Tricked

I think part of my interest began with having a bad experience with Shakespeare. I was made to read The Merchant of Venice *aloud in class. And it made no sense to me, it was like reading the telephone directory. About four years later, I worked with a different teacher, who said that the English theatre class we were about to take was going to concern itself solely with sex, adolescent sex, and gang violence. We were very interested in that. About half way though the lecture, he mentioned* Romeo and Juliet, *and we went 'Oh, nooo! We've been tricked!'*   (Kenneth Branagh, 'Making Love', *The Daily Telegiraffe*, on the making of *Love's Labour's Lost*)

Confusing twins

Twins provide a fruitful source of comedy in several plays: having been separated by some accident, each twin then causes confusion among the people they meet. Viola and Sebastian in *Twelfth Night* are so alike that they are described as 'an apple cleft in twain'. The plot of *The Comedy of Errors* is unique in using two pairs of twins – the two masters (both named Antipholus) and the two servants (both named Dromio).

False friends: revolting

MODERN SENSE: repulsive, disgusting

OBSOLETE SENSE (with people): rebellious, mutinous, insurgent

♣ Cardinal Pandulph describes King John as a 'revolting son' to his mother the Church (*King John*, III.1.257).

♣ The Lieutenant talks to Suffolk about 'the false revolting Normans' (*Henry VI Part II*, IV.1.87).

OBSOLETE SENSE (with objects): as above

♣ Bedford appeals to comets to 'scourge the bad revolting stars / That have consented unto Henry's death' (*Henry VI Part I*, I.1.4).

♣ Richard hopes that his tears will 'make a dearth in this revolting land' (*Richard II*, III.3.163).

Multiplying errors

Reprints of an Elizabethan book would usually be made from a copy of the previous edition, rather than the original manuscript, with the result that typesetting errors would increase with each copy. A long chain of reprints was possible. In the case of *Henry IV Part I* the first Quarto, called Q0, was followed by five reprints, Q1, Q2, Q3, Q4 and Q5, each one based on the one before. The text used in the First Folio was based on Q5.

Living with Shakespeare

I have lived with Shakespeare all my thinking life – the greatest dramatist of all time; to some the greatest poet, philosopher, man. With a flick of his pen he can twist an audience from laughter to tears. His genius is unparalleled. He writes roles that any actor worth his salt would find the means to play by hook or by crook. He is matchless in wit, power, imagination, fire, philosophy ... I could go on for ever. But what he has above all is a magical sense of theatre.

(Laurence Olivier, *On Acting*, 1986, p. 43)

The meaning of 'nothing'

At first sight, the title of *Much Ado About Nothing* seems misplaced. The plot turns on a vicious slander which leads to an apparent death. This is hardly 'nothing'. But the title may not be referring to this aspect of the plot. It is the story of Beatrice and Benedick which has always captured the imagination, and the play has often been informally referred to by their names. A famous title-changer was King Charles I, who took a copy of the Second Folio into imprisonment, and altered the title of this play to *Benedick and Beatrice*. Some therefore think that the title has to be interpreted with reference to the love-plot between the two main characters. *Nothing* was Elizabethan slang for female genitalia – Hamlet refers to Ophelia's use of the word as 'a fair thought – to lie between maids' legs' (*Hamlet*, III.2.127). Would that have been the allusion here?

The late plays

Four plays written between *c.*1608 and *c.*1612, alone or in collaboration, are often referred to as 'romances'.

Pericles
The Winter's Tale
Cymbeline
The Tempest

If the term is altered to 'last plays', *Henry VIII* and *The Two Noble Kinsmen* (1613–14) must be added to the list.

Varying names

Many Shakespearian names turn up in more than one form, usually because the alternatives suit different metres. Marc Antony is usually called *Antony* in *Antony and Cleopatra* (138 times), but he is called *Antonio* twice. In this extract (II.2.5), we see both forms used in quick succession, satisfying the demands of the iambic metre:

> Let Antony look over Caesar's head
> And speak as loud as Mars. By Jupiter,
> Were I the wearer of Antonio's beard,
> I would not shave 't today.

Similarly, in *Troilus and Cressida*, we might think that the heroine of the play is called *Cressida* – but when she is talked about, she is so named only thirteen times; she is usually referred to as *Cressid* (thirty-four times), a much easier name to fit the metre. Similarly, *Diomedes* is used twice, and *Diomed* thirty-three times. The alternative is not always a shortening. *Priam* turns up eighteen times, and *Priamus* twice.

False friends: ecstasy

MODERN SENSE: intense delight, rapture

OBSOLETE SENSE: any point on a scale of emotional intensity

❧ The weak end of the scale is illustrated in the description of Venus: 'Thus stands she in a trembling ecstasy' (*Venus*, 895), where it means little more than 'emotion' or 'feeling'.

❧ The middle of the scale is illustrated by the Courtesan's description of the increasingly confused and angry Antipholus of Ephesus: 'Mark how he trembles in his ecstasy' (*The Comedy of Errors*, IV.4.49), where it means 'mental fit' or 'frenzy'.

❧ The strong end of the scale is illustrated when Gertrude talks to Hamlet (*Hamlet*, III.4.139): 'This bodiless creation ecstasy / Is very cunning in' – to which Hamlet immediately replies: 'Ecstasy?' and denies it, making the strong sense perfectly clear: 'It is not madness that I have uttered'.

Dominating parts

Eleven characters speak more than a quarter of the lines in the play in which they appear. In some cases, the differential with the next speaking part is huge. Prospero has five times more lines than the next largest part, Caliban, and Henry V has four times more than Fluellen.

Play	Character	Number of lines	% of play
Hamlet	Hamlet	1506	39
Timon of Athens	Timon	850	36
Macbeth	Macbeth	716	34
Henry V	Henry	1031	32
Richard III	Richard	1151	32
The Tempest	Prospero	656	32
Measure for Measure	Duke	847	31
King Edward III	Edward	748	30
Titus Andronicus	Titus	711	28
Richard II	Richard	756	27
As You Like It	Rosalind	685	25

Long lines

Some plays make a great use of long lines – longer, that is, than the routine five-foot rhythm of the iambic pentameter (p. 50). There are over seventy six-foot lines ('alexandrines') in *Othello*, as seen in these two instances (II.3.47 and III.3.131).

As <u>my</u> young <u>mistress'</u> <u>dog</u>. Now <u>my</u> sick <u>fool</u> Rode<u>ri</u>go ...
As <u>thou</u> dost <u>ru</u><u>min</u>ate, and <u>give</u> thy <u>worst</u> of <u>thoughts</u> ...

The ten longest scenes

Number of lines	Number of words	Play
920	7137	Love's Labour's Lost, V.2
838	6856	The Winter's Tale, IV.4
602	4688	Hamlet, II.2
598	4677	King John, II.1
540	4198	Timon of Athens, IV.3
538	4278	Richard III, IV.4
536	4216	Measure for Measure, V.1
534	4402	Henry IV Part I, II.4
502	4076	The Tempest, I.2
498	3769	Titus Andronicus, I.1

Shakespeare praised

In *Palladis Tamia* (1598), Francis Meres includes Shakespeare in his lists of the best poets of the time:

> as one in whom 'the English tongue is mightily enriched, and gorgeously invested in rare ornaments and resplendent habiliments';
>
> for being one of 'the best lyric poets';
>
> for being one of 'our best [poets] for tragedy';
>
> for being one of 'the best [poets] for comedy';
>
> for being one of 'the most passionate among us to bewail and bemoan the perplexities of love'.

For more on *Palladis Tamia*, see p.143.

The ten shortest scenes

Number of lines	Number of words	Play
4	28	Antony and Cleopatra, III.9
4	33	The Merry Wives of Windsor, V.4
4	34	Antony and Cleopatra, IV.11
6	32	Antony and Cleopatra, III.8
6	45	Julius Caesar, V.2
6	46	Othello, III.2
7	44	Coriolanus, V.5
7	62	Coriolanus, I.7
9	68	Antony and Cleopatra, IV.10
9	69	Pericles, IV.5

Earliest manuscript

The earliest known manuscript of a Shakespeare play is a conflated and abridged version (to almost half the length) of the two parts of *Henry IV*. It is known as the Dering manuscript, as it was discovered in 1845 in the private library of the baronet Sir Edward Dering (1598–1644). It was written *c.*1613 and revised *c.*1623, probably for private performance. Two unidentified hands can be detected in the writing. The manuscript is now in the Folger Shakespeare Library.

The Master of the Revels

The Master of the Revels was an immensely powerful man. No play could be performed without his authorization. The aim was to ensure that the Court received the best possible entertainment from the array of companies and works brought forward for acceptance (although by 1606, he controlled the plays performed in the public theatres too). This is how a contemporary record describes the job:

> *the office resteth in skill of device, in understanding of historyes, in judgment of comedies, tragedies and showes, in sight of perspective and architecture, some smacke of geometry and other things; wherefore the best help is to make a good choice of cunnynge artificers severally, according to their best quality.*

Philostrate has a similar task to perform, in *A Midsummer Night's Dream* (V.1). From 1579 until 1610 the post was held by Edmund Tilney. It is possible to see him at work in the deleted lines in the manuscript of *Sir Thomas More* (p. 26).

Hall on Henry

Peter Hall, after watching Olivier's *Henry V* in 1977 'for the umpteenth time':

> *It's still beautifully shot; silly remark — it always will be. But I still dislike all the Elizabethan theatre scenes, so patronizing and bad. Why do we have to assume that our theatrical ancestors were crass, vulgar and untalented, particularly when they fostered and produced Shakespeare?*

> (*Peter Hall's Diaries*, 8 June 1977)

Magpie

Shakespeare was a magpie with the knack of the literary alchemist.
(Adrian Noble, *New York Times*, 23 April 2000)

No rest for the wicked

Terry [Hands] *... believes it is the play in which Shakespeare made all his mistakes. 'For a start he doesn't give Richard a rest. Macbeth has the England scene, Hamlet has all that Ophelia stuff, Lear's got the whole Edmund sub-plot, but Richard is on throughout. With the terrible physical strain, of course, of sustaining a crippled position all evening ... it's a little known historical fact, but apparently after the original production Burbage said to Shakespeare, 'If you ever do that to me again, mate, I'll kill you.'*

(Antony Sher on Richard III, in *Year of the King*, 1985, p. 42)

The return of Falstaff

The character of Falstaff was evidently a great success, for in the epilogue to *Henry IV Part II* Shakespeare promises to bring him back in *Henry V*:

our humble author will continue the story, with Sir John in it ...

However, there we hear only of Falstaff's death. There is a tradition that Queen Elizabeth herself asked Shakespeare to write a play about Falstaff in love, which resulted in *The Merry Wives of Windsor*. The story is first recorded in 1702 by the playwright John Dennis, who had written an adaptation of the Shakespeare play, and it is he who says that *Merry Wives* was written in fourteen days (or, in another place, ten days). According to the 1602 Quarto, the play was indeed performed before Elizabeth, but the other points are unsubstantiated.

The top ten speakers in Twelfth Night

343*	Sir Toby	220	Orsino
335	Viola	161	Sir Andrew
314	Olivia	149	Maria
306	Feste	124	Sebastian
281	Malvolio	113	Fabian

* These are the line totals in the New Penguin Shakespeare. Prose line totals vary greatly between editions.

Disputed divisions

Editors do not always agree on the way a play divides into acts and scenes. An example is *Cymbeline*. There are six scenes in Act 1 in the Oxford Shakespeare edition, whereas in the Arden Shakespeare there are seven.

How many words did Shakespeare invent?

The true figure will not be known until far more texts from the Elizabethan period come to be documented. For the present, we have to rely on the way the *Oxford English Dictionary* has recorded the first usages of words.

- ❧ There are 357 instances where Shakespeare is the only recorded user of a word in one or more of its senses (see p. 108).
- ❧ There are 1035 instances where Shakespeare is the first of several people using a word, in one or more senses, but the later usages do not occur until at least twenty-five years later, making it likely that he introduced the word (see p. 114).
- ❧ There are a further 642 instances where Shakespeare is the first of several people using a word, in one or more senses, but other usages of the word occur within twenty-five years, making it much less likely that he introduced it.

If all words are accepted as Shakespearian coinages, the total is 2034. However, only the first two categories are really strong candidates: 1392. About 800 of these have survived to the present day.

Anti-jigs

In 1612, the magistrates of Middlesex issued 'An Ordre for suppressinge of Jigges att the end of Playes' at the Fortune theatre:

> *by reason of certayne lewde Jigges songes and daunces used and accustomed at the playhouse called the Fortune in Gouldinglane, divers cutt-purses and other lewde and ill-disposed persons in greate multitudes doe resorte thither at th'end of everye playe, many tymes causing tumultes and outrages wherebye His Majesties peace is often broke and much mischiefe like to ensue thereby.*

Jigs also feature after plays in the modern Globe in London, but only as dances, and without the bawdry and mischief.

How many left?

Around 1000 copies of the First Folio were printed. Today, the number of surviving copies is thought to be 229, but the figure is debatable. Few copies are in perfect condition, and many are so damaged or dismembered that it is a decision whether to count them as a copy at all. The Folger Shakespeare Library in Washington owns seventy-nine copies. Undiscovered copies undoubtedly exist (see p.189).

An apprentice glover?

Did Shakespeare work in his father's shop, after he left school? John Shakespeare is identified several times in Stratford records as a glover – an important business, for gloves were fashionable status symbols – and there are many references to hides and skins in the plays. For instance, cheveril (kid-skin) was used for making the finer gloves because it was so soft and flexible. 'O, here's a wit of cheveril', says Mercutio, 'that stretches from an inch narrow to an ell broad' (*Romeo and Juliet*, II.4.82). And Feste comments in *Twelfth Night* (III.1.11): 'A sentence is but a cheveril glove to a good wit; how quickly the wrong side may be turned outward!' Scholars have been impressed by the technical character of such references, and many have seen behind them the training of an apprentice glover.

False friends: doubt

MODERN SENSE: be uncertain about, hesitate to believe
OBSOLETE SENSE: fear, be afraid

- ♣ A messenger approaches Macduff's wife to say 'I doubt some danger does approach you nearly' (*Macbeth* IV.2.67). He thinks that danger *is* approaching, not that it isn't.
- ♣ Hamlet says 'I doubt some foul play' (*Hamlet*, I.2.256). He thinks that there *has* been some foul play, not that there hasn't.

All the men and women merely players

The sign hung at the entrance to the original Globe theatre is said to have portrayed Hercules supporting the world on his shoulders, with the motto: *Totus mundus agit histrionem* (literally, 'the whole world presents an actor'). A free translation gives the opening line of Jaques' speech in *As You Like It* (II.7.140): 'All the world's a stage'.

On playing Henry V

I was intensely shy of a great deal of it, being influenced by the 1930s *dislike of all heroism, and I tried to find ways round the problem by playing against the declamatory style and undercutting it; it was hopeless, of course. I went to Ralph* [Richardson] *with the problem. 'I know he's a boring old scout-master on the face of it,' Ralph said, 'but being Shakespeare he's the exaltation of all scout-masters. He's the cold bath king, and you have to glory in it.'*

(Laurence Olivier, *On Acting*, 1986, p. 79)

Most frequent productions

What Shakespeare plays are most often performed? Tastes and budgets vary, around the world, but here is the top ten, from 1879 to the end of 2004, produced by the Shakespeare Memorial Theatre and (in its later incarnation) the Royal Shakespeare Company. The list, taken from the Shakespeare's Birthplace Trust online archive (www.shakespeare.org.uk), includes transfers, rehearsed readings, regional tours and world tours. It is interesting to note there are no history plays in the top ten:

Hamlet	82
Twelfth Night	81
As You Like It	80
The Taming of the Shrew	79
A Midsummer Night's Dream	77
Much Ado About Nothing	76
The Merchant of Venice	75
Macbeth	64
The Merry Wives of Windsor	66
Romeo and Juliet	61

And the others?

Richard III	54
Julius Caesar	54
Henry V	51
Richard II	49
King Lear	46
Othello	45
The Tempest	45
The Winter's Tale	41
Measure for Measure	36
The Comedy of Errors	32
Coriolanus	30
Antony and Cleopatra	30
Henry IV Part II	28
Henry IV Part I	26
Cymbeline	25
Love's Labour's Lost	25
Troilus and Cressida	24
The Two Gentlemen of Verona	23
All's Well that Ends Well	21
King John	20
Henry VIII	17
Henry VI Part I	14
Pericles	13
Titus Andronicus	12
Timon of Athens	11
Henry VI Part II	10
Henry VI Part III	9
King Edward III	7
The Two Noble Kinsmen	4

Dating Henry V

The Chorus to Act V of *Henry V* contains a topical reference which allows us to date the play's composition with some precision:

> Were now the General of our gracious Empress —
> As in good time he may — from Ireland coming,
> Bringing rebellion broached on his sword,
> How many would the peaceful city quit
> To welcome him!

The general has to be the Earl of Essex, sent by Elizabeth to Ireland on 27 March 1599 to subdue the rebels, following the massive English defeat at Yellow Ford in August 1598. However, the expedition was a failure, and Essex returned in disgrace on 28 September. The passage would have made no sense after the news of the failure became public, and problems had been anticipated long before September. So the play was very likely written — allowing for 'in good time' — in the first half of 1599.

False friends: mutiny

MODERN SENSE: refusal to obey military superiors

OBSOLETE SENSE: riot, state of discord, civil disturbance

♣ The opposed families in *Romeo and Juliet* 'From ancient grudge break to new mutiny' (Prologue.3).

OBSOLETE SENSE (metaphorical): rebellion, quarrel

♣ King Henry says of Cardinal Wolsey 'There is a mutiny in's mind' (*Henry VIII*, III.2.120).

Shaxberd plays at Court

The King's Men played at Court on 160 occasions between 1603 and the end of 1615. The Master of the Revels lists several of Shakespeare's plays as being performed 'by his Ma^tis [majesty's] plaiers' over the Christmas season in 1604–5:

Othello (1 November)
The Merry Wives of Windsor (4 November)
Measure for Measure (26 December)
The Comedy of Errors (28 December)
Henry V (7 January)
The Merchant of Venice (twice, on 10 and 12 February)

Occasionally, the Master of the Revels lists in the right-hand column of his records 'The poets who mayd the plaies'. Shakespeare is named several times — but in an unusual spelling: Shaxberd.

Brooke or Broome?

In *The Merry Wives of Windsor*, the jealous husband of Mistress Ford disguises himself as 'Master Brooke', to gain evidence of Falstaff's wrongdoing. But in the First Folio, the name is altered to Broome – despite the change destroying some of the puns in the play. On being told by Bardolph that a 'Master Broome below would fain speak with you', Falstaff ripostes (II.2.147):

> such Broomes are welcome to mee, that ore'flowes such liquor.

Only brooks can overflow. The wordplay does not work with 'Broome'. So why was the name changed? Very likely the company remembered the Oldcastle incident (p. 42), when someone – probably Lord Cobham – objected to the name of his ancestor being presented as a buffoon in *Henry IV Part I*, and caused it to be changed to Falstaff. The Cobham family name was Brooke.

Being heard

One encouraging thing I learned from our tour of the Globe is that the plaster used around the walls is mixed with goat hair. Many of our grand old provincial theatres have horsehair under their gilded decoration and this (or so I was told years ago) gives exactly the right resonance to the human voice. Walk on to the stage of any of those big old theatres and you know at once that you are going to be heard with very little effort. (Alec Guinness,
My Name Escapes Me, 1996, p. 53)

In praise of Henry

Henry VI Part I was evidently a very popular play – if we can judge from a reference to one of its characters by Thomas Nashe in *Pierce Pennilesse* (1592):

> *How would it have joyed brave Talbot (the terror of the French) to thinke that after he had lyne two hundred yeares in his Tombe, hee should triumphe againe on the Stage, and have his bones newe embalmed with the teares of ten thousand spectators at least (at severall times), who, in the Tragedian that represents his person, imagine they behold him fresh bleeding.*

The audience total Nashe had in mind is unclear, but with the largest theatres allowing an attendance of up to 3000, it suggests many successful performances.

Garrick's role

This book – along with several thousand others – would probably not have been written, were it not for the actor David Garrick (1717–79). Until 1769, Shakespeare achieved little national prominence; his standing was not recognized even in his home town. Garrick turned the tide and made Shakespeare famous in Stratford by beginning an annual jubilee in his honour. The first year's celebrations did not go well, but it would be fair to say it started something of a trend.

Bawds and players

The word *bawd* is found in thirteen of the plays and two of the poems. A character in *Pericles* is actually called Bawd. Seventeen of the forty-one uses of the word are in a single play, *Measure for Measure*, which deals with the nature of immorality, the banning of brothels and the use of double standards. The play is set in Vienna, but the sexual situation could just as easily have been contemporary London. Research data would not have been hard to come by. Theatre manager Philip Henslowe and his son-in-law/actor Edward Alleyn were both in the brothel-owning business.

Hate away

Shakespearian sonnets usually have a predictable structure – fourteen lines of ten syllables, iambic pentameter, three *abab* quatrains, a final rhyming couplet. But not Sonnet 145, which is in eight-syllable lines. Sonnet performer Will Sutton thinks it is best performed as a present-day rap.

Some think that the final couplet is a punning reference to his wife, Anne Hathaway (= 'hate away'):

> 'I hate' from 'hate' away she threw,
> And saved my life, saying 'not you'.

The words were pronounced more alike then than they are now. The *th* sound in the middle of a proper name could have been pronounced as *t*, and the vowel of *hate* would have been more like present-day *het*. Moreover, the *d* of *and* was often not pronounced (it is often written *an'* in contemporary texts), suggesting a second pun on *Anne*.

Thinking about Hamlet

I have never ceased to think about Hamlet at odd moments.
(Laurence Olivier, *On Acting*, 1986, p. 79)

The dark lady

The woman addressed in many of Shakespeare's sonnets, especially from Sonnet 127 onwards, has been called 'the dark lady' because of the repeated references to her colouring and character:

- ♣ In the old age black was not counted fair … (127.1)
- ♣ Therefore my mistress' eyes are raven black (127.9)
- ♣ If snow be white, why then her breasts are dun;
  If hairs be wires, black wires grow on her head (130.3–4)
- ♣ In nothing art thou black save in thy deeds (131.13)
- ♣ Then will I swear beauty herself is black,
  And all they foul that thy complexion lack (132.13–14)

No woman has been identified, but several have been proposed, notably:

- ♣ Mary Fitton, a lady-in-waiting at Queen Elizabeth's court
- ♣ Emilia Bassano Lanier, the daughter of a court musician from Venice, and the mistress of Henry Carey, Lord Hunsdon, Shakespeare's company patron
- ♣ Lucy Morgan, abbess of Clerkenwell and a courtesan
- ♣ The wife of John Davenant, vintner at the Crown Tavern, Oxford, whose son William claimed to be Shakespeare's illegitimate son
- ♣ The wife of John Florio, Italian secretary to the Earl of Southampton

There is also the possibility that the lady could have been a literary creation, a composite.

Kinda difficult

But you're not going to come to me if you want to do Shakespeare. I'm not really interested in Shakespeare. I'm interested in the absolute naturalness of movies and to do that in iambic pentameter is kinda difficult.   (Michael Caine, *indieLondon* interview, 2003)

The Roman plays

This is the name given to the four plays set in or around classical Rome:

Antony and Cleopatra	Coriolanus
Titus Andronicus	Julius Caesar

Roman history is also a part of *Cymbeline*. Shakespeare obtained his plots, and often his descriptive detail, from Plutarch's *Lives of the Noble Grecians and Romans*, as translated by Sir Thomas North from a French original in 1579.

Break a leg

It is bad luck, in the theatrical world, to wish an actor 'good luck' before a performance. It has become customary to say 'break a leg'. The origin of this blessing is unknown, but some have attributed it to David Garrick's first breakthrough role, Richard III. It has been said that during one performance he was so involved in playing the famous crookback he didn't notice he had suffered a fracture.

Anne Shakespeare

The tourist popularity of the name Anne Hathaway makes us forget that for most of her life she was actually Anne Shakespeare. The name occurs just once – in the will of the Hathaway family shepherd, Thomas Whittington, dated 25 March 1601:

> *I geve & bequeth unto the poore people of Stratford xl^s* [40 shillings] *that is in the hand of Anne Shaxpere Wyf unto m^r Wyllyam Shaxspere ...*

Theatre expires, Globe rises

In the mid-1590s the Chamberlain's Men performed in public chiefly at the Theatre, which had been leased from Giles Allen by James Burbage until 1597. When the lease ran out, Allen – a puritan, and no lover of plays – increased the rent by 60 per cent and made unacceptable demands on the company, which therefore moved to the nearby Curtain, leaving the Theatre empty. After James's death in 1597, his sons Cuthbert and Richard continued the negotiations, but when they learned that Allen was planning to tear the Theatre down and put the materials 'to some better use', they made their own plans. A clause in their old lease gave them permission to dismantle the building. While Allen was out of town, a team of carpenters arrived at the Theatre one night, dismantled it and carried it across the Thames to build a new playhouse – the Globe. Allen complained furiously about the 'outragious' behaviour of the 'ryotous persons' to the Star Chamber in 1601, and sued repeatedly for damages, but to no avail.

Adlibs

Adlibbing is difficult enough in a modern play but to succeed with it in Shakespeare requires a touch of genius.

(John Mills, *Up in the Clouds, Gentlemen Please*, 1980, p. 100)

The middle 'e'

All five versions of Shakespeare's signature have one thing in common: they have no middle 'e'. The familiar form, Shakespeare, first appears in print in the 1593 letter of dedication which preceded his first published work, the poem *Venus and Adonis*; and printers thereafter generally retained it. Why? A likely reason is the nature of Elizabethan typesetting practice. Adding extra symbols was a way of separating pieces of type which would otherwise be awkwardly juxtaposed. A noticeable feature of printed works at the time was the way some letters had long curling ascenders or descenders. Two of these, side by side, would often clash, and this would have been the case when a *k* with a long curling right-hand leg came up against the left-curling foot of the Elizabethan 'long s'. We can see an instance of the problem below in the memorial by I.M. at the beginning of the Folio, where Shakespeare's name is printed in italics, and both a letter e and a hyphen are needed to keep the descenders apart. We have the printers to thank, it seems, for the name that has come down to us.

To the memorie of M. *W*.Shake-speare.

Marriage

There is no documentary evidence of Shakespeare between his baptism and his marriage. According to the Episcopal Register of the Diocese of Worcester, a marriage is recorded 'inter Willelmum Shaxpere et Annam Whateley de Temple Grafton' – between William Shakespeare and Anne Whateley of Temple Grafton. The date is 27 November 1582. The clerk is known to have made other mistakes in his Register entries that day, and as another of his cases involved a William Whateley, a 'slip of the brain' can explain the confusion over the surname. But the reference to Temple Grafton has remained a puzzle, for Anne Hathaway came from Stratford. The marriage bond, which was drawn up the following day, has the names correct: 'William Shagspere ... and Anne Hathwey of Stratford'.

Ending well?

I've always said this play should be called All's Well that Ends Well? *– with a question mark.*

(Royal Shakespeare Company director, Gregory Doran, RSC Website)

False friends: naughty

MODERN SENSE: badly behaved [of children], improper [playfully, of adults], sexually suggestive [of objects, words, etc.]

OBSOLETE SENSE: wicked, evil, vile

❧ Said of people, as when Gloucester describes Regan as a 'naughty lady' (*King Lear*, III.7.37) or Falstaff (pretending to be King Henry) calls Hal a 'naughty varlet' (*Henry IV Part I*, II.4.420).

❧ Said of concepts, such as the world, the times and the earth – as in Portia's description of a candle flame in the darkness: 'So shines a good deed in a naughty world' (*The Merchant of Venice*, V.1.91).

❧ Said of sexual situations, where there is always a note of real moral impropriety, as in Elbow's description of Mistress Overdone's abode as 'a naughty house' (*Measure for Measure*, II.1.74).

False friends: nice

MODERN SENSE: agreeable, pleasant

OBSOLETE SENSE: lustful

❧ Mote talks of 'nice wenches' in *Love's Labour's Lost* (III.1.21).

OBSOLETE SENSE: foolish

❧ Sick Northumberland shouts at his 'nice crutch' as he throws it down (*Henry IV Part II*, I.1.145).

OBSOLETE SENSE: fastidious

❧ Henry talks to Katherine about 'the nice fashion of your country' (*Henry V*, V.2.270).

OBSOLETE SENSE: uncertain

❧ Hotspur talks about a 'nice hazard' (*Henry IV Part I*, IV.1.48).

OBSOLETE SENSE: trivial

❧ Benvolio describes the quarrel between Romeo and Tybalt as 'nice' (*Romeo and Juliet*, III.1.154).

OBSOLETE SENSE: minutely detailed

❧ The narrator in *The Rape of Lucrece* talks about the ability of a painter as 'nice' (l.1412).

OBSOLETE SENSE: subtle

❧ Richard accuses Edward of standing 'on nice points' (*Henry VI Part III*, IV.7.58).

OBSOLETE SENSE: skilful

❧ Leonato talks about Claudio's 'nice fence' (i.e. fencing ability, in *Much Ado About Nothing*, V.1.75).

The one thing the word never means is just 'I like it'.

The least female

Timon of Athens is the play with the fewest female lines – eleven, given to the two camp-followers, Phrynia and Timandra. *As You Like It* has the most – nearly 40 per cent of the play. (See the complete list on p. 99.)

Ending with -eth or -s?

In the sixteenth century, there were two endings in the present tense of verbs where today we have only one: *-th* and *-s*, as in *readeth* and *reads*. The *-th* form was dying out, though it was still routine in *doth* and *hath*; but with most verbs there was still a choice. So, what would lead Shakespeare to choose one form rather than the other? One factor is that *-s* seems to have conveyed a more colloquial tone (it is the normal form in prose), whereas *-th* was more formal (it is often used in the 'official' language of stage directions). But that explanation will not do for the many cases in the poetry, where we find both endings. The choice there seems to depend on the way the *-th* ending often provides a useful extra syllable to make up the metre of a line. In this example from *Henry VI Part II* (II.4.52), both endings are used with the same verb.

> For Suffolk, he that can do all in all
> With her that hateth thee and hates us all …

Only the sequence of *hateth* followed by *hates* preserves the regular rhythmical beat; the alternative order would not work.

Hoo!

I saw a great drunken one, it was Wilfred Lawson and Trevor Howard and they were bombed in a Shakespeare matinee, and it got very bad with the lines, and someone shouted out, 'You're pissed!' and one of them said, 'If you think I'm pissed wait until you see the Duke of Norfolk. (Michael Caine, interview for *Phase 9 Movies*, 28 September 2004)

Sequels

Sequels are written to continue a story, typically because of popular demand. Unless we view the history cycle of plays as a 'series of sequels', the only Shakespearian sequel is *The Merry Wives of Windsor*, written to keep the character of Falstaff alive. But John Fletcher wrote a sequel to *The Taming of the Shrew*, in which Petruchio is humbled by his second wife, Maria: *The Tamer Tamed*. These two plays were performed together in Gregory Doran's 'Jacobethan' series in Stratford in 2002.

Daniel Day-Lewis

In 1989 Daniel Day-Lewis, renowned for his method approach to acting, went to the Royal National Theatre to play Hamlet, but walked off stage, half-way through a performance, unable to continue. Myths abounded – especially that he was so 'in' the role that he saw his dead father's ghost. Day-Lewis later recounted:

I had a very vivid, almost hallucinatory moment in which I was engaged in a dialogue with my father … yes, but that wasn't the reason I had to leave the stage. I had to leave the stage because I was an empty vessel. I had nothing in me, nothing to say, nothing to give. I depleted myself to the point where I had nothing left.

In Ian Holm's *Acting My Life*, Day-Lewis's director, Sir Richard Eyre, concurred:

Dan's problem wasn't really with the ghost or the ghost of his father, but with everything else the play deals with … Mothers, fathers, suicide, death, love … you know, everything. Hamlet touches on the lot, and I think Dan was knocked out by it all. He battled with the issues until they just overwhelmed him.

Distractions

When Richard Burton gave his Hamlet in Toronto it wasn't at the [Royal Alexandra Theatre] but at the vast O'Keefe Centre. The opening coincided with a Big Fight – I can't remember who was thumping whom. There was electricity in the air; the theatre fairly crackled with an extraordinary sound, which turned out to be about 2000 of the male members of audience glued to the fight on their transistor radios with their eyes politely turned towards the stage: their spouses had their heads turned away from Hamlet, their eyes fixed on Elizabeth Taylor, who was sitting among them, glittering in real emeralds and green glass beads. (Alec Guinness,
My Name Escapes Me, 1996, p. 68)

Melancholy humours

People sometimes say that actors give us their own Hamlets, and not Shakespeare's … In point of fact, there is no such thing as Shakespeare's [Hamlet]. If Hamlet has something of the definiteness of a work of art, he has also all the obscurity that belongs to life. There are as many Hamlets as there are melancholies.

(Oscar Wilde, *The Critic As Artist*, 1891)

Send in the Clowns

There are twelve characters named 'clown' in Shakespeare: six in the Comedies, six in the Tragedies. There are none so named in the Histories. The 'mechanicals' are also referred to as clowns in the stage direction at the beginning of Act III Scene 1 of *A Midsummer Night's Dream*.

Play	Name	First Entrance
All's Well that Ends Well	Clown [Lavatch]	I.3.1
Antony and Cleopatra	Clown	V.2.241
As You Like It	Clown [Touchstone]	I.2.42
Hamlet	Clown, First [Gravedigger]	V.1.1
	Clown, Second [Gravedigger]	V.1.1
Measure for Measure	Clown [Pompey]	I.2.84
The Merchant of Venice	Clown [Launcelot Gobbo]	II.2.1
Othello	Clown	III.1.3
Romeo and Juliet	Clown	I.2.1
Titus Andronicus	Clown	IV.3.77
Twelfth Night	Clown [Feste]	I.4.1
The Winter's Tale	Clown	III.3.77

Unplayable?

In Nigel Hawthorne's autobiography, there is a wry comment about a Shakespearian character:

> *Touchstone in* As You Like It *is just about unplayable ... The trouble is that the lines are little or no help, laced as they are with jokes which may have had them rolling in the aisles in Shakespeare's Day, but now fall flatter than pancakes on Shrove Tuesday.* (*Straight Face* (2002), p. 229.)

Shakespeare's original clowns

Shakespeare seems to have written parts specifically for his clown-actors. William Kemp was the Chamberlain's (and so Shakespeare's main) clown between 1594 and 1599. He played Dogberry in *Much Ado About Nothing*, the often-cut Peter in *Romeo and Juliet*, and possibly Costard in *Love's Labour's Lost* and Falstaff in *Henry IV Part I* and *II* (though John Lowin and Thomas Pope have also been suggested).

Robert Armin took over from Kemp in 1599, and was the first Touchstone, Feste, Lavatch, Thersites and Fool (in *As You Like It*, *Twelfth Night*, *All's Well that Ends Well*, *Troilus and Cressida* and *King Lear*, respectively).

The 1564 plague

The plague reached Stratford in July 1564. Alongside a burial entry for
11 July in Stratford Parish Register we read *hic incepit pestis* – here the
plague began. It killed some 200 people before abating towards the end
of that year. Roger Green in Henley Street lost four of his children.
Many a bardolator has reflected on the fortune that the disease did not
carry off the newest member of the Shakespeare household, further
along the same street.

Humours

Several Shakespearian characters are described in terms of 'humours' –
the combination of fluids within the body which governed a person's
physical and mental disposition. Four humours were recognized, and
good health was thought to come from having these in balance.
However, characters often display the predominance of one or the other,
and their actions are interpreted accordingly. 'You are altogether governed by humours', complains Lady Percy of her hot-headed husband
(*Henry IV Part I*, III.1.228).

Humour	Typical disposition	Seen in character	Example
blood	optimistic, passionate, amorous, courageous	Hotspur (as described by his wife)	In military rules, humours of blood, / He was the mark and glass, copy and book, / That fashioned others (*Henry IV Part II*, II.3.30)
phlegm	dull, indifferent, indolent, idle, apathetic	Falstaff and his companions (as described by Prince Hal)	I know you all, and will awhile uphold / The unyoked humour of your idleness (*Henry IV Part I*, I.2.194)
choler (or yellow bile)	angry, irascible, bad-tempered	Cassius (as described by Brutus)	Go show your slaves how choleric you are ... Must I stand and crouch / Under your testy humour? (*Julius Caesar*, IV.3.43)
melancholy (or black bile, black choler)	sad, gloomy, sullen, depressed	Jaques (as described by Rosalind)	They say you are a melancholy fellow. JAQUES: I am so: I do love it better than laughing (*As You Like It*, IV.1.3)

═══ Thou *or* you: *Polonius and his children* ═══

In *Hamlet*, when Polonius talks to his children, we would expect him to use *thou*-forms, and for them to use *you*-forms in return. In fact he varies, depending on the topic of the conversation.

❧ Talking to Laertes (I.3.55), he begins with *you*, suiting the business-like nature of his greeting, then switches to *thou*, when he starts offering intimate advice:

> The wind sits in the shoulder of your sail,
> And you are stayed for. There – my blessing with thee ...

He changes back to *you* when he finishes:

> My blessing season this in thee! ...
> The time invites you. Go. Your servants tend.

❧ Talking to Ophelia, he uses *you*, suiting his tone of serious advice. But there are two exceptions.

  ❧ In II.1.85 he replies to her report of the distracted Hamlet coming before her by saying 'Mad for thy love?' Perhaps it is the forceful implication of intimacy which prompts the use of *thy*, or perhaps it is because he is imagining the situation in which Ophelia has found herself. (*Thou*-forms are regularly used when people talk to those who are absent.)

  ❧ In II.2.141 he tells Claudius what he said to Ophelia: 'Lord Hamlet is a prince, out of thy star'. Polonius would have said 'out of your star' at the time, but when he recalls the moment, the pronoun changes to the *thy* of imaginary intimacy.

═══════ *Reputation* ═══════

In 1598, Francis Meres published a review of the contemporary literary scene, *Palladis Tamia*, in which he refers to Shakespeare as a dramatist comparable to the great classical writers Plautus and Seneca, and sees in his poetry a reincarnation of Ovid. Shakespeare's literary reputation was consolidated when anthologies began to appear containing excerpts from his work. Many extracts appear in three collections all published in 1600 – John Flasket's *England's Helicon*, John Bodenham's *Belvedere or The Garden of the Muses*, and Robert Allot's *England's Parnassus*, whose subtitle was 'The Choysest Flowers of our Moderne poets'.

═══════ *That* thing ═══════

For Americans, what is that, that thing that gets between us and Shakespeare, that makes some of our best actors just stop when it comes to Shakespeare? (Al Pacino, *Looking for Richard*, 1996)

False friends

False friends ('*faux amis*') are words in one language which look the same as words in another. We therefore think that their meanings are the same, and get a shock when we find they are not. Generations of French students have believed that *demander* means 'demand' (whereas it means 'ask') or *librairie* means 'library' (instead of 'bookshop'). It is a sign of a mature understanding of a language when one can cope with the false friends, which can be some of its most frequently used words. Having a good grasp of the false friends is a crucial part of 'learning to speak French' – and the same applies to Early Modern English. Shakespeare has false friends, too. Some sixteenth-century words may look the same as their Modern English equivalent, but their meaning may have radically changed. *Naughty* doesn't mean 'naughty'. *Revolve* doesn't mean 'revolve'. *Ecstasy* doesn't mean 'ecstasy'. Some of these words occur so often in the plays and poems that they can be a regular source of misunderstanding. This book contains some of the most important ones (see Index).

False friends: lover

MODERN SENSE: someone with whom one has an (often illicit) sexual relationship
OBSOLETE SENSE: companion, comrade, dear friend

♣ Menenius refers to Coriolanus as 'my lover' (*Coriolanus*, V.2.14).
♣ Ulysses says to Achilles 'I as your lover speak' (*Troilus and Cressida*, III.3.214).
♣ Brutus harangues the crowd with 'Romans, countrymen, and lovers, hear me for my cause' (*Julius Caesar*, III.2.13).

False friends: gale

MODERN SENSE: storm, tempest
OBSOLETE SENSE: wind (without any connotation of severity or danger); breeze

♣ Gales can be 'merry' (in *King Edward III*, III.1.77), 'happy' (*The Taming of the Shrew*, I.2.47) and 'auspicious' (*The Tempest*, V.1.315).
♣ In *Henry VI Part III*, King Edward has been worrying about the 'black cloud' of the enemy. 'A little gale will soon disperse that cloud', says his brother George to him (V.3.10). The concept of a 'little gale' seems paradoxical, until we remember the milder meaning of the word.

Change of hands

Playwrights had little control over their works once they were finished. Copyright, as we know it today, did not exist. When a play was ready, the author would sell it to a company (prices varied, but £5 or £6 per play was normal) and the work would become the actors' joint property. The company would then cut the play as it saw fit, often to keep its duration or costs down, then send it to the Master of Revels for a licence. There was a reluctance to have plays printed, for then another company could steal them; and those which *were* printed rarely had an author involved (a famous exception is Ben Jonson, who carefully supervised his *Works* in 1616). There is no record of Shakespeare being involved in the publication of any of his plays.

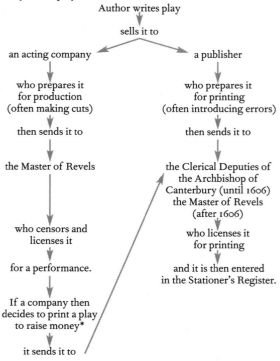

Author writes play

sells it to

an acting company ⟵⟶ a publisher

who prepares it
for production
(often making cuts)

who prepares it
for printing
(often introducing errors)

then sends it to

then sends it to

the Master of Revels

the Clerical Deputies of
the Archbishop of
Canterbury (until 1606)
the Master of Revels
(after 1606)

who censors and
licenses it

who licenses it
for printing

for a performance.

and it is then entered
in the Stationer's Register.

If a company then
decides to print a play
to raise money*

it sends it to

*Some Quartos of Shakespeare's plays were published in 1593–4, when the theatres were closed due to plague; and four more were published in 1600, probably to raise money for the Globe project.

Retrieving your own play

Once a playwright had sold a play to an acting company, he would have a hard time getting it back. This was evidently Thomas Middleton's experience, who refers to the problem in 1624, when he dedicates his play *The Witch* (written originally *c*.1615) to Thomas Holmes:

> *As a true testimony of my ready inclination to your service, I have, merely upon a taste of your desire, recovered into my hands, though not without much difficulty, this ignorantly ill-fated labour of mine.*

Shakespeare would have had the same problem.

Shakespeare abroad

European translations of Shakespeare play-titles are usually transparent to speakers of English with a modicum of European language learning:

> *La Comedia degli Equivoci* (Italian)
> *Songe d'une Nuit d'Été* (French)
> *Ein Sommernachtsraum* (German)
> *Die Lustigen Weiber von Windsor* (German)
> *Sogno di una Notte d'Estate* (Italian)
> *Racconto d'Inverno* (Italian)
> *Conte d'Hiver* (French)

Occasionally, the conventions of a different alphabet or transliteration get in the way, as in Italian *Amleto* or Russian *Gamlet*. And sometimes, there is a real problem. Which play is *Dente per Dente* (Italian, literally 'Tooth for Tooth')? [See bottom of page.*]

Triple negating

In Shakespearian English we often find sequences of negative words whose function is to intensify the negative meaning of an utterance.

> You know my father hath no child but I, *nor none* is like to have (*As You Like It*, I.2.16)

Such forms are sometimes criticized in standard English today, but in the sixteenth century they were normal everyday usage (as they still are in most modern dialects). Even longer negative sequences were routine. Here is Viola, using a triple negative to talk about her heart (*Twelfth Night*, III.1.156):

> And that no woman has, nor never none
> Shall mistress be of it, save I alone

*Measure for Measure

False friends: distracted

MODERN SENSE: unable to think clearly, unfocused, anxious

OBSOLETE SENSE: (of people) perplexed, confused, near madness*

♣ Hamlet, having just met his father's ghost, refers to his head going round and round as a 'distracted globe' (*Hamlet*, I.5.97).

OBSOLETE SENSE: (of things) divided, torn apart

♣ The King of France says 'to the brightest beams / Distracted clouds give way' (*All's Well that Ends Well*, V.3.35).

*Shakespeare is the first recorded user of *distracted* in this sense, in the *Oxford English Dictionary*.

Imogen or Innogen?

The name of the heroine of *Cymbeline* is spelled 'Innogen' in Shakespeare's source for the story, Holinshed's *Chronicles*, and when Simon Forman saw the play in 1611 his account names her as 'Innogen'. Shakespeare also used the name in a non-speaking part in *Much Ado About Nothing*, where Innogen is the wife of Leonato. The name 'Imogen' is found only in the First Folio, where the misreading of two *n*s as an *m* would have been an easy error in the typesetting process – especially if the text was being set from a manuscript handwritten by Shakespeare, whose rendition of an *m* in *William* in his 1612 signature is little more than a squiggle (p. 131). The authority of the Folio has kept the name 'Imogen' in use over the centuries, but 'Innogen' is restored by Stanley Wells and Gary Taylor in the Oxford Shakespeare.

Barbarous

It is a vulgar and barbarous drama which would not be tolerated by the vilest populace of France or Italy.
(Voltaire on *Hamlet*, in *Dissertation sur la Tragédie*, 1748)

Moving to Blackfriars

In August 1608 Shakespeare's company took over the lease of the Blackfriars theatre, in the centre of London near St Paul's. It was an indoor theatre, much smaller than the Globe, capable of taking an audience of around 700. Everyone had seats, and – at sixpence a time – people paid for their comfort. Some scholars have seen in this move to a more intimate venue the motivation for a change of direction in the stagecraft and content of Shakespeare's later plays. But the primary purpose of the move was to provide the company with a winter base for its work. It would be back at the Globe when the weather improved.

Final exit

The stage direction at *The Winter's Tale* (III.3.58) tests the ingenuity of all Shakespeare directors. The courtier Antigonus has to

Exit, pursued by a Beare.

Whatever the manner in which someone presents Bear, we can be thankful that the ingestion of poor Antigonus invariably takes place off-stage.

Shakespeare non-stop

On 1 May 2000, students of the University of Leicester performed the entire works of Shakespeare to raise funds to take their production of *As You Like It* to the Shakespeare Youth 2000 Festival in Vilnius, Lithuania. It took them over 106 hours, starting on a Monday and ending on the following Friday, reading the plays chronologically twenty-four hours a day, including the poems and sonnets, and finishing with Shakespeare's will. They included *Two Noble Kinsmen*, *King Edward III* and the 250-line fragment of *Sir Thomas More*.

In 1984, outside the Royal Shakespeare Theatre, actor Antony Sher notes a similar event in his *Year of the King* diaries (p. 241):

A group of university students are reading the entire works of Shakespeare non-stop, as a stunt to raise money. There are about four of them and a pile of cloaks, hats and wooden swords. They have been at it for over forty-eight hours. Currently on Much Ado, they are already staggering and giggling, voices gone, heavy eyes – drunk on Shakespeare.

The Royal Shakespeare Company are planning to perform the complete works of Shakespeare in one season, beginning April 2006. It is expected to be played over seven months, in theatres in Stratford-upon-Avon, with theatre companies from around the world taking part.

History or not?

Richard II and *Richard III* are classed as history plays in the First Folio. But in their 1597 Quarto versions they are both called tragedies:

The Tragedy of King Richard the Second
The Tragedy of King Richard the Third

A real bear?

I wonder if, in The Winter's Tale, *a real bear was borrowed from the adjacent bear-baiting pit to chase Antigonus near the end of Act III: 'Exit, pursued by a bear' – every actor's favourite stage direction.*

(Alec Guinness, *My Name Escapes Me*, 1996, p. 52)

Cibber's Richard III

The actor David Garrick, most famous for his performance of Richard III, never spoke the lines modern readers most readily associate with the play, 'Now is the winter of our discontent / Made glorious summer by this son of York'. Like virtually all other eighteenth- and nineteenth-century actors, Garrick performed using Colly Cibber's 1700 adaptation. Cibber (1671–1757) was an English actor, playwright, theatre manager and poet laureate, and his adaptation of *Richard III* was favoured over Shakespeare's original text for 170 years. Even in 1821, when the English actor William Macready was playing Richard and attempted to reintroduce more of Shakespeare's text, he was met with general disapproval. As well as cutting the opening lines of Shakespeare's opening speech, Cibber made other alterations and additions, including 'Off with his head! so much for Buckingham!' added to Act 4 Scene 3, famously used by Laurence Olivier in his 1955 film. The original text of the play was restored by the actor Henry Irving in his 1871 production.

Preparing for Richard

Unable to get back to sleep, I find my copy of the play and have a proper look at the speech. 'Now is the winter ...'

God. It seems terribly unfair of Shakespeare to begin his play with such a famous speech. You don't like to put your mouth to it, so many other mouths have been there. Or to be more honest, one particularly distinctive mouth. His poised, staccato delivery is imprinted on those words like teeth marks.

I sit in shock, in the middle of the night, staring at the text.

'Now is the winter ...'

God. It's as hard as saying 'I love you', as if you had just coined the phrase for the first time.

(Antony Sher, of Olivier, *Year of the King*, 1985, p. 27)

False friends: want

MODERN SENSE: desire, wish, need, require

OBSOLETE SENSE: * lack, be without

- ♣ Cordelia says to Lear, 'I want that glib and oily art / To speak and purpose not' (*King Lear*, I.1.224)
- ♣ In the Epilogue to *The Tempest* (line 14), Prospero says 'Now I want / Spirits to enforce, art to enchant'

*Over half of Shakespeare's uses of *want* have this sense.

Wherefore wherefore?

If there were a competition for the most widely misunderstood word in Shakespeare, the winner would probably be *wherefore*, when Juliet says:

O Romeo, Romeo – wherefore art thou Romeo

(Romeo and Juliet, II.2.33)

The force of modern *where* overrides the older meaning, which is an emphatic 'why'. Juliet is asking in frustration: '*Why* are you called Romeo?' It is one of 148 instances of the word in Shakespeare. Other instances can be even more misleading, when heard spoken aloud. When Cassio tells Bianca to leave him (*Othello*, III.4.188), she replies:

Leave you! Wherefore?

To modern English ears, that sounds very much like 'Where for?'

Will guarantee cheques

Since 1 October 1990, an image of William Shakespeare, as a hologram or a printed logo, has been used as a theme for the UK's Domestic Cheque Guarantee Card Scheme. The hologram, when moved from side to side, shows Shakespeare frowning, then warmly smiling.

Male Rosalinds?

Jan Kott, the Polish poet and critic, published his *Shakespeare Our Contemporary* in 1965. Inspired by long-haired hippies kissing on a street corner in Stockholm, he saw *As You Like It* as the best Shakespeare play to explore sexual ambiguity, and that it could be most fully explored with an all-male cast. He wrote that a boy actor

disguised as a girl plays a girl disguised as a boy. Everything is real and unreal, false and genuine at the same time. And we cannot tell on which side of the looking glass we have found ourselves. As if everything were mere reflection.

Since, there have been a few all-male *As You Like It*s – the most famous English productions are:

Date	Director	Company	Rosalind played by:
1967 *revived 1974*	Clifford Williams	National Theatre	Ronald Pickup
1991 *revived 1994*	Declan Donnellan	Cheek By Jowl	Adrian Lester

All-male productions of other plays did not end with women being allowed to act on-stage after the Restoration. The reconstructed Globe has given all-male productions, and a New York theatre company, Splinter Group, gave a four-man production of *Romeo and Juliet*, which transferred to London in September 2003.

MODERN SENSE: woman in domestic charge of a public institution, especially a hospital

OBSOLETE SENSE: married woman, especially one who has a dignified position in society

♣ When Timon expostulates to Alcibiades about matrons, he does not have hospitals in mind: 'Strike me the counterfeit matron' (*Timon of Athens*, IV.3.113).

♣ 'Enter ... an ancient matron' (*Cymbeline*, V.4.30).

Idle hours

What did Shakespeare do during the plague years? Some have thought he spent time travelling abroad. But in the Dedication to the Earl of Southampton at the beginning of *Venus and Adonis* he talks about vowing 'to take aduantage of all idle houres, till I haue honoured you with some grauer labour'. This would be *The Rape of Lucrece*. It suggests that, at least for some of the period, he stayed working at home.

Thou *or* you: *Lady to Macbeth*

The relationship between Macbeth and his wife is reflected in their pronouns. To begin with, the forms suggest closeness.

♣ When she reads his letter to her (I.5.1–12), there are four *thou*-forms in it.

♣ When she talks to him in her imagination, after reading it (13–28), she uses *thou*-forms repeatedly – fourteen times.

♣ When he arrives later in the scene, she shows both intimacy ('Thy letters have transported me ...', line 54) and formality ('Your face, my thane, is as a book ...', line 60).

Two scenes later, everything changes.

♣ In I.7.29, she meets him outside the dining chamber, and addresses him coldly: 'Why have you left the chamber?'

♣ When Macbeth replies 'We will proceed no further in this business' she rounds on him with seven contemptuous *thou*-forms in rapid succession: 'From this time / Such I account thy love. Art thou afeard ...'

♣ She then switches to *you*: 'What beast was't then / That made you break this enterprise to me?'

Macbeth tries to maintain a *thou*-relationship with his wife, using these forms a further nine times in later scenes; but they are not reciprocated. After I.7.43, Lady Macbeth never uses *thou*-forms to her husband again.

Happier endings

The Bowdlers (p. 152) were not the first to adapt Shakespeare. In the 1740s, David Garrick's *Romeo and Juliet* suited the eighteenth-century mood for propriety by omitting the coarse dialogue between Gregory and Sampson, increasing Juliet's age to an acceptable eighteen, omitting any mention of Rosaline, excluding the bedroom scene and not having Romeo descend from the balcony. He also gave them an extra conversation in the tomb, before both die (p. 16).

The Manningham story

John Manningham was a student in Middle Temple in 1602, when he was told a story about Shakespeare. He wrote it in his diary for 13 March:

> *Vpon a tyme when Burbidge played Rich. 3. there was a citizen greue [grew] soe farr in liking with him, that before shee went from the play shee appointed him to come that night vnto hir by the name of Ri: the 3. Shakespeare overhearing their conclusion went before, was intertained, and at his game ere Burbidge came. Then message being brought that Rich. the 3.d was at the dore, Shakespeare caused returne to be made that William the Conquerour was before Rich. the 3.*

And then, as if to make sure the point is not missed, Manningham adds:

Shakespeare's name William.

It is a good story, and if it is not true, it ought to be.

Folio word-forms

Estimates of the size of Shakespeare's vocabulary are inevitably vague (see p. 41), even in a single text, such as the First Folio. Given the vagaries of Elizabethan typesetting, counting the number of different word-forms can give only an approximate indication of the range of the vocabulary found there. The text includes many hyphenated units, both within lines and at line-endings, which editors analyse differently – such as 'rascally-yea-forsooth-knaue'. Words are also run together for no apparent reason, such as 'shalbe'. If a count is made of *every* different graphic unit surrounded by spaces – including all spelling variants, capitalized and uncapitalized forms, hyphenations, abbreviations, stage directions and proper names (including speaker names) – the result is 43,219. If capitalization is ignored, this reduces to 35,274 – the difference largely accounted for by the use of an opening capital at the beginning of a poetic line.

Being natural

Many modern actors, I believe, are inclined to think that Shakespeare must be spoken naturalistically at all costs. But when Shakespeare wants to be naturalistic he writes: 'Pray you, undo this button', 'Dost thou not see my baby at my breast that sucks the nurse asleep', 'All the perfumes of Arabia will not sweeten this little hand.' Such lines are extraordinarily simple, and every audience will find them moving.

(John Gielgud, *Stage Directions*, 1963, p. 5)

Sonnets in plays

The vogue for writing love-poetry in sonnet form was at its height in the mid-1590s, and many people think that most of Shakespeare's sonnets were composed at around that time. But the form is not restricted to the group of 154 independent poems we now call 'The Sonnets'; it appears also in several plays. The Chorus in the Epilogue to *Henry V* is written as a sonnet, as is Helen's letter to the Countess in *All's Well that Ends Well*. But the form is especially notable in the plays about love written in the mid-1590s – *Love's Labour's Lost* and *Romeo and Juliet*. The latter begins with a sonnet – the Prologue – and the Chorus uses the form again at the beginning of Act II. The first conversation between the two lovers (I.5.93) is actually a sonnet duet: Romeo speaks four lines, then Juliet speaks four; they share the next four and the final couplet, and then they kiss each other. Indeed, they enjoy the experience so much that they immediately start off on another sequence, but after the first four lines the Nurse calls Juliet, and the moment is lost. Several characters in the play also speak a 'half-sonnet' – a six-line combination of quatrain and couplet – Benvolio (I.2.45), Romeo (I.2.87), Paris (V.3.12), and Escalus (V.3.305) – poetically ending the play as it began.

Fifteen lines a sonnet?

Sonnets usually have fourteen lines of iambic pentameter (p. 50). Sonnet 99 has fifteen. An extra line, with an unusual rhythm, precedes the first quatrain, making the rhyme-scheme *ababa*:

> *The forward violet thus did I chide:*
> *'Sweet thief, whence didst thou steal thy sweet that smells,*
> *If not from my love's breath? The purple pride*
> *Which on thy soft cheek for complexion dwells*
> *In my love's veins thou hast too grossly dyed.'*

The first line is really outside the structure of the poem. It is the only sonnet to begin with a reporting clause introducing some direct speech.

False friends: rude

MODERN SENSE: * impolite, offensive; mildly obscene (sexual)

OBSOLETE SENSE: (of people) violent

❧ Ulysses says 'the rude son should strike his father dead' (*Troilus and Cressida*, I.3.115).

OBSOLETE SENSE: (of people) uncultured, ignorant

❧ Puck calls the rustics 'rude mechanicals' (*A Midsummer Night's Dream*, III.2.9).

OBSOLETE SENSE: (of things) rough, wild

❧ King Philip describes a city walls as having a 'rude circumference' (*King John*, II.1.262).

OBSOLETE SENSE: (of the wind and waves) stormy

❧ King Richard tells Aumerle, 'Not all the water in the rough rude sea / Can wash the balm off from an anointed king' (*Richard II*, III.2.54).

*The modern 'impoliteness' sense also features in the canon, as when Duke Senior tells off Orlando for being 'a rude despiser of good manners' (*As You Like It*, II.7.93). But the sexual sense of 'rude' never occurs in Shakespeare.

Character lengths compared

In the first three plays below, it is often thought that the character on the right speaks more than the one on the left. The opposite is the case.

Play	Character	Number of lines	Character	Number of lines
The Merchant of Venice	Portia	574	Shylock	352
Othello	Iago	1088	Othello	880
Much Ado About Nothing	Benedick	430	Beatrice	279
The Two Noble Kinsmen	Palamon	595	Arcite	523
Troilus and Cressida	Troilus	537	Cressida	301
Romeo and Juliet	Romeo	617	Juliet	542

False friends: excrement

MODERN SENSE: waste matter discharged from the bowels

OBSOLETE SENSE: outgrowth (of hair, nails, or feathers)

❧ Don Armado boasts to Holofernes that the King would 'with his royal finger thus dally with my excrement, with my mustachio' (*Love's Labour's Lost*, V.1.98).*

❧ Autolycus says 'Let me pocket up my pedlar's excrement' (*The Winter's Tale* IV.4.709).

*Shakespeare is the first recorded user of *excrement* in this sense, in the *Oxford English Dictionary*.

Professional recognition

In his account book for 15 March 1595, the Treasurer of the Queen's Chamber lists a payment made for plays performed before her Majesty at the palace in Greenwich the previous December:

> *To William Kempe, William Shakespeare, and*
> *Richarde Burbage, seruantes to the Lord chamberleyne.*

This is the first official record of Shakespeare belonging to a theatre company – the Chamberlain's Men – and the only extant record of his name being linked to specific performances. It also indicates that, by 1595, he had become one of its leading members – presumably seen as an actor, along with the clown Kempe and the tragedian Burbage. In the First Folio, the actor who heads the cast-list is William Shakespeare.

An Elizabethan actor's day

* Wake at dawn, eat breakfast, get to the theatre.
* Learn and run through any fights or dances needed. Check you have all your props and costume.
* Perform around 2 o'clock in the afternoon.
* Get your scroll for the play to be performed tomorrow (see cue-scripts, p. 13).
* Find your props and costume for that play, and learn (or finish off learning) your scroll. Ensure that this is done by nightfall, because the poor-quality smoky candles afforded by actors would make it difficult or impossible to read at home.
* Visit an ale-tavern (some things don't change).
* To bed, then the same again.

Short-line endings

The plays whose final lines are written in poetry generally use one of two methods: either a couplet consisting of two full rhyming lines or two full non-rhyming lines. There are just five exceptions which use short lines of one, two or three metrical feet:

> *Hamlet*: Go, bid the soldiers shoot.
> *Coriolanus*: Assist.
> *Timon of Athens*: Let our drums strike.
> *The Two Noble Kinsmen*: And bear us like the time.
> *Henry IV Part II*: Come, will you hence?

In each case, the tone is peremptory, terse. But perhaps this is not surprising, for all the speakers are generals – respectively, Fortinbras, Aufidius, Alcibiades, Theseus and Prince John.

Epitaph

Shakespeare's epitaph is carved on his tombstone in the chancel of Holy Trinity Church, Stratford. The word 'the' in the third line, and the two uses of 'that', are written in an abbreviated form on the stone.

> GOOD FREND FOR IESVS SAKE FORBEARE,
> TO DIGG THE DVST ENCLOASED HEARE.
> BLESTE BE Y^E MAN Y^T SPARES THES STONES,
> AND CVRST BE HE Y^T MOVES MY BONES.

There is a tradition, dating from the late seventeenth century, that the words are Shakespeare's. The inscription we see today is thought to be a copy, made in the eighteenth century when the original stone was in an advanced state of decay. The curse is not aimed at the curious passer-by, but at the church staff, who would routinely move bones to make room for more burials. It seems to have been respected.

Through a glass darkly

Reading Shakespeare is sometimes like looking through a window into a dark room. You don't see in. You see nothing but a reflection of yourself unable to see in. An unflattering image of yourself blind.

(Antony Sher, *Year of the King*, 1985, p. 36)

Playing fair

Nigel Playfair produced *As You Like It* for the opening night of the Shakespeare Festival at Stratford-upon-Avon in April 1919. It was a radical departure. Inspired by the innovative ballet company the Ballets Russes, his uncut version was bright, dynamic and musical, with young actors. The stuffed Charlecote stag, routinely on stage in previous productions, was conspicuous by its absence. Many critics now call it the first modern production of the play, but at the time theatre-goers found it hard to stomach. In his book *Story of the Lyric Theatre, Hammersmith*, Playfair recounts an incident that happened to his designer:

> *When Lovat Fraser was walking in the street, a woman came up to him and shook her fist in his face. 'Young man,' she said impressively, 'how dare you meddle with our Shakespeare!'*

What is a petard?

The phrase 'to be hoist with one's own petard' is familiar today, and it is always one of the examples in any list of modern idioms coming from Shakespeare. It is used when Hamlet refers to the way he will anticipate treachery by Rosencrantz and Guildenstern: 'For 'tis the sport to have the enginer / Hoist with his own petar' (III.4.208) – they will be 'blown up by their own device'. It was a daring usage, for the petard had not been around for long when *Hamlet* was written (*c.*1600). It was the first major gunpowder siege weapon, 'lately invented', according to the scholar John Minsheu, in 1599. It was also an evocative term: it comes from French *péter* 'to break wind', presumably reflecting the muffled sound of an underground explosion.

Tower of fun

As Hastings leads the Princes off to the tower, I hear [Brian] *Blessed mutter to them, 'Come on lads, lots of fun in the Tower, video games and everything ...'*   (Antony Sher, *Year of the King*, 1985, p. 173)

New Place

On 4 May 1597, Shakespeare bought New Place in Stratford-upon-Avon, a large house – the second-largest in Stratford – set in spacious grounds at the corner of Chapel Street and Chapel Lane. He paid £60 for it. How could a young playwright afford it? His position as a share-holder in his acting company meant that he received a proportion of all its receipts, and evidently this had brought him sufficient income to be able to invest in property. The house was demolished in 1759 (the owner, annoyed by constant Shakespeare fans and a rise in Land Taxes, razed the property to the ground, and was driven out of Stratford by angry Stratfordians). The site was bought by the Shakespeare Birthplace Trust in 1892. The present-day gardens contain several bronze sculptures of the plays and some foundations of the original property.

A London property

On 10 March 1613 Shakespeare paid £140 for a gate-house in London, in Blackfriars, near the theatre. It seems to have been a property investment, with three trustees in support, for there is no record of his ever living there. His signature is on the conveyance, and also on a subsequent mortgage deed (see p.131).

Acting clues

How did Shakespeare's actors know how to play their parts? Were they directed? Did they rehearse? And if they did, for how long? Patrick Tucker, in *Secrets of Acting Shakespeare*, thinks the general estimate of two weeks' rehearsal time is wrong. Given the extensive repertoire of plays the company had to put on, he suggests that the actors would have had no time at all to rehearse (see p. 90), and would have found their directions in Shakespeare's writing. Both John Barton and Peter Hall believe Shakespeare used his text to tell his actors how to perform.

> *Shakespeare is his text. So if you want to do him justice, you have to look for and follow the clues he offers. If an actor does that then he'll find that Shakespeare himself starts to direct him.*
>
> (John Barton, *Playing Shakespeare*, 1984, p. 168)

> *Shakespeare tells the actor when to go fast and when to go slow; when to come in on cue, and when to accent a particular word or series of words. He tells the actor much else; and he always tells him* when *to do it (provided the actor knows where to look). But he never tells him* why. *The motive, the* why, *remains the creative task of the actor … For instance, the words may tell the actor to speak slowly because they are monosyllabic; but they will not tell him* why. *The actor's emotions must do that.*
>
> (Peter Hall, *Shakespeare's Advice to the Players*, 2003, p. 13)

The name

Stratford comes from the Old English word *stræt* 'road, highway' + *ford* 'water crossing'. Stratford-upon-Avon was thus the place where a road crossed the River Avon by means of a ford. The location has been settled at least since the Bronze Age. In Anglo-Saxon times a monastery is known at *Stretforde*. Later, in the Domesday Book, the name is recorded as a manor owned by Wulfstan, Bishop of Worcester.

False friends: curst or cursed

MODERN SENSE: under a curse, deserving a curse
OBSOLETE SENSE: (of a person's disposition) cantankerous, angry, bad-tempered

♣ 'Be curst and brief' says Sir Toby to Sir Andrew in *Twelfth Night* (III.2.40).
♣ The Clown in *The Winter's Tale* (III.3.126) talks about bears: 'They are never curst but when they are hungry'.

A fatal stage duel

On 2 April 1891, the St James's Gazette reported an extraordinary accident which occurred during an amateur production of *Romeo and Juliet* by the Manchester Cathedral Schools. The production had reached the Mercutio / Tybalt fight, but after Romeo had parted the fighters and Mercutio fell to the floor, blood was seen flowing from his nose and mouth, and he died on his way to hospital. The post-mortem examination showed that the sword had penetrated his chest to a depth of seven inches. The actor playing Tybalt reported that Romeo came in between the two fighting actors, instead of knocking the swords out of the way as normal. Tybalt thrust around Romeo, but did not feel any resistance to the point of the sword and did not put the weight of his body behind the blow. When he saw Mercutio fall, he realized he must have hurt him.

In the investigation, the coroner informed the jury that 'with a stiff arm and a slight lunge forward they could send any of the swords used in the performance through a man's body or through a door without feeling any resistance'. He added it was probably an accident, but there had been 'some degree of negligence on the part of everyone who took part in the performance'. The jury returned a verdict of 'Death from loss of blood from a wound received while taking part in a dramatic performance'.

The top ten speakers in
A Midsummer Night's Dream

Number of lines*	Character	Number of lines*	Character
255	Bottom	179	Lysander
235	Theseus	165	Hermia
229	Helena	141	Titania
225	Oberon	136	Demetrius
206	Puck	121	Quince

*These are the totals in the New Penguin Shakespeare. Prose line totals vary greatly between editions.

Making a folio

A folio is a book consisting of large sheets of paper which have been folded in half to make two leaves (four pages). The First Folio has 454 leaves, including the preliminary pages, each 13.4 x 8.5 inches (34 x 21 cm). In the play texts, the page is divided into two columns. On the bottom right-hand side of each page is a 'catchword' – the first word of the text starting on the following page.

History plays

Shakespeare wrote or contributed to eleven history plays. Here they are in historical order:

King John, King Edward III, Richard II, Henry IV Part I and II, Henry V, Henry VI Part I, II and III, Richard III, Henry VIII.

Eight fall naturally into two groups of four, each presenting a historical sequence of events, and are sometimes referred to as 'tetralogies'.

*Richard II, Henry IV Part I and II, Henry V
Henry VI Part I, II and III, Richard III*

They were not, however, all written in historical sequence.

Near to history

The monarchs of Britain and France, covering the period of the history plays. Characters who appear in the plays are in italics.

Britain		France	
Monarch	*Dates*	*Monarch*	*Dates*
John	1199–1216	*Philippe II (Philip)*	1180–1223
Henry III	1216–1272	*Louis VIII ('the Lion') (Lewis)*	1223–1226
		Louis IX (St Louis)	1226–1270
Edward I	1272–1307	Philip III ('the Bold')	1270–1285
Edward II	1307–1327	Philip IV ('the Fair')	1285–1314
		Louis X ('the Quarrelsome')	1314–1316
		Jean (John) I	1316
		Philip V ('the Tall')	1316–1322
Edward III	1327–1377	Charles IV ('the Fair')	1322–1328
		Philippe VI	1328–1350
		Jean II ('the Good')	1350–1364
Richard II	1377–1399	*Charles V ('the Wise')*	1364–1380
Henry IV	1399–1413	*Charles VI ('the Foolish')*	1380–1422
Henry V	1413–1422		
Henry VI	1422–1461	Charles VII	1422–1461
Edward IV	1461–1470	*Louis XI (Lewis)*	1461–1483
Henry VI	1470–1471		
Edward IV	1471–1483		
Edward V	1483	Charles VIII ('the Affable')	1483–1498
Richard III	1483–1485		
Henry VII	1485–1509	Louis XII	1498–1515
Henry VIII	1509–1547	François I	1515–1547
Edward VI	1547–1553	Henri II	1547–1559
Mary I	1553–1558		
Elizabeth I	1558–1603	François II	1559–1560
		Charles IX	1560–1574
		Henri III	1574–1589
James I	1603–1625	Henri IV	1589–1610
		Louis XIII	1610–1643

Struggling Hamlet

In every actor is a Hamlet struggling to get out. In fact, in most directors, too.   (Steven Berkoff, *I Am Hamlet*, 1989, p. vii)

The other 'to be'

The so-called 'bad' Quarto of *Hamlet* (1603), probably compiled by a few of the actors from memory, contains an alternative version of Hamlet's famous soliloquy (III.1.56ff., with lines numbered here for reference):

1 To be, or not to be, I [ay] there's the point,
2 To Die, to sleepe, is that all? I all:
3 No, to sleepe, to dreame, I mary [marry] there it goes,
4 For in that dreame of death, when wee awake,
5 And borne before an euerlasting Iudge,
6 From whence no passenger euer retur'nd,
7 The vndiscouered country, at whose sight
8 The happy smile, and the accursed damn'd.

Apart from the opening line, the only close correspondence with the 'good' Quarto of 1604 is between lines 2–4 above and its lines 64–6 and lines 6–7 with its lines 79–80. There is nothing remotely like the phrasing of lines 5 and 8 in the 1604 speech – or anywhere else in Shakespeare. Whoever the actors were, it would seem their memories were not of the best.

The first Hamlet

Richard Burbage was probably the first to play Hamlet, Lear and Othello, judging by an elegy written for him in *c*.1619:

> *No more young Hamlet, old Hieronimo,** *
> *Kind Lear, the grieved Moor, and more beside,*
> *That lived in him, have now forever died.*

*A character in Thomas Kyd's *The Spanish Tragedy*.

Female Hamlets

Sarah Siddons, the sister of the eighteenth-century actor John Kemble, was in 1775 the first of many women to play Hamlet. Over the next hundred years the list included Kitty Clive, Charlotte Cushman, Julia Gloves, and Sarah Bernhardt. In the twentieth century, Judith Anderson notably took on the role – notably, as she was seventy-three at the time.

Unusual names

Some Shakespearian names are repeatedly used in the plays: there are five *Antonio*s, for instance, and four *Balthasar*s. Others are unique, and often unusual, and scholars have always been interested in discovering sources for them. It turns out that there were two students named Rosenkrantz and Gyldenstjerne on the rolls of the University of Wittenberg between 1586 and 1595 (*Hamlet* was written around 1600).

Hamlet on film

Film-makers have rung the changes on *Hamlet*, in a search for new angles. Here are a few of the titles:

Hamlet, Scène de Duel (1900, France)
Être Ou Être Pas (1914, France, 'To Be or Not to Be')
A Sagebrush Hamlet (1919, USA)
Hamlet at Elsinore (1951, Ireland; 1964, UK)
Der Rest ist Schweigen (1959, Germany, 'The Rest is Silence')
Inmolacion de Hamlet (1967, Spain, 'The Sacrifice of Hamlet')
Ofelias Blomsters (1968, Denmark, 'Ophelia's Flowers')
H for Hamlet (1993, Ireland)

Thou *or* you: *friend vs soldier*

The opening scene of *Hamlet* displays an interesting *thou-/you-* switch.

BARNARDO: Who's there?
FRANCISCO: Nay, answer me. Stand and unfold *yourself.*

A formal usage: Barnardo does not know who he is talking to.

BARNARDO: Long live the King!
FRANCISCO: Barnardo?
BARNARDO: He.
FRANCISCO: *You* come most carefully upon *your* hour.
BARNARDO: 'Tis now struck twelve. Get *thee* to bed, Francisco.

A courtesy acknowledgment followed by a friendly suggestion.

FRANCISCO: For this relief much thanks. 'Tis bitter cold,
    And I am sick at heart.
BARNARDO: Have *you* had quiet guard?

Why the *you*, when Barnardo was saying *thou* to Francesco a second before? This is the professional soldier speaking now, not the friend. Francisco is sick at heart, so maybe there's been some trouble. He has to check it out, officially. He could have said, 'Hast *thou* had quiet guard?', but that would have been a casual chatty remark, inappropriate for a tone of military inquiry.

Workers at the Revels

Documents from the Office of the Revels show a wide range of people employed in the business of preparing a play for production, in addition to the Master of the Revels and his clerks:

Apothecaries
Armourers
Basket-makers
Bootiers [boot-makers]
Buskin-makers [makers of boots reaching to the calf or knee]
Chandlers [candle-makers]
Coffee-makers
Deckers [decorators]
Drapers
Feather-makers
Furriers
Haberdashers
Horse-shoers
Hunters
Ironmongers
Joiners
Linen-drapers
Mercers [textile dealers]
Messengers
Milliners
Painters
Plasterers
Porters
Property-makers
Silk-weavers
Silkwomen [women working with silk]
Smiths
Stationers
Tailors
Upholsterers
Wagon-makers
Wire-drawers [wire-makers]

Spear-carrier?

John Gielgud, who would become one of the most acclaimed Shakespearian actors, won a scholarship to London's Royal Academy of Dramatic Art, and made his professional debut in 1921 in *Henry V*.

He had one line.

Largest male roles

Number of lines	Character	Play
1506	Hamlet	Hamlet
1151	(King) Richard	Richard III
1088	Iago	Othello
1031	King Henry	Henry V
880	Othello	Othello
877	Coriolanus	Coriolanus
850	Timon	Timon of Athens
847	Duke	Measure for Measure
839	Antony	Antony and Cleopatra
756	(King) Richard	Richard II
749	Lear	King Lear
748	King Edward	King Edward III
721	Brutus	Julius Caesar
716	Macbeth	Macbeth
711	Titus	Titus Andronicus
686	Leontes	The Winter's Tale
656	Prospero	The Tempest
641	Falstaff	Henry IV Part II
617	Romeo	Romeo and Juliet
602	Falstaff	Henry IV Part I

If the totals for a character who appears in more than one play are combined, three names outrank Hamlet: Prince Hal/Prince Henry/Henry V (1915), Falstaff (1681) and Richard of Gloucester/Richard III (1531).

Largest female roles

Number of lines	Character	Play
685	Rosalind	As You Like It
678	Cleopatra	Antony and Cleopatra
594	Innogen	Cymbeline
574	Portia	The Merchant of Venice
542	Juliet	Romeo and Juliet
478	Helena	All's Well that Ends Well
424	Isabella	Measure for Measure
391	Desdemona	Othello
374	Emilia	The Two Noble Kinsmen
335	Viola	Twelfth Night
332	Paulina	The Winter's Tale
329	Mistress Page	The Merry Wives of Windsor
324	Daughter	The Two Noble Kinsmen
322	Julia	The Two Gentlemen of Verona
316	Queen Margaret	Henry VI Part II
314	Olivia	Twelfth Night
311	Volumnia	Coriolanus
301	Cressida	Troilus and Cressida
291	Countess	All's Well that Ends Well
290	Princess	Love's Labour's Lost

How do we know what Elizabethan pronunciation sounded like?

There are three main ways.

1) English spelling had not yet standardized, and many people still spelled as they spoke. So, when we see a word spelled in a semi-phonetic way, it is good evidence for its contemporary pronunciation. For example, in *Romeo and Juliet* we find Mercutio describing Queen Mab (I.4.66):

Her whip, of cricket's bone; the lash, of film

The Folio and most of the Quartos spell *film* as *Philome*. It must have been a two-syllable word (as in modern Irish). Or how should we take *poppering-pear* (II.1.38)? The First Folio spells it *Poprin Peare*. This tells us that *poppering* must have had just two syllables, and there was no -*g* sounded in the -*ing* ending.

2) Several authors wrote detailed accounts of how words were to be pronounced. Ben Jonson was one, in his *English Grammar*. How do we know that *r* was pronounced after vowels in Elizabethan English? Because he tells us so, using a vivid description (the *grrr* of a dog):

> *The dog's letter hirreth in the sound, the tongue striking the inner palate, with a trembling about the teeth. It is sounded firme in the beginning of the words, and more liquid in the middle, and ends; as in* rarer, riper.

This not only tells us that *r* was pronounced after vowels, it also indicates that its pronunciation at the beginning of words was different from that at the end.

3) Above all, we can use the rhythms, rhymes and puns used by the writers. We can deduce the stress pattern of a word from the metre of a line, the value of a vowel from the way words rhyme, and whether a consonant was sounded from the way puns work. For instance, how should we pronounce the last syllable of Romeo's first love, *Rosaline* – to rhyme with *fin* or with *fine*? The text makes it clear (II.3.77):

ROMEO: Thou chidst me oft for loving Rosaline.
FRIAR: For doting, not for loving, pupil mine.

Trippingly

Shakespeare is easier to understand spoken at speed
rather than slowly spelt out.
(Cicely Berry, quoted in Antony Sher, *Year of the King*, 1985, p. 196)

Pronouncing th

There are many spellings in Shakespearian texts to show that, in Elizabethan English, a common pronunciation of the *th* sound in the middle or end of words was a *t* or *d*, as in *Henry the fift* and *fadoms* (for *fathoms*). This was the usual sound in proper names and in words of foreign origin, such as *Arthur*, *Balthasar*, *lethargy* and *apothecary*. Interesting echoes between words, missed in modern pronunciation, can result. 'Valiant Othello', says the Duke of Venice (*Othello*, I.3.48), 'we must straight employ you / Against the general enemy Ottoman'. If we pronounce the name as 'Otello', we obtain an interesting resonance with *Ottoman*, which the modern pronunciation obscures.

On Shakespeare in a South African accent

What's it going to be like, playing Shakespeare in an accent like this? – an accent that isn't all smooth and rounded, but full of muscles and edges. An earth accent, a root accent, instead of one that floats and flitters around in the air. (Antony Sher and Gregory Doran, *Woza Shakespeare!*, 1996, p. 45)

Original pronunciation

There have been few attempts to perform a Shakespeare play using a reconstruction of the accents thought to be current in Elizabethan England (Early Modern English). John Barton directed a production of *Julius Caesar* in original pronunciation at Cambridge in 1952, but it was over fifty years before it was tried again. Shakespeare's Globe devoted a weekend of three performances to it during Tim Carroll's production of *Romeo and Juliet*, in June 2004. David Crystal, who provided the transcription, tells the story of the production in *Pronouncing Shakespeare: the Globe Experiment* (2005).

Music of the line

When I started work on Shakespeare, I did believe to a limited extent in the possibility of classical word music, that each verse had a sound that was correct, with only moderate variations; then through direct experience I found that this was absolutely and totally untrue. The more musical the approach you bring to Shakespeare, which means the more sensitive you are to music, the more you find that there is no way, except by sheer pedantry, that can fix a line's music. It just can't exist. (Peter Brook, *The Shifting Point*, 1987, p. 94)

Fines

It was a disciplined business, being a member of an acting company in Jacobethan England. The Lady Elizabeth's Men (she was the daughter of James I) were for a while financed by Philip Henslowe, and he laid down strict rules. In 1614, an actor, Robert Dawes, is known to have taken up a three-year contract with the company, promising to pay fines if:

he was late for rehearsal	12 pence
he missed a rehearsal	2 shillings
he was late for a performance	3 shillings
he arrived drunk before a performance	10 shillings
he missed a play entirely	20 shillings

Times do not change. We are aware of at least two occasions in the past few years where a performance of a Shakespeare play has had to be cancelled because of the 'indisposition' of the leading actor. Whether fines were levied, on these occasions, we have been unable to establish.

In for a penny …

The Swiss traveller Thomas Platter described a theatre he visited 'in the suburb, as far as I remember, in Bishopsgate' in late 1599. It would have been the Curtain, as the Theatre had been dismantled by then (p. 71). Here is a translation of what he saw:

The places are built so that they act on a raised stage, and everyone is able to see everything. There are, however, separate galleries and places where you can stand more comfortably, and also sit, though it costs more. If you remain standing below you pay only one English penny, but if you want to sit you are let in at another door, where you pay another penny. But if you want to sit on a cushion in the best place, where you can not only see everything clearly but also be seen, then you pay another English penny at another door. And when there is a break in the play, food and drink is carried around …

You can hire a cushion at the reconstructed Globe, too – though not for a penny.

No delete

With most plays the lines do stick until the run's over and you can lose them – you just press 'delete'. Apart from Shakespeare, which stays for ever.
(Michael Gambon, *The Daily Telegraph*, 17 February 2004)

Only two doors

In a letter written by John Chamberlain to Sir Ralph Winwood, 8 July 1613, in which the Globe fire is mentioned, we learn that the theatre had only two doors:

> *The burning of the Globe or playhouse on the Bankside on St. Peter's day cannot escape you; which fell out by a peal of chambers, (that I know not upon what occasion were to be used in the play,) the tampin or stopple of one of them lighting in the thatch that covered the house, burn'd it down to the ground in less than two hours, with a dwelling-house adjoyning; and it was a great marvaile and a fair grace of God that the people had so little harm, having but two narrow doors to get out.*

Early editions

Date	Text	Editors
1623	First Folio	John Heminge, Henry Condell
1632	Second Folio	unknown
1663	Third Folio	unknown
1685	Fourth Folio	unknown
1709	6 octavo volumes	Nicholas Rowe
1725	6 quarto volumes	Alexander Pope
1733	7 octavo volumes	Lewis Theobald
1744	6 quarto volumes	Thomas Hanmer
1747	8 octavo volumes	William Warburton
1765	8 octavo volumes	Samuel Johnson
1768	10 octavo volumes	Edward Capell
1773	10 octavo volumes	George Steevens
1790	10 octavo volumes	Edmond Malone
1803	First Variorum 21 volumes	Isaac Reed

A 'variorum' edition is one which brings together the editorial decisions and notes of different editors. For the distinction between folio, quarto and octavo, see p. 104.

Rural folk

Edgar's meeting with Oswald in *King Lear* (IV.6.226) is the only time Shakespeare represents a rustic dialect. His country people, such as the shepherds in *As You Like It*, are honest, dignified folk, and use styles of English not far removed from those of upper-class speakers. Other regional speakers, such as Fluellen (Welsh), McMorris (Irish) and Jamy (Scots) in *Henry V*, or Evans (Welsh) and Caius (French) in *The Merry Wives of Windsor*, are all, in their different ways, professional people.

Ghosts *

The most famous Shakespearian ghost is Hamlet's father, but he is not alone.

Spirits of murdered people in	Hamlet
	Julius Caesar
	Macbeth
	Richard III
Apparitions (supernatural appearances, whether friendly or malevolent) in	Cymbeline
	Henry VI Parts I and II
	Henry VIII
	Macbeth

*Ghosts should not be confused with 'ghost characters' – people named in a text who do not actually appear, such as Innogen (Leonato's wife), mentioned only in the stage directions of *Much Ado About Nothing*.

Folio vs quarto vs octavo

There were three main book sizes produced by Elizabethan printers.
* A folio is a book made from sheets of paper that have been folded once, making two leaves (four pages).
* A quarto is a much smaller book, because the sheets of paper are folded twice, making four leaves (eight pages).
* An octavo has the sheets of paper folded three times, making eight leaves (sixteen pages).

Nineteen of Shakespeare's plays were issued as quartos before the First Folio edition of 1623. *The Passionate Pilgrim* was published in octavo, as were several later editions of *The Rape of Lucrece* and *Venus and Adonis*.

Size isn't everything

There is not always a correlation between the size of a part (in lines) and the 'presence' of the character in a play. Especially in the case of female characters, there are several instances where the character has less than 200 lines, yet their role is great.

Play	Character	Number of lines
King Lear	Cordelia	117
The Winter's Tale	Perdita	130
Julius Caesar	Caesar	151
The Tempest	Miranda	154
Hamlet	Ophelia	173
The Merchant of Venice	Antonio	188
Pericles	Marina	190

There are a number of plays attributed to Shakespeare. *The Two Noble Kinsmen* was entered into the Stationer's Register in 1634 as being 'by John ffletcher and William Shakespeare' but was not included in any of the Folios. Seven plays were added to the second impression of the Third Folio, in 1664, 'never before Printed in Folio':

Pericles Prince of Tyre
The London Prodigall
The History of Thomas Ld. Cromwell
Sir John Oldcastle Lord Cobham
The Puritan Widow
A Yorkshire Tragedy
The Tragedy of Locrine

These had all been printed as Quartos, and attributed to W.S. or Shakespeare, but *Pericles* is the only one now thought to be partly written by him. Several other proposed attributions followed. They include *Faire Em*, *The Merry Devil of Edmonton*, and *Mucedorus*, which were bound together in King Charles II's library and labelled 'Shakespeare Vol. I'. Most likely they were attributed to Shakespeare by booksellers or publishers wanting to make money out of the name. Later attributions include *Arden of Feversham*, *Sir Thomas More* and *King Edward III*. *Sir Thomas More* is thought to contain an extract of Shakespeare's handwriting (p. 26). *King Edward III* was included in the New Cambridge Shakespeare series in 1998 (p. 107).

======= *Shakespeare the land investor* =======

Shakespeare made several property investments, when he was living in Stratford.

* On 1 May 1602 he paid £320 to William Combe and his nephew John for roughly 107 acres of arable land and 20 acres of pasture land in Old Stratford, to the north of the town.
* On 28 September 1602 he bought a cottage and garden opposite New Place in Chapel Lane.
* On 24 July 1605 he paid £440 to buy a half-interest in tithes of crops from Old Stratford, Welcombe and Bishopton, as well as certain tithes in Stratford parish.*

*A tithe is a tenth part of the value of agricultural produce. Originally a payment to the Church, in the sixteenth century such payments became available to secular landowners and the Crown.

Thou *or* you: *Lear to his daughters*

In the opening scene of *King Lear*, Lear divides his land into three parts and plans to give one part to each of his daughters, Goneril, Regan and Cordelia. We would expect a father to use *thou*-forms to daughters, and they to use *you*-forms back, and that is how the dialogue begins. Goneril speaks first, with flattering words:

GONERIL: Sir, I love you more than word can wield the matter ...

Lear then gives her a third of his kingdom, using *thee*.

LEAR: Of all these bounds ... We make thee lady.

Regan speaks next, outdoing her sister, and Lear replies with *thee / thine*:

REGAN : ... I am alone felicitate
   In your dear highness' love.

LEAR : To thee and thine hereditary ever
   Remain this ample third of our fair kingdom ...

But when Lear turns to his favourite, Cordelia, he uses *you / your*:

LEAR :   ... what can you say to draw
   A third more opulent than your sisters?

Evidently, if *thou* is normal for 'ordinary' daughters, then *you* conveys a different value. By reversing the normal usage, Shakespeare suggests a special intimacy between Lear and Cordelia. But when Cordelia doesn't reply in the way Lear is expecting, he switches to *thy*:

LEAR: But goes thy heart with this?
   ... Thy truth then be thy dower.

Once again, the reversal conveys a different value. Now the *thou*-forms are being used not as a marker of affection, but of anger.

Queen Lear

One theory I came up with for explaining the King's mood in the first scene was the death of the Queen — Queen Lear. Not a character who normally features. There must have been one. Perhaps her coffin could dominate the stage, everyone in mourning ... No ... the scene was celebratory. (Nigel Hawthorne, *Straight Face*, 2002, p. 310)

King Vultan

People talk about the difference between radio acting, TV acting, and stage acting, but I think it's all the same. For instance, when I played Vultan in Flash Gordon, I put as much energy into it as I would with King Lear — it's all part of the same thing.
(Brian Blessed, interview in *Metro Cafe*, 18 April 2002)

Riddles

The dedication to the Sonnets, written by the publisher T.T. (Thomas Thorpe), raises one of the most enduring riddles of the whole canon:

TO.THE.ONLIE.BEGETTER.OF.
THESE.INSVING.SONNETS.
M^r.W.H. ALL HAPPINESSE.
AND.THAT.ETERNITIE.
PROMISED.

BY.

OVR.EVER-LIVING.POET.

WISHETH.

THE.WELL-WISHING.
ADVENTVRER.IN.
SETTING.
FORTH.

T.T.

What does the dedication, with its curious punctuation, spacing, and ambiguous syntax, mean? Who was W.H.? Many names have been suggested, notably the Earl of Southampton, Henry Wriothesley (with initials reversed), William Herbert the 3rd Earl of Pembroke (though both of these are unlikely to have been addressed as 'Mr') and Sir William Harvey, the third husband of the Countess of Southampton.

King Edward III

King Edward III is first mentioned in the Stationer's Register in 1595, and the view that it was written by Shakespeare can be traced back to 1656. It is described in the New Cambridge Shakespeare series in 1998 as 'a major new addition to the Shakespearean canon', and it was given a production by the Royal Shakespeare Company in 2002, with David Rintoul as King Edward. Its status remains controversial, however. There are a number of passages and dramatic moments which are thought to be undoubtedly Shakespearian in style and approach, and others which seem quite different. Several theories have been proposed: Shakespeare might have collaborated with one or more of his contemporaries; he might have revised someone else's work, or someone might have revised his; or the play might have been written by him throughout, but at different stages in his development as a writer.

Only recorded user

On the opposite page there are 357 cases where the *Oxford English Dictionary* has Shakespeare as the *only* recorded user of a word, in a particular sense, on one or more occasions. The abbreviations refer to word-class (part of speech): for example, he is the only one recorded as using *attorney* as a verb, though the noun usage dates from long before. Hyphenation, spacing and spelling practice are as found in the *OED*. A gloss is given where this is needed to find the right sense in the *OED*. (For Shakespeare as the *first* recorded user of a word, see p. 114.)

Shakespeare spelling

Over seventy variations have been found in the spelling of the Shakespeare family name – a name which can be traced back to the thirteenth century. Among them we find Sakesere (in 1248), Shaksper, Chacsper, Schakespere, Scakespeire and Saksper. It was a common surname, meaning 'spearman'. US academic David Kathman collected as many variants as he could find for William Shakespeare's surname between 1564 and 1616, finding twenty-five variants in 342 instances. Just over 60 per cent of the cases are Shakespeare or Shake-speare.

Schaksp	Shake-speare	Shakspere
Shackespeare	Shakespere	Shaxberd
Shackespere	Shakespheare	Shaxpeare
Shackspeare	Shakp	Shaxper
Shackspere	Shakspe~	Shaxpere
Shagspere	Shakspear	Shaxspere
Shakespe	Shakspeare	Shexpere
Shakespear	Shak-speare	
Shakespeare	Shaksper	

a-doing

Many words in Shakespearian texts begin with *a-* used as a grammatical particle (an element which affects the meaning of other words but without any dictionary meaning itself). The commonest use is before a verb ending in *-ing* (*com*ing, *go*ing), to which it is usually shown linked with a hyphen. Historically a form of *on*, it came to be used as a particle emphasizing various aspects of the verb's durative meaning, such as the repeated nature of an action or the length of time it takes. On this basis, to be 'a-feasting' (in *The Merry Wives of Windsor*, II.3.80) means 'to be engaged in the time-consuming activity of feasting'.

abrook, acture, adoptedly, adoptious, a-hold, allayment, allottery, anthropophaginian, apathaton, appertainment, askance (v.), attask, attemptable, attorney (v.), attributive (adj.), auguring (adj.), ballow, barful, bass (v.), becomed, becoming, bedroom, belee, belock, beloving (adj.), bepray, besort (n.), besort (v.), bestill, betumbled, birthdom, bitter-sweeting, bitume, boggler, bold-beating, bonnet (v.), bragless, braid (adj.), brooded, bubukle, budger, candle-holder, capocchia, carlot, casted, caudie, cern (v.), chapeless, charge-house, chirurgeonly, cital, cloistress, cloy (v., 'claw'), cloyment, cockled, codding, co-mart, compulsative, conceptious, concernancy, concupy, confineless, confirmity, congreet, congrue, considered, conspectuity, continuantly, convive, copataine, correctioner, counter-caster, counter-seal, crack-hemp, cubiculo, curdy (v.), cyme, Dansker, demi-puppet, demure (v.), derogately, despised, directitude, discandy, dishabit, disliken, disproperty, disvouch, dotant, down-gyved, eft (adj.), emballing, embarked, embrasure, empatron, empiricutic, emulate (adj.), emure, enacture, encave, enridged, enschedule, ensear, enshield (adj.), ensteep, escot (v.), evil (n., ?'hovel'), exceptless, expiate (adj.), exposture, exsufflicate, extincture, extracting, eye-glass, fashion-monging, fated, fathomless, fedarie, felicitate, fig (v.), fit (v.), fitment, flap-dragon (v.), fleshment, foxship, frutify, fustilarian, gibbet (v.), gnarling, gratulate (adj.), gull-catcher, half-cap, half-checked, hardock, hay (n., 'home-thrust'), heartling, hewgh, high-borne, Hobbididance, hob nob, hodge-pudding, incardinate, immask, immoment, immure (n.), impair (adj.), imperceiverant, implorator, importless, inaidable, infamonize, inherce, inhoop, injoint, insisture, insultment, intenible, interjoin, intrenchant, intrince, invised, irregulous, jaded, jure, kickie-wickie, kitchen (v.), labras, land-damn, Lethied, looped, marcantant, meal (v.), mered, mid-season, misadventured, misbehaved, misdread (n.), misgraffed, misprized, mistership, Moorship, moraller, mose (v.), moulten, moy (n.), nayward, near-legged, necessitied, non-come, non-regardance, oathable, obliquie, observing (adj.), obstruct (n.), offendress, offering, omittance, oneyers, out-burn, out-crafty, outdwell, over-dyed, overgreen, over-office, overperch, overpost, over-ripen, over-stain, overstink, overweathered, pannell (v.), parling, pauser, phantasim, phese, phraseless, pilcher, please-man, plighter, portage, practisant, precipit, precurrer, predict (n.), probal, protester, pugging (adj.), quatch, questant, questrist, razorable, recollected, recomforture, recountment, rejoindure, reputeless, restem, revengive, right-drawn, rug-headed, salt rheum, scamel, scandalled, scrimer, sea-wing, sedged, self-abuse, self-offence, self-substantial, sessa, sharded, signeur, signeury, skains mate, sleided, slish, so-forth, soil (n.), sola, solidare, sortance, speciously, spectatorship, squire-like (adv.), sternage, stranger (v.), stricture, subcontract, substractor, successantly, suffered, superscript (n.), supervise (n.), suppliant (adj.), suraddition, suum, swoltery, sympathized, tallow catch, temperality, testern, tetter (n.), thoughten, torcher, tranect, twilled, [for coinages with <u>un-</u>, see p. 118], undercrest, under-fiend, under-hangman, under-honest, uplocked, uprighteously, upswarm (v.), vail (n., = 'sunset'), varletto, vastly, vizament, wappened, water-rug, wealsman, well-allied, well-dealing, well-derived, well-desired, well-entered, well-forewarning, well-labouring, well-noted, well-possessed, well-sailing, well-saying, well-seeing, well-seeming, well-took, well-weighing, well-wished, wenchless, window (v.), windring, wragged, wreakless, wroath

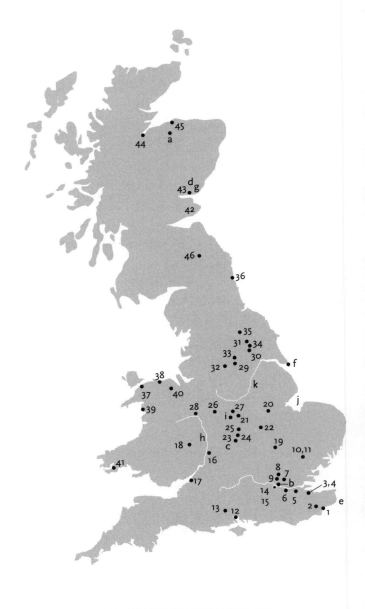

There are 184 scenes set in Britain outside London in Shakespeare's plays, though not all in specified or identifiable locations. In particular, there are few named settings in the 'ancient Britain' plays, *Cymbeline* and *King Lear*. In this table, counties are given in their names prior to local government reorganization in 1976. The map also shows a few of the other places mentioned in the plays.

Area	Location	Play	Scene	Map Number
Berkshire	Windsor	Richard II	II.2, V.3–4, 6	14
Berkshire	Windsor	The Merry Wives of Windsor	I, II, III.2–5, IV, V	14
Berkshire	Frogmore	The Merry Wives of Windsor	III.1	15
Gloucestershire	Tewkesbury	Henry VI Part III	V.4–5	16
Gloucestershire	unspecified	Henry IV Part II	III.2, V.1, 3	—
Gloucestershire	unspecified	Richard II	II.3	—
Gloucestershire	Bristol	Richard II	III.1	17
Hampshire	Southampton	Henry V	II.1	12
Herefordshire	Mortimer's Cross	Henry VI Part III	II.1	18
Hertfordshire	Barnet	Henry VI Part III	V.2–3	7
Hertfordshire	St Albans	Henry VI Part II	II.1, V.2–3	8
Hertfordshire	(King's) Langley	Richard II	III.4	9
Huntingdonshire	Kimbolton	Henry VIII	IV.2	19
Kent	Rochester	Henry IV Part I	II.1	3
Kent	Gadshill	Henry IV Part I	II.2	4
Kent	Dover	Henry VI Part II	IV.1	1
Kent	Dover	King Lear	IV.3–4, 6–7, V	1
Kent	nr Ashford	Henry VI Part II	IV.10	2
Kent	Dartford-Blackheath	Henry VI Part II	V.1	5
Kent	Blackheath	Henry VI Part II	IV.2–3	6
Leicestershire	Leicester?	King Lear	I.1	21
Lincolnshire	Swinstead Abbey	King John	V.6–7	20
Northamptonshire	Northampton	King John	I.1, ?IV.1–3, V.1	22
Northumberland	Warkworth	Henry IV Part I	II.3	36
Northumberland	Warkworth	Henry IV Part II	I.1, II.3	36
Scotland	Forres, Morayshire	Macbeth	I.1–4, III, IV.1	45
Scotland	Inverness	Macbeth	I.5–7, II	44
Scotland	Fife	Macbeth	IV.2	42
Scotland	Dunsinane	Macbeth	V	43
Scotland	Roxborough Castle	King Edward III	I.2, II	46
Shropshire	Shrewsbury	Henry IV Part I	IV.1, 3, V	28
Staffordshire	Tamworth	Richard III	V.2	26
Staffordshire	Bosworth	Richard III	V.3–5	27
Suffolk	Bury St Edmund's	Henry VI Part II	III.1–2	10
Suffolk	St Edmundsbury	King John	V.2–5	11
Wales	Bangor	Henry IV Part I	III.1	37
Wales	Flint	Richard II	III.3	40
Wales	Conwy?	Richard II	II.4	38
Wales	Harlech? (Barkloughly)	Richard II	III.2	39

(continues)

(continued from p.111)

Area	Location	Play	Scene	Map Number
Wales	Milford Haven	Cymbeline	III.4	41
Wales	unspecified	Cymbeline	III.3, IV.1, 2, 4	–
Warwickshire	Warwick	Henry VI Part III	IV.2–3	23
Warwickshire	Kenilworth	Henry VI Part II	IV.9	24
Warwickshire	Coventry	Henry VI Part II	IV.1	25
Warwickshire	Coventry	Henry IV Part I	IV.2	25
Warwickshire	Coventry	Richard II	I.3	25
Wiltshire	Salisbury	Richard III	V.1	13
Yorkshire	Pontefract (Pomfret)	Richard II	V.5	29
Yorkshire	Pontefract (Pomfret)	Richard III	III.3	29
Yorkshire	Bishopthorpe, nr York	Henry IV Part I	IV.4	30
Yorkshire	Bishopthorpe, nr York	Henry IV Part II	I.3	30
Yorkshire	Gaultree Forest, nr York	Henry IV Part II	IV.1–3	31
Yorkshire	Sandal Castle, nr Wakefield	Henry VI Part III	I.2–4	32
Yorkshire	Towton, Saxton	Henry VI Part III	II.3–6	33
Yorkshire*	York	Henry VI Part III	II.2, IV.7	34
Yorkshire	Middleham Castle	Henry VI Part III	IV.5	35
Britain	unspecified	Cymbeline	I.1–3, 5–6, II.1–2, III.1, 2, 5, IV.3, V	–
Britain	unspecified	King Lear	I, II, III, IV.1, 2, 5	–

Also shown:

a Cawdor (Macbeth)
b Datchet (The Merry Wives of Windsor)
c Forest of Arden (As You Like It)
d Glamis (Macbeth)
e Goodwins (The Merchant of Venice)
f Ravenspur (Richard II)
g Scone (Macbeth)
h Severn (Henry IV Part I)
i Sutton Coldfield (Henry IV Part II)
j The Wash (King John)
k Trent (Henry IV Part I)

*Surprisingly, no scene in the 'Wars of the Roses' history plays (*Henry VI Part II* and *III*) is set in Lancaster, though several are set in York.

════ *Shakespeare's pronunciation* ════

Shakespeare must have spoken with the Warwickshire accent of his day, but after many years in London this would have been modified in the direction of the city. Moving between Stratford and London, his accent would have accommodated to the people around him – a facility everyone has, but one which is especially sensitive in people who have to listen and speak for a living, such as actors.

Play Settings

Twenty-two of Shakespeare's plays are not set in Britain.
This map shows where they are located.

1 Antony and Cleopatra
2 All's Well that Ends Well
3 The Comedy of Errors
4 Coriolanus
5 Hamlet
6 Julius Caesar
7 Love's Labour's Lost
8 Measure for Measure
9 The Merchant of Venice
10 A Midsummer Night's Dream
11 Much Ado About Nothing
12 Othello
13 Pericles
14 Romeo and Juliet
15 The Tempest
16 Timon of Athens
17 Titus Andronicus
18 Troilus and Cressida
19 Twelfth Night
20 The Two Gentlemen of Verona
21 The Two Noble Kinsmen
22 The Winter's Tale
23 English history plays

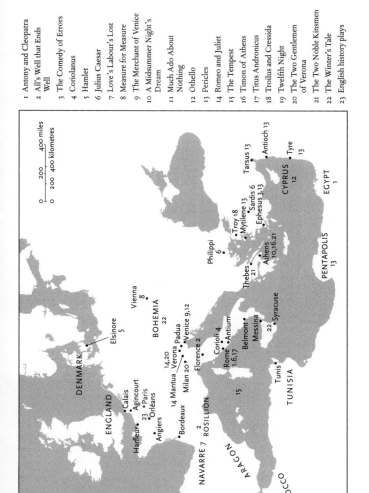

There are 1035 cases where the *Oxford English Dictionary* has Shakespeare recorded as the *first* of several people to use a word, in one or more senses, with the next recorded use not occurring until at least a generation – twenty-five years – later, suggesting that others did not employ the usage before him. A gloss is given where this is needed to find the right sense in the *OED*. (For Shakespeare as the *only* recorded user of a word, see p. 108.)

abhorred, abjectly, abodement, abruption, abutting, Academe, accessible, accoutred, accuse (n.), accused, Acheron, acorned, acquired, acutely, added, adjunct (adj.), admiringly, Adon, adsum, advantaged, adversely, advertising (adj.), affrighted, after-supper, agued, aidance, aidless, airless, alarm-bell, alarmed, allaying, allegiant, allicholly, amazedly, amazing, anchoring, anear, an-hungry, annexment, antre, appearer, apperil, applauding (adj.), apple-john, argal, aroint, arouse, arrivance, asinego, askant (preposition), assailable, assassination, assembled, assubjugate, atomy, attending, attest, avouch, awakening, back-sword-man, bail (v.), ballad-monger, bandying, barber (v.), barefaced, baring, barky, barn (v.), based (adj.), baseless, bass-viol, basta, basting, bated, batler, battered, batty, baubling, bawcock, beached, be-all, bear-like, bedabble, bedazzle, beetle (v.), befortune, beggared, beguiling, behaved, behowl, Bellona, belonging, bemad, bemeet, bemock, bemoil, bescreen, besmirch, besmirched, bethump, betrayed, betrim, bettering, betting, bewailing (adj.), bewitchment, biddy, bifold, birthplace, blabbing, black man, black-browed, blastment, bloodied, blood-stained, blue-cap, blue-eyed, blue-veined, blusterer, bodikin, boding, bold-faced, bona-roba, bonded, bookful, botch (n.), bottled, bow-wow, boys'-play, breaking, briareus, brimfulness, brisky, brooch (v.), broomstaff, bully-rook, bumbailiff, burdened, butchered, caged, calumniating, camping (adj.), canary (v.), cannibally, canopy (v.), caparison (v), caper (v.), capriccio, cased, casing, castigate, Cataian, cater, cat-like, caudle, censuring (adj.), centure, cerement, ceremoniously, chaffless, chaliced, champion (v.), changeful, channel (v.), chanson, chapless, characterless, cheerer, cheese-paring, chidden, childness, chimney-top, chop-fallen, choppy, churchlike, Cimmerian, circummure, climate (v.), clod-poll, closing (adj.), clot-poll, cloud-capped, cloyless, coign, cold-hearted, collected, collied, combless, co-mingle, committed, commutual, companion (v.), compassion, compelling (adj.), comply, compunctious, condoling, confirmer, confix,

===== *Who has more lines?* =====

Portia or Shylock? (See p. 89.)

conflicting, congregated, conquering, consanguineous, consigned, contaminated, contending, contentless, contriving (adj.), control (n.), copper-nose, corragio, corresponsive, couching (adj.), counted, counterfeiting (adj.), coursing (adj.), court-hand, cowed, crank (v.), craven (v.), creating (adj.), creating (n.), credent, crestless, crimeful, crimeless, crimson (v.), crushed, cuckoo-bud, cudgel (v.), cudgelling, culled, cullionly, curbed, cursing (adj.), daisied, dangling, Dardan, Dardanian, darting (adj.), dateless, dauntless, dawn, dawning, dead man's fingers, deafened, deafening, deceptious, deep-mouthed, defeated, definement, defunctive, delighted, deluding, depositary, deracinate, derived, despairing, destined, dewdrop, dey-woman, diable, dialogue (v.), differency, ding (n.), disbench, discarded, disedge, dislimn, disorb, disproportion, dispurse, disquantity, disquietly, dissembly, disturbed, disturbing, divest, dobbin, dog-weary, domineering, double-lock, doughy, dower (v.), dowerless, downstairs, dragon's tail, droplet, dropsied, drug (v.), duello, duteous, East Indies, ecce, Edward, effectless, effuse (n.), elbow (v.), elf (v.), embound, embrace (n.), employer, emptying, enchafed, enchantingly, encompassment, encrimsoned, encroaching, end (v.), end-all, enfranchisement, enhearse, enmesh, enrapt, ensky, enswathe, entame, enthrone, entwist, Erebus, even-handed, eventful, exacting, excitement, expertness, expressure, extolment, eye-beam, eye-wink, facinorious, fairyland, fanged, fangless, fap, far-off, fathered, fat-witted, featureless, fee-faw-fum, fern-seed, festinate, festinately, fielded, fiendlike, fill (n.), film (v.), fineless, finless, fishify, fitful, fives, fixture, flame-coloured, flaw (v.), flawed, fleckled, fleer (n.), footfall, foppish, foregone, forgetive, forging, foul-mouthed, founded, foutre, Franciscan (adj.), Frenchwoman, fronting (adj.), full-hearted, futurity, Galen, gallian, galloping (n.), gally (v.), gentlefolk, ghastly, gibber (v.), girded, glass eye, glaze, glib (v.), glow (n.), gnarled, go-between, goldenly, gormandizing, grannam, grass-plot, gravel-blind, graveless, graze, green-eyed, grey-coated, grumbling (adj.), grumbling (n.), guessing (adj.), guiding (adj.), guiltily, half-cheek, halt (n.), hatch (n.), heart-sore, heart-struck, heaving (adj.), hedge-pig, hell-born, Hellespont, herblet, herb-woman, hic jacet, high-day (interjection), highmost, high-pitched, high-reaching, high-wrought, hillo, hinge (v.), hoarding (adj.), hoarding (n.), home-keeping, homo, honoured, hoo (interjection), horridly, hostile, hot-blooded, hum (interjection), hunchbacked, idle (v.), ignobly, ill-boding, ill-got, ill-starred, ill-tempered, illume, ill-used, immediacy, imminence, impaint, impartment, impede, *(continues)*

Who has more lines?

Palamon or Arcite? (See p. 89.)

impleach, import (n.), importantly, impress (n.), impress (v.), impressed, inaudible, inauspicious, incarnadine, inched, inclip, incorpsed, increasing (adj.), indart, indirection, indistinguishable, indistinguished, inscroll, insculpture (n.), inshell, instinctively, insulter, insulting, insuppressive, interchangement, intertissued, intruding, inurn, inventorial, inviting (adj.), irreconciled, iterance, jaunce (n.), jaunce (v.), jig (v.), jointress, joint-ring, judgement-day, juiced, Juno-like, kecksy, keech, kingdomed, king-killer, kissing, kitchen-wench, label (v.), lack-lustre, lagging, languageless, lapse (v.), laughable, leaky, leap-frog, leer (n.), lengthened, lethargy (v.), lewdster, logger-headed, lonely, loo (interjection), looked (adj.), looking, lovered, love-token, lower (v.), low-spirited, lune, lustihood, majestically, malignancy, mammock (v.), mangling, manifested, mansionry, marriage-bed, melted, mended, merited, miching malicho, militarist, milk-livered, millioned, minimus, minutely, miracle (v.), misplaced, misquote, mistaking, mistful, mist-like, mistreading, moble, mockable, monster (v.), monumental, moonbeam, morris, mortifying, motionless, mountain snow, mountebank (v.), mousing (adj.), moved, muddy (v.), mull (v.), multipotent, narrow-mouthed, nayword, neat's tongue, neglected, neglection, neighbouring, Nemean, nervy, Nessus, Nestor, never-dying, new-create, new-devised, new-fallen, new-form, new-risen, newsmonger, new-sprung, night-fly, night-owl, night-walking, night-wandering, nodding, noiseless, nook-shotten, Norweyan, notedly, novum, oar (v.), obduracy, obscenely, obscured, observingly, offenceful, onwards, operant, operate, opposeless, opposing, oppugnancy, opulency, orbed, Ottomite, outbreak, outbreathed, outdared, outfrown, outgrow, out-Herod, outlustre, outpeer, outpray, out-prize, outroar, outscold, outsleep, outstay, outswear, outsweeten, outswell, out-talk, out-villain, outvoice, outweigh, overcanopy, over-credulous, over-eye, overglance, overgrowth, overhang, over-kind, over-leaven, overname, overparted, overpay, over-picture, overpower, overrate, over-red, overscutched, oversize, oversnow, over-tedious, overteem, overview, ox-head, pageant (v.), pageantry, paiocke, pale-faced, pander (v.), parkward, parti-, partner (v.), pash (n.), pebbled, pellet (v.), pelting (n.), peregrinate, persistency, persistive, personating, perusal, petition (v.), Phoebe, pibble-pabble, pig-nut, pioned, placcate, plantage, pleached, plodder, plodding, plumpy, posied, pouncet-box, prabble, preceptial, precurse, predecease, predeceased, preformed, preparedly, presented, preyful, primogenitive, primy, prison-gate, profitless, promising, prompture, propertied, property (v.), prophetic, proposer, protesting (n.), protractive, published, pudency,

═══════ *Who has more lines?* ═══════

Troilus or Cressida ? (See p. 89.)

pulpiter, pupil age, puppy-dog, purr (v.), push-pin, qualifying, quartering, queen (v.), radiance, ransomless, ranting (adj.), rat-catcher, rated, ratifier, raw-boned, recanting, receiving, reclusive, regardfully, regreet, relenting, reliance, relume, remarked, remediate (adj.), repair (n.), repasture, repeated, replenished, reprobance, required, resurvey (v.), revealing, rev., reverted, reviving, revokement, revolted, reword, right (n.), riveted, rondure, rooky, rootedly, rose-cheeked, rose-lipped, routed, rubied, rubious, rumination, rumourer, runnion, sacked, sacrificial, satisfying, savagery, scaffoldage, scarfed, scholarly (adv.), schooldays, scrippage, scuffle (n.), sea-like (adv.), seamy, seated, sect, seemer, self-killed, self-slaughter, self-slaughtered, semblative, sepulchre (v.), sequestered, servant (v.), seven years, severing, shard-born, sheeted, sheltered, sherris, shifted, shipwrecking, should (n.), shudder (n.), shunless, sickly (v.), silliness, silverly, silver-white, sire (v.), sister (v.), sistering, skimble-skamble (adj.), skim-milk, skirted, skyey, skyish, slab (adj.), sledded, slickly, slightness, slippered, sliver (v.), slug-a-bed, sluggardize, smirched, smutch (v.), snail-slow, sneak-cup, sneap (n.), sneaping, soaring (adj.), soiled, solicit (n.), soliciting (adj.), soundless, sowl, sphered, spilth, spirit-stirring, spleenful, splitting (adj.), sprag, springhalt, squabble (v.), squeaking (n.), stealthy, still-stand, stitchery, stone jug, streaked, strewment, struck, successfully, sucked, sufficing, suffocating, suggesting, sully (n.), sumless, summer-cloud, superflux, superserviceable, surfeited, surviver, surviving, sustaining (adj.), swag-bellied, swallowed, swan's-down, swelled, sweltered, tamely, tangled, tanling, tardily, tardiness, Tarpeian, tearing (adj.), tempest-tossed, tender-minded, tented, tested, testril, Thessalian (adj.), thick-sighted, threateningly, three-foot, three-inch, three-legged, threnos, throw (v.), thumb-ring, thunder-bearer, time-honoured, Timon, tirrit, tithed, tod (v.), toged, tortive, trade-fallen, tranced, triplex, trippingly, triumviry, true-born, true-bred, twin-brother, umbered, [for coinages with un-, see p. 118], underpeep, under-skinker, up-pricked, uproar (v.), uproused, upstairs, upturned, urging, useful, useless, ushering, vagrom, valueless, varied, varletry, vastidity, vaulting, versal, viewless, villagery, violated, visiting (adj.), votary, vulnerable, wafture, waned, war-proof, warranted, warring, war-worn, watch-case, watch-dog, water-drop, water-fly, waverer, weather-fend, week (interjection), well-accomplished, well-behaved, well-bred, well-composed, well-descended, well-divided, well-educated, well-famed, well-fitted, well-flowered, well-married, well-painted, well-reputed, well-respected, well-saved, well-warranted, well-won, wenching (adj.), wheeled, whereuntil, white-bearded, wifelike (adj.), wrack, writing, Xantippe, yellow (v.), yelping, yoking, young-eyed

=== *Who has more lines?* ===

Romeo or Juliet ? (See p. 89.)

Shakespeare's uns

Shakespeare seems to have had a penchant for coining words beginning with the prefix *un-*. Several, such as *uncurse* and *unshout*, are among the more dramatic of his creations.

As only user (see p. 108)

unbraided, uncape, uncheck, uncolted, uncomprehensive, uncuckolded, uncurbable, uncurse, undeeded, unfair (v.), unfolding, ungenitured, unhacked, unhaired, unimproved, unowed, unpay, unpinked, unplausive, unprovoke, unqualitied, unrecalling, unrecounted, unrecuring, unseeming, unseminared, unshout, unshrubbed, unsisting, unspoke, unsured, untempering, unweighing, unwit (v.), unwrung

As first user (see p. 114)

unaching, unaneled, unauspicious, unbefitting, unbless, unbloodied, unbonneted, unbookish, unbreeched, unbuild, unchanging, uncharmed, unchary, unclaimed, unclew, unclog, unconfinable, undeaf, undeserver, undinted, undistinguishable, undivulged, undreamed, unduteous, unearthly, uneducated, unexperient, unexpressive, unfamed, unfathered, unfilial, unfix, unfool, unforfeited, unfrequented, ungained, ungalled, ungored, ungravely, ungrown, unhand, unhatched (adj. 'unhacked'), unhelpful, unhidden, unkinged, unkinglike, unlicensed, unlicked, unlink, unmeritable, unmitigated, unmusical, unmuzzle, unnerved, unpitifully, unpolicied, unpolluted, unpossessing, unpregnant, unpremeditated, unprevailing, unprofited, unpruned, unraked, unreal, unreversed, unrivalled, unscratched, unsex, unshrinking, unshunnable, unshunned, unslipping, unsmirched, unsolicited, unsphere, unstooping, unsullied, unswayable, unswear, untalked, untender, untented, unthread, untimbered, untreasure, unvarnished, unvulnerable, unwedgeable, unwept, unwhipped, unyielding

MacHomer

At the Edinburgh Festival Fringe in 2000, Canadian impressionist Rick Miller cast Homer Simpson as Macbeth. The play follows the Shakespeare plot but the roles are taken by the cast of *The Simpsons*, voiced by Miller. Marge plays Lady Macbeth, Mr Burns plays Duncan. Barney plays Macduff. The text is not always true to the First Folio. Macbeth's speech at II.1.33 begins:

> Is this a dagger I see before me or a pizza?
> Mmmmmm … pizza.

Schwarzenegger Shakespeare

When we typed 'schwarzenegger shakespeare' into the Internet search engine Google, we got 39,200 results. The links between the two are not as doubtful as you might think. Schwarzenegger apparently got his first part in an American film (*Hercules in New York*, 1970) because his friend and promoter Joe Weider convinced the film's producers that he had been a great Shakespearian actor in Austria. The two Ss are often compared in news items, and Shakespeare has entered Schwarzenegger's films. In *Last Action Hero* (1993), the world's biggest fan of the world's best action hero imagines Schwarzenegger as a Terminator-style Hamlet. 'Don't talk. Just do it!' he calls to the screen …

HAMLET: Hey Claudius! You killed my father! Big mistake!
NARRATOR: Something is rotten in the state of Denmark, and Hamlet is taking out the trash!
OLD MAN: Stay thy hand, fair prince.
HAMLET: [*shooting him*] Who said I'm fair?
NARRATOR: No one is going to tell this sweet prince good night.
HAMLET: To be or not to be? Not to be.

Which is certainly *one* way of dealing with Claudius.

Move over, Arnie

In its day it was the most popular Shakespeare, the absolute pot-boiler of this period. I showed it for inner-city high school students early on. They went crazy over it. They said, 'Move over, Schwarzenegger, here comes Titus.' (Julie Taymor, on why make a film of *Titus Andronicus,* in *Written By*, February 2000)

Monosyllabic words

Around a quarter of Shakespeare's poetic lines consist entirely of monosyllabic words, increasing the impression of pace, and drawing the verse in the direction of everyday speech. Some examples:

For who would bear the whips and scorns of time
(*Hamlet*, III.1.70)

O then I see Queen Mab hath been with you
(*Romeo and Juliet*, I.4.53)

I pray you give me leave to go from hence
(*The Merchant of Venice*, IV.1.392)

O how I faint when I of you do write
(Sonnet 80, 1)

Men only

In Elizabethan England it was illegal for women to perform on stage. Actresses were not permitted until the Restoration (1660). Boys, with their higher voices, would usually take the younger female roles. Shakespeare's Globe in London has presented several all-male productions, with Mark Rylance giving acclaimed performances as Cleopatra (in *Antony and Cleopatra*, 1999) and Olivia (in *Twelfth Night*, 2002). The Globe has also redressed the balance: their all-female productions include *Richard III* and *The Taming of the Shrew* (both 2003) and *Much Ado About Nothing* (2004).

A question of gender

Throughout our tour [an all-male production] *I would be asked, 'Why are the women's roles played by men?' yet, though I'd waffle on about purity and clarity, I was never able to persuade them that it was anything other than a gimmick. We know that female roles were played by boys in Shakespeare's time, but to have a man with five o'clock shadow striding about pretending to be Rosalind or Phoebe and talking in a rich baritone must have been, to the average man in the street, somewhat disconcerting.*

(Nigel Hawthorne, *Straight Face*, 2002, p. 33)

Girls vs swots

By the age of fifteen, though, Shakespeare had still taken no special hold of my imagination. I was interested in soccer and girls. Shakespeare was for swots.

(Kenneth Branagh, interview in *The Daily Telegiraffe*, 30 October 1995)

Great parts

When I first started acting, and we would all sit down and talk about Shakespeare and how great it was, I thought well, I suppose it is. It is if you get to play Macbeth or Hamlet. But who wants to play bloody Lady Macbeth or Ophelia? And it struck me that most women seem to be required to pit themselves against men in dramatic situations, and the men get to pit themselves against ideas or God.

(Judy Davis, quoted in the Judy Davis site at perfectpeople.net)

Who has more lines?

Beatrice or Benedick? (See p. 89.)

False friends: revolve

MODERN SENSE: perform a circular motion
OBSOLETE SENSE: consider, ponder, meditate

♣ Tarquin lies 'revolving / The sundry dangers of his will's obtaining' (*The Rape of Lucrece*, 127).
♣ Queen Margaret advises Queen Elizabeth to listen carefully to what she's been saying: 'Revolving this will teach thee how to curse' (*Richard III*, IV.4.123).
♣ Belarius says to his sons: 'you may then revolve what tales I have told you' (*Cymbeline*, III.3.14).
♣ Malvolio reads the letter which tells him 'If this fall into thy hands, revolve' (*Twelfth Night*, II.5.139).

Actors playing Malvolio have been known to turn themselves around when saying this line – but that sense didn't arrive in English until a century after Shakespeare.

Note also the related word used by King Richard when darkly musing: 'The deep-revolving witty Buckingham / No more shall be the neighbour to my counsels' (*Richard III*, IV.2.42).

Siblings

William was one of eight children born to John and Mary Shakespeare:

Name	Birth	Death	Biography
Joan	1558	?	death year unknown, but presumably early, as the same name was given to their fifth child – not an unusual practice, in those days
Margaret	1562	1563	died age one
William	1564	1616	died age fifty-two (p. 161)
Gilbert	1566	1612	died age forty-eight
Joan	1569	1646	died age seventy-seven, married William Hart of Stratford
Anne	1571	1579	died age eight
Richard	1574	1613	died age thirty-nine
Edmund	1580	1607	died age twenty-seven, followed William into the theatre, becoming an actor; a brother Edmund features in *King Lear* (1605–6)

New editions

New editions of Shakespeare appear regularly, but never more so than during the nineteenth century. Between 1800 and 1900 a new complete edition appeared on average every six weeks.

Some modern editions

Edition	Dates	Editors
Arden	1891–1924	W. J. Craig, then R. H. Case
Arden Second Series (the 'New Arden')	1951–95	Una Ellis-Fermor, then Harold Brooks, Harold Jenkins, later with Brian Morris, Richard Proudfoot
Arden Third Series	1995–	Richard Proudfoot, Ann Thompson, David Scott Kastan
Cambridge Shakespeare	1863–6	W. G. Clark, J. Glover, W. A. Wright
New Cambridge	1921–66	J. Dover Wilson, Arthur Quiller-Couch
New Cambridge	1984–	Philip Brockbank, then Brian Gibbons
Oxford Shakespeare	1982–	Stanley Wells
Oxford Shakespeare (1 vol.)	1986	Stanley Wells, Gary Taylor
Pelican Shakespeare	1956–67	Alfred Harbage
New Penguin Shakespeare	1967–2005	T. J. B. Spencer, Stanley Wells
Penguin Shakespeare	2005–	Stanley Wells
Riverside Shakespeare (1 vol.)	1974, 1997	G. Blakemore Evans

Too much punctuation

Shakespeare's text is always absurdly over punctuated: generations of scholars have tried to turn him into a good grammarian. Even the original printed texts are not much help – the first printers popped in some extra punctuation. When punctuation is just related to the flow of the spoken word, the actor is liberated. (*Peter Hall's Diaries*, 21 August 1975)

Leading parts

A Shakespeare play does not usually have more than eight important speaking parts. This was as much a consequence of the company management system as of dramatic artistry: there were eight sharers in Shakespeare's company. The company then hired several men and boys for other parts. The total cast might have reached fifteen – the impression given by Swiss traveller Thomas Platter, when he watched *Julius Caesar* at the Globe in 1599. As that play has over forty parts, the amount of doubling must have been considerable.

Anti-playing

Not everyone liked acting companies. When in 1596 the citizens of Blackfriars heard that James Burbage planned to turn a local hall into a 'comon playhouse', they drew up a petition of complaint to the Privy Council. It will, they said,

> grow to be a very great annoyance and trouble, not only to all the noblemen and gentlemen thereabout inhabiting, but allso a generall inconvenience to all the inhabitants of the same precinct, both by reason of the great resort and gathering togeather of all manner of vagrant and lewde persons that, under cullor [colour] of resorting to the playes, will come thither and worke all manner of mischeefe ...

That was not all:

> ... and allso to the great pestring and filling up of the same precinct, yf it should please God to send any visitation of sickness as heretofore hath been, for that the same precinct is allready growne very populous ...

And still more:

> ... and besides, that the same playhouse is so neere the Church that the noyse of the drummes and trumpetts will greatly disturbe and hinder both the ministers and parishioners in tyme of devine service and sermons ...

The petition was upheld. James Burbage moved on.

Death-knell

The Queen's Men, created by royal command in 1583, were primarily a touring company, and they visited Stratford several times. William Knell was their chief tragedian – until 13 June 1587, when he died in a duel with a fellow-actor. During that summer, the company was therefore a man short – and this has fuelled the hypothesis that they took on the young Shakespeare as an actor, who then returned with them to London. There is no evidence – and it would have been unusual for a company whose actors were routinely recruited in the capital – but the idea has support.

A comment from Mr Curdle

Mr Curdle in Charles Dickens' *Nicholas Nickleby* (Chapter 24), had proved to his own satisfaction 'that by altering the received mode of punctuation, any one of Shakespeare's plays could be made quite different, and the sense completely changed'.

Central Park

In New York's Central Park on Literary Walk, there is a full-standing statue of Shakespeare. It was made by John Quincy Adams Ward (1830–1910) and unveiled on 23 May 1872. The statue was planned ten years earlier by a group of actors which included the great Shakespearian actor Edwin Booth. They received permission to lay the cornerstone, but nothing was done until after the Civil War in 1866. There has been a reading of *Julius Caesar* at the statue on the Ides of March every year since the late 1890s (that play was used to originally raise funds for the statue). Central Park has been home to a Shakespeare Festival since 1962.

Which acts have most scenes?

Five plays have acts containing ten scenes or more:

Antony and Cleopatra, IV	15	Henry VI Part II, IV	10
Antony and Cleopatra, III	13	Troilus and Cressida, V	10
Coriolanus, I	10		

He that plays the king ...

The Anglo-Welsh poet known as John Davies of Hereford wrote *The Scourge of Folly* in 1610. In it there is an epigram addressed to 'our English Terence [see p. 4], Mr Will: Shake-speare':

> *Some say (good Will) which I, in sport, do sing*
> *Had'st thou not plaid some Kingly parts in sport,*
> *Thou hadst bin a companion for a King ...*

No one knows which kingly parts Shakespeare played, though Nicholas Rowe in 1709 asserts that he played the Ghost in *Hamlet*, and others have suggested Duncan and some of the Henrys. Other reports mention him playing Adam in *As You Like It*. And Ben Jonson lists him along with other actors as a player in *Every Man in his Humour* (1598) and as a 'principall Tragœdian' in his play about Sejanus, *Seianvs his Fall* (1603).

The new plays

Eighteen of Shakespeare's plays were published for the first time in the First Folio: *All's Well that Ends Well*; *Antony and Cleopatra*; *As You Like It*; *The Comedy of Errors*; *Coriolanus*; *Cymbeline*; *Henry VI Part I*; *Henry VIII*; *Julius Caesar*; *King John*; *Macbeth*; *Measure for Measure*; *The Taming of the Shrew*; *The Tempest*; *Timon of Athens*; *Twelfth Night*; *The Two Gentlemen of Verona*; *The Winter's Tale*.

A quick-fire exchange

In rare cases, a single line of five feet (p. 50) is split into five separate units, with one unit given to each of the speakers in rapid succession. An example is in *King John* (III.3.64), when the King intimates to Hubert that Arthur should be killed:

KING JOHN:
    Thou art his keeper.
HUBERT: And I'll keep him so
    That he shall not offend your majesty.
KING JOHN:
    Death.
HUBERT: My lord.
KING JOHN: A grave.
HUBERT: He shall not live.
KING JOHN: Enough.

Latin grammar

Shakespeare remembers his school Latin grammar several times.

In *Titus Andronicus* (IV.2.20), Demetrius reads aloud a Latin verse, and Chiron replies:

O, 'tis a verse in Horace, I know it well;
I read it in the grammar long ago.

'The', not 'a', grammar: William Lily's was the only one in universal use.

In *Henry IV Part I* (II.1.96), Gadshill ends an exchange of pleasantries with the Chamberlain by saying 'Go to, homo is a common name to all men.' This too is directly from Lily:

A noun substantive is proper to the thing it betokeneth, as Eduardus is my proper name, or else is common to more, as Homo is a common name to all men.

Best known is the scene in *The Merry Wives of Windsor* (IV.1.20, 29) when Sir Hugh Evans examines young William on his Latin.

EVANS: William, how many numbers is in nouns?
WILLIAM: Two ...
EVANS: What is lapis, William?
WILLIAM: A stone.

Why does he choose this word? It is Lily's choice of example.

In nouns be two numbers, the singular and the plural. The singular number speaketh of one, as lapis, a stone. The plural number speaketh of more than one, as lapides, stones.

Prologues

Eight plays have a character introducing the events which are to be portrayed:

Henry IV Part II, spoken by Rumour

Henry V, spoken by Chorus before each act

Henry VIII, unnamed

Pericles, spoken by Gower before each act

Romeo and Juliet, spoken by Chorus before both Acts I and II

Troilus and Cressida, unnamed

The Two Noble Kinsmen, unnamed

The Winter's Tale, where Time bridges the gap of sixteen years after Act III

There is also a Prologue in the 'play within a play' in *Hamlet*.

Copying

In a modern repertory company, each member will have a copy of an entire play to read. This was not the procedure in Shakespeare's time: the actors had only their own parts. There would be one main copy of the play, held by the book-keeper (see p. 155), and used on-stage to prompt the actors if they lost their lines. The reasons were chiefly practical – the cost and time it would take to make copies – but there was a side-benefit. The absence of complete copies meant, in an age where copyright did not exist, that it would be difficult for rival theatre companies to steal each other's work. This did not stop the members of a company going to see a rival production and trying to copy down the lines. Some of the badly remembered Quarto versions of Shakespeare's plays doubtless had this origin (see p. 96).

Using you *and* thou

Of all uses of second-person pronouns in Shakespeare, 60 per cent are *you*-forms. *You* exceeds *thou* in a ratio of 3:2.

You-forms		*Thou*-forms	
you	14,244	thou	5942
ye	352	thee	3444
your	6912	thy	4429
yours	260	thine	510
yourself	289	thyself	251
yourselves	74		
Total	22,131		14,576

How many books did Shakespeare read?

Is it possible to work out how many books influenced Shakespeare when he was writing his plays and poems? Stuart Gillespie's dictionary of Shakespeare sources, *Shakespeare's Books*, lists around 200 works which we 'can on current evidence suppose Shakespeare read in whole or in part, and which affected his writing in some way'. They include his historical sources, notably Raphael Holinshed's *Chronicles* and Thomas North's translation from Plutarch, Latin authors such as Ovid and Horace, the Bible and the *Book of Common Prayer*, and many smaller texts such as Aesop's *Fables*.

Payment for not performing?

In the 1622 accounts of the Borough Chamberlain of Stratford-upon-Avon, there is this curious entry:

> *To the King's Players*
> *for not playing in the Hall, 6/-* [six shillings]

The event relates to a visit by some of Shakespeare's fellows that year — perhaps to see the new monument at his tomb. Stratford had banned the performance of plays, but the King's Players had a royal licence 'freely to use and exercise the arte and facultie of playing ... stage-plaies'. The Council's dilemma seems to have been resolved by paying them compensation. A cynic would say they had been paid not to play!

Epilogues

The epilogue was a conventional expression of humility at the end of a play, apologizing for any inadequacy in the performance and asking for applause. It also sometimes informed the audience about future plays by the company. Ten of Shakespeare's plays have one, all comedies or histories:

> *All's Well that Ends Well*, spoken by the King
> *As You Like It*, spoken by Rosalind
> *Henry IV Part II*, unnamed
> *Henry VIII*, unnamed
> *A Midsummer Night's Dream*, spoken by Puck
> *Pericles*, spoken by Gower
> *The Tempest*, spoken by Prospero
> *The Two Noble Kinsmen*, unnamed
> *Troilus and Cressida*, spoken by Pandarus
> *Twelfth Night*, sung by Feste

Venus and Adonis

The plague closed London's theatres for a time in 1593. What was an aspiring dramatist to do? Doubtless Shakespeare carried on writing plays, but it also provided an opportunity to write a long erotic poem, *Venus and Adonis*, consisting of 1194 lines written in six-line stanzas with the rhymes following an *ab ab cc* pattern. In the dedication that precedes the poem, we read that it is 'the first heir of my invention'. It may have been his first complete work as a writer.

A thousand pounds?

Nicholas Rowe, in an early life of Shakespeare (1709), reports that Shakespeare received £1000 from the Earl of Southampton for his work – a huge sum, in those days (a Stratford schoolteacher's salary would be about £20 a year). The report has often been doubted. Shakespeare may have received some money – why dedicate a poem otherwise? – but the benefits may have taken other forms, such as access to the Earl's library.

Dedications

In 1593, Shakespeare dedicated his first major poem, *Venus and Adonis*, to Henry Wriothesley, the 3rd Earl of Southampton (1573-1624), then a young man of nineteen. It must have been well received, for in 1594 he dedicated *The Rape of Lucrece* to him as well. He is one of many claimants for the identity of 'W.H.' in the Sonnets.

Richard, the first

Venus and Adonis was entered on the Stationer's Register on 18 April 1593. In his diary for 12 June, a London civil servant, Richard Stonley, records two book purchases:

> *for the Survey of Ffraunce, with the Venus and Adhonay p^r Shakspere, xii.d*

Twelve pence – sixpence each (the other book was a topographical description of France, also published in 1592). Doubtless others bought *Venus and Adonis* before him, but Stonley is the first known purchaser.

Relevance

I think it's totally relevant. The terrible thing is that if people see one bad production, they tend to never want to see a Shakespeare play again. But the reverse is true too.

(Judi Dench, asked if Shakespeare is still relevant, RSC Interview, 2003)

Butchery

A story is told of Shakespeare's birthplace in Henley Street, when it was later owned by a butcher. He is reported to have written over his door:

> **SHAKESPEARE**
> **WAS BORN HERE.**
> **N.B. A HORSE AND CART TO LET.**

V, X or XX poems

The Passionate Pilgrim is another Miscellany – of twenty poems brought together and printed by William Jaggard as a publishing 'potboiler' in two editions in 1599 under the name of W. Shakespeare. It includes:

♣ Items I and II: pirated versions of two of Shakespeare's Sonnets (138, 144)
♣ Items III, V, and XVI: three poetic extracts from *Love's Labour's Lost* (IV.3.56–69, 2.101–14, 3.96–115)
♣ Poems by Richard Barnfield, Bartholomew Griffin and various unnamed writers.

Only five poems are definitely by Shakespeare, and the quality of the remainder has gained them few supporters as candidates for his authorship, but they have traditionally been printed together.

'Pirated' may seem to be a strong word, but this is the accusation made by Thomas Heywood in 1612, when Jaggard printed a third edition, also under Shakespeare's name, only this time including some of Heywood's poems. In his *Apologie for Actors* (1612), Heywood complained about the 'manifest injury' done to himself by printing his poems

> *in a lesse volume, vnder the name of another, which may put the world in opinion I might steale them from him; and hee to doe himselfe right, hath since published them in his owne name: but as I must acknowledge my lines not worthy his patronage, vnder whom he* [Jaggard] *hath publisht them, so the Author I know much offended with M. Jaggard (that altogether vnknowne to him) presumed to make so bold with his name.*

Why did Jaggard do it? Shakespeare's other poems were selling very well – *Venus and Adonis* had fifth and sixth editions in 1599. There was money in poetry. But the criticism seems to have had an effect, for a title-page exists where Shakespeare's name has been removed.

What religion was Shakespeare?

PROTESTANT

❧ Records of his baptism, marriage and burial show him as a member of the Church of England.

❧ Allusions in the plays to religious works include the Protestant Geneva Bible, *Book of Common Prayer* and the Homilies.

❧ What we know of his life-style suggests Protestantism: he lived for at least six years in London at the house of a refugee French Huguenot, Christopher Mountjoy; in 1608 the Stratford parish register shows him acting as godfather to a child of Henry Walker; in 1614 he entertained a preacher at New Place.

❧ None of the legatees and executors of his will can be identified as Catholics.

❧ He was intimate with Ben Jonson, despite the latter's apostasy from Catholicism.

❧ There is a strongly anti-papal tone in several passages in the plays, notably in *King John*.

CATHOLIC

❧ The late seventeenth-century Anglican archdeacon Richard Davies inherited papers which led him to claim that Shakespeare 'dyed a Papyst'.

❧ His parents had strong Catholic connections: his mother, Mary Arden, belonged to a family that remained Catholic during the reign of Elizabeth; John Shakespeare held public offices in Stratford-on-Avon during the Catholic Queen Mary's reign, when Protestants were excluded from such posts; also, in 1592 he is referred to as one of the 'recusants* heretofore presented who were thought to forbear coming to church for fear of process of debt'; and a spiritual testament found in the roof of the Henley Street house in 1757 is a Catholic profession of faith in fourteen articles, each headed John Shakespeare.

❧ Many recusants lived in the Stratford area; for example, the Catesbys (of Gunpowder Plot fame) lived at Bushwood Park in Stratford parish.

❧ Some biblical allusions in the plays seem to come from the Catholic Rheims Bible.

❧ There is a generally sympathetic portrayal of Catholicism, notably in the characters of the friars in *Romeo and Juliet*, *Much Ado About Nothing* and *Measure for Measure* – a marked contrast to the usual antipathetic portrayals of friars in Shakespeare's day.

❧ Many intimate details of Catholicism, such as confessions, purgatory and the last sacraments, are found in the plays. The reference to 'evening mass' in *Romeo and Juliet* (IV.I.38) is sometimes cited as ignorance, as the practice had been forbidden by the Pope; however, it was still continued in many places – including Verona.

*'An Act for restraining Popish Recusants to some certain place of abode' was passed in 1593. The statute defines a recusant as one 'Convicted for not repairing to some Church, Chapel, or usual place of Common Prayer to hear Divine Service there'.

Signatures

There are six Shakespearian signatures thought to be authentic – all in legal documents, including three in his will – and they display no less than five spellings. They are:

[a] *Shakp*, 1612, Belott-Mountjoy Deposition

[b] *Shakspe(r)*, 1613, Gatehouse Conveyance

[c] *Shaksper*, 1613, Gatehouse Mortgage

[d, e] *Shakspere*, 1616, first and second sheet of will

[f] *Shakspeare*, 1616, third sheet of will

It's the characters

Someone asked me why I liked Shakespeare. Without really thinking, I said 'It's because of the characters.' The range of Shakespeare's characters is enormous. He could write about the employer and the employee, about the king and the subject, about men and women, about young people and old people, people in love, people who are ready to kill. There is no area of human life that Shakespeare didn't seem to be in total contact with.

(Ian McKellen, 'On Acting Shakespeare',
Shakespeare Quarterly, Summer 1982)

Adaptations

There have been a number of stage adaptations of Shakespeare's plays, probably the best known being Tom Stoppard's *Rosencrantz and Guildenstern Are Dead*. The play takes place 'behind the scenes' of Shakespeare's *Hamlet*, with the two friends lost and confused while the events of Elsinore take place around them. Other adaptations of *Hamlet* include *Green Eggs and Hamlet*, *Gertrude and Claudius*, a novel by John Updike.

Bible translations

Scholars have identified thousands of allusions to biblical verses in the works, but it is often not clear which translation Shakespeare used, because the various Tudor versions are linguistically very close to each other. There are three main sources. The translation of the Bible used officially in churches was the Bishops' Bible of 1568, which became an authorized version in 1571. Some churches, however, continued to use the Geneva Bible of 1560, the first English Bible to be printed in roman type. The Catholic equivalent was the Rheims New Testament, which appeared in 1582. The Geneva was printed in small quartos, and its portability made it popular, especially for use in the home, so it is likely that this was Shakespeare's main source. There is some evidence to suggest he used the Bishops' version in the early plays (up to about 1598) and the Geneva in the later.

Exertion

The exertion of playing that massive role for a long time – it's never just a short spurt – was too daunting even to think about.

(Nigel Hawthorne on playing Lear,
Straight Face, 2002, p. 304)

Hamnet and Hamlet

The name Hamnet is unusual today, but it was common in the sixteenth and seventeenth centuries, when it was used both as a first name and as a surname. It has related forms in Hamlin, Hamblyn, Hamelot, Hamonet, Hammond and others – and also Hamlet. Hamlet too was a common first name – a seventeenth-century clergyman, Hamlet Marshall, named his son Hamlet, lived with his nephew Hamlet Joyce and in his will left legacies to two more Hamlets. Shakespeare's Dane has a somewhat different history: it is an Anglicized version of Amleth, the Germanic name used in the tale of the same name as told by the twelfth-century historian Saxo Grammaticus.

False friends: safe

MODERN SENSE: unharmed, secure, free from risk

OBSOLETE SENSE: sure, certain

♣ Macbeth asks the First Murderer 'But Banquo's safe?'
(*Macbeth*, III.4.24). It is not a polite inquiry after Banquo's health. Macbeth means: 'Is he definitely dead?'

OBSOLETE SENSE: safely out of the way

♣ Miranda tells Ferdinand that her father 'is safe for these three hours' (*The Tempest*, III.1.21).

OBSOLETE SENSE: harmless, not dangerous

♣ King Henry, talking alone with Aumerle, is warned by York that Aumerle is a traitor. 'Villain, I'll make thee safe!' says Henry, turning on Aumerle (*Richard II*, V.3.40).

Rogero

In *The Winter's Tale*, the Second Gentleman who brings the first account of the reconciliation between the characters towards the end of the play (V.2.21) is addressed as 'Rogero'. The name means nothing now, but *Rogero* was a ballad tune in Shakespeare's time, and its subject – paralleling the plot of the play – was a jealous husband who kills his innocent wife.

Tennyson's last read

Hallam Tennyson's account of his poet-laureate father – *Alfred, Lord Tennyson: a Memoir* (1897) – records that he died on 8 October 1892 with Shakespeare's *Cymbeline* open before him at Act V Scene 5, where Posthumus says to Innogen: 'Hang there like fruit, my soul, / Till the tree die' (V.5.264). The book was laid in his coffin.

An easy part

Frankly Lear is an easy part, one of the easiest parts in Shakespeare apart from Coriolanus. We can all play it. It is simply bang straightforward. Not like Romeo for instance, where you spend the whole evening searching for sympathy. But then anyone who lets an erection rule his life doesn't deserve much sympathy, does he?

(Laurence Olivier, *On Acting*, 1986, p. 93)

Drowning the storm

Shakespeare didn't want the actor playing Lear to drown out the storm. A Gentleman reports that Lear 'Strives in his little world of man to outscorn / the to and fro conflicting wind and rain.' He's in his eighties. All he can do in his impotent frustration is to wave his pathetic old fists at the elements. 'Strives' — he doesn't succeed. That's what is so wonderful about the scene.

(Nigel Hawthorne, *Straight Face*, 2002, p. 318)

Climbing Everest

Every night I referred to it as 'climbing on board the juggernaut' or 'climbing Everest', but certainly climbing, and there was a real sense of the verse and the drama pulling you forward with great compulsion and urgency. After each performance I would feel drained and exhausted, though consumed in a very different way from a Pinter play. With Lear there was a physical weariness that was similar to the feebleness one experiences after extreme exercise.

(Ian Holm, *Acting My Life*, 2004, p. 280)

Best line in the play

Laura Partridge, played by Judy Holliday, describing her short career as a Shakespearian actress:

No one's allowed to sit down unless you're a king.

(In George S. Kaufman's 1956 play and film *The Solid Gold Cadillac*)

Everything negotiable

The first and most important lesson she teaches is that there are no rules about how to do Shakespeare, just clues. Everything is negotiable. (Antony Sher and Gregory Doran, *Woza Shakespeare!*, 1996, p. 80, on Cicely Berry, RSC's head of voice 1970–92)

Missing persons

There are several missing people in Shakespeare's plays – Queen Lear, Lady Polonius, the children of Cleopatra and Lady Macbeth. Some Shakespearian scholars have as a result questioned Shakespeare's opinion of women, but the real reason may well have been practical: there were fewer women's parts written because women weren't allowed to act on stage, and few younger roles because there were only a couple of boy actors in the company at any one time.

A twelve-line sonnet

Sonnet 126 is an exception to the rule that sonnets have a predictable fourteen-line structure. It has only twelve lines, of six couplets. In the original 1609 Quarto edition, two pairs of empty italic parentheses mark where the final couplet should be.

> Her *Audite* (though delayd) answer'd must be,
> And her *Quietus* is to render thee.
> (   )
> (   )

The reason for their presence has occasioned much debate. Some think that they symbolize a silence, as a kind of farewell or 'envoi', as it is the last poem in the sequence devoted to the 'fair youth'.

The 'real' Richard III

The Richard III Society was founded in 1924 in England by a Liverpool surgeon, Saxon Barton, and originally called The Fellowship of the White Boar (the white boar was Richard's emblem). Its aim is to promote the 'real' Richard III, asserting that Richard was a good king and not the evil tyrant portrayed in the play.

The biased account presented in Shakespeare, it is claimed, comes from Holinshed, whose source was Thomas More's *The History of Richard III*. More, who was still a child when Richard died, was writing under the Tudor dynasty, which wanted to support the claim to the throne of Richmond, the man who deposed Richard in 1485 and became the first Tudor king as Henry VII.

The Society argues that Tudor writers exaggerated Richard's villainy and portrayed him in the worst possible light, such as by making him a hunchback – something that writers in the 1480s never mentioned. There are over 4000 members of the Society worldwide.

Anachronisms

It is not difficult to find anachronisms in Shakespeare. Historical accuracy was not a critical consideration for Elizabethan playwrights, who manipulated time and distance to meet dramatic demands, and routinely interpreted situations in contemporary terms. Many of Shakespeare's plays are set in other centuries and countries, but present a picture of life that would have been immediately recognizable in sixteenth-century Europe.

♣ 'Let's to billiards' (*Antony and Cleopatra*, II.5.3) Cleopatra could not have played billiards, which evolved in France in the late Middle Ages.

♣ 'The clock hath stricken three' (*Julius Caesar*, II.i.192) Cassius could not have heard a clock strike in ancient Rome, if he had a mechanical clock in mind; these were an invention of the early fourteenth century.

♣ 'If it be nothing I shall not need spectacles' (*King Lear*, I.2.36) Gloucester could not have had spectacles in ancient Britain; they were a thirteenth-century Italian invention.

♣ 'In going back to school in Wittenberg, / It is most retrograde to our desire' (*Hamlet*, I.2.113) Hamlet, supposedly a twelfth-century character, could not have gone back to school in Wittenberg University, which was not founded until 1502.

♣ 'A good sherris-sack hath a twofold operation in it' (*Henry IV Part I I*, IV.3.95) Falstaff could not have drunk sack in the reign of Henry IV, as this sweet wine from Jerez, Spain, was not introduced until around the time of Henry VII.

♣ 'I'll broach the tadpole on my rapier's point.' (*Titus Andronicus*, IV.2.84) Demetrius, living in Roman times, could not have killed Aaron's baby with a rapier, which was a sixteenth-century invention.

♣ 'young men whom Aristotle thought / Unfit to hear moral philosophy' (*Troilus and Cressida*, II.2.167) Hector, involved in the Trojan War (thirteenth century BC) could not have read Aristotle, who wrote in the fourth century BC.

For all time

History is a way of looking at things, but not one that interests me very much. I'm interested in the present. Shakespeare doesn't belong to the past. If his material is valid, it is valid now.

(Peter Brook, *The Shifting Point*, 1987, p. 95)

Penalty for improper use?

There should be an injunction, like the warning about pulling the communication cord, against performing Shakespeare unless absolutely necessary. People should only do Shakespeare because they want to, not because they have to.

(Richard Eyre, *National Service*, 2004, p. 200)

Cause of death?

According to the diary of John Ward, the vicar of Stratford-upon-Avon from 1662 to 1681, 'Shakespear Drayton and Ben Jhonson had a merry meeting and it seems drank too hard for Shakespear died of a feavour there contracted.' The story lacks evidence, but it could be true, given that there was an occasion for jollity not long before his death – his daughter Judith's marriage to Thomas Quiney on 10 February 1616. Ward also knew Judith, who did not die until 1662, so he could have heard the story from her mouth – or, of course, from the report of other old Stratfordians recalling an event which had taken place only forty-six years before.

False friends: silly

MODERN SENSE: * foolish, stupid

OBSOLETE SENSE: helpless, defenceless

♣ Henry VI's Queen calls herself a 'silly woman' (*Henry VI Part III*, I.1.243).

OBSOLETE SENSE: lowly, humble

♣ A captain describes the disguised Posthumus as being 'in a silly habit' (*Cymbeline*, V.3.86).

OBSOLETE SENSE: simple

♣ Orsino reflects to Viola/Cesario that Feste's sad song is 'silly sooth' (the simple truth) (*Twelfth Night*, II.4.46).

*The modern sense was coming into the language in Shakespeare's time – 'This is the silliest stuff that ever I heard' says Hippolyta to Theseus (*A Midsummer Night's Dream*, V.1.207).

To be nude ...

My being naked was Roman's idea. In Macbeth's time, he said, people didn't wear nightgowns.

(Francesca Annis, on her nude sleepwalking scene for Roman Polanski's film, *The Philadelphia Enquirer*, 17 May 1981)

How long are the plays?

On the opposite page are the lengths, ordered in terms of the number of lines, of all the plays in the New Penguin Shakespeare series, with the addition of *King Edward III*. Note that if the plays were to be ordered by number of words the sequence would be slightly different.

All play-lists giving line totals should be taken with a pinch of salt, as length obviously depends on the editions used and on the width of the page in which prose text is set. To illustrate the variation, we give the line lengths for two other editions: the First Folio, using the Norton numbering (p. 36) and the Riverside Shakespeare, on which Martin Spevack based his Concordance (p. 32). The Riverside editions print conflated texts of plays, where alternative versions exist, which is why, for example, *King Lear* and *Hamlet* are so much longer. The Folio versions are sometimes very different, because of the idiosyncratic typesetting practices: for example, some texts have pages in which the lines had to be crammed into a page to fit; and several poetic passages are printed as prose, such as Mercutio's Queen Mab speech in *Romeo and Juliet*.

Nonetheless, on all counts, *Hamlet* is the longest play and *The Comedy of Errors* the shortest.

Bardolatry

This blend of 'bard' + 'idolatry' was coined in 1901 by George Bernard Shaw, angered by those whom he perceived to be excessively devoted to Shakespeare – such as the authors of this Miscellany. He didn't have much time for what he called 'bardolaters'. 'The word "pity"', he said in a review a few years later, 'does not reach even the third row of the stalls, much less the gaping bardolatrous pit'. Other coinages followed. We now have 'bardoholics'.

False friends: subsidy

MODERN SENSE: grant, financial aid – perceived to be a good thing
OBSOLETE SENSE: special tax granted by parliament to meet a particular need (as much as four shillings in the pound on land) – perceived to be a bad thing

- ♣ A defensive King Henry says, 'I have not ... much oppressed them [his subjects] with great subsidies' (*Henry VI Part III*, IV.8.45).
- ♣ Rebel Jack Cade is told that Lord Say 'made us pay ... one shilling to the pound, the last subsidy' (*Henry VI Part II*, IV.7.20).

Total lines	Total words	Play	First Folio	Riverside
3834	29,844	Hamlet	3906	4042
3602	28,439	Richard III	3887	3667
3387	25,730	Troilus and Cressida	3592	3531
3331	26,479	Coriolanus	3838	3752
3295	26,876	Cymbeline	3819	3707
3247	25,737	Henry IV Part II	3350	3326
3232	26,003	Othello	3685	3551
3212	25,623	Henry V	3381	3297
3210	25,341	King Lear	3302	3487
3083	24,490	Henry VI Part II	3355	3130
3026	23,726	Antony and Cleopatra	3636	3522
3003	24,023	Romeo and Juliet	3185	3099
2998	24,126	Henry IV Part I	3180	3081
2981	24,597	The Winter's Tale	3369	3348
2900	23,318	Henry VI Part III	3217	2915
2809	23,333	Henry VIII	3463	3221
2803	22,537	All's Well that Ends Well	3078	3013
2795	23,388	The Two Noble Kinsmen	not in	3261
2752	21,884	Richard II	2849	2796
2708	21,290	The Merry Wives of Windsor	2729	2891
2696	21,269	Measure for Measure	2938	2891
2691	21,477	As You Like It	2796	2810
2678	20,541	Henry VI Part I	2931	2695
2671	20,881	Love's Labour's Lost	2900	2829
2610	20,767	Much Ado About Nothing	2684	2787
2576	20,911	The Merchant of Venice	2737	2701
2574	20,552	The Taming of the Shrew	2750	2676
2569	20,472	King John	2729	2638
2514	19,888	Titus Andronicus	2708	2538
2493	19,406	King Edward III	not in	not in
2481	19,592	Twelfth Night	2579	2591
2452	19,149	Julius Caesar	2730	2591
2344	17,728	Pericles	not in	2459
2334	17,796	Timon of Athens	2607	2488
2208	16,936	The Two Gentlemen of Verona	2298	2288
2126	16,305	A Midsummer Night's Dream	2222	2192
2083	16,372	Macbeth	2529	2349
2050	16,047	The Tempest	2341	2283
1782	14,415	The Comedy of Errors	1918	1787

Royal reflection

Each time I have seen or read [Henry V], *it has been the humanity of the King that has moved me most ... When I re-read this play nearly twenty years after performing in it at school, I found myself wondering in amazement at Shakespeare's insight into the mind of someone born into this kind of position.*

(Prince Charles, introduction to *The Prince's Choice*, 1995, p. 2)

Royal grooms

London was in the grip of the plague, when James I arrived in London in 1603, and he was unable to hold his coronation until March 1604. The King's Men named in the Patent then became members of the royal household, Grooms of the Chamber, and the Master of the Great Wardrobe issued each man with four-and-a-half yards of red cloth for his livery.

The Office of the Revels

The scope of the Office of the Revels was very wide, as we can see from the description made by one of the clerks:

The Office of the Revells comprising all maskes, triumphes, Plaies, and other shewes of Disporte, with Banqueting howses and like devises to be used for the Amusemente of the Queens Maiesties most roiall Court and her highness recreacion and pastyme.

The aim was to keep the Queen amused and unoffended. The aim was censorship but not suppression. Although many puritan members of the city wanted the theatres closed, it would not have been in the Master's interest to stop plays being performed. Apart from anything else, much of his income came from licensing fees levied on the theatre companies.

The Jacobethans

It is always a problem deciding what to call the period in which Shakespeare lived. 'Elizabethan' England takes us only to 1603, at which point 'Jacobean' England takes over. A compromise is the term 'Jacobethan' – first used in the context of architecture by John Betjeman in 1933. The label achieved some publicity when RSC director Gregory Doran used it for a series of plays by Shakespeare's contemporaries produced during the Stratford season in 2002. A second Jacobethan series followed in 2005.

Shakespearian pictures

Many portraits are supposed to be of Shakespeare. The five primary candidates are listed below. Each has attracted controversy over its claims to authenticity.

❧ The *Droeshout* portrait is the picture at the front of the First Folio, made by the English engraver Martin Droeshout probably from another painting or drawing now lost. It is one of only two representations thought to be an authentic likeness, the other being the monument in Holy Trinity Church. Other early portraits were made from it, notably one by William Faithorne for the frontispiece of the 1655 edition of *The Rape of Lucrece* and one by William Marshall for the 1640 edition of the poems.

❧ The *Chandos* portrait is probably the one most often seen by the public, for it hangs in London's National Gallery. Named after its owners, the Dukes of Chandos, it dates from the early seventeenth century.

❧ The *Flower* portrait is probably a copy of the Droeshout engraving. Named after its former owner, Mrs Charles Flower, it is now in the Royal Shakespeare Theatre Picture Gallery.

❧ The *Soest* portrait is a mid-seventeenth-century painting by Dutch artist Gerard Soest. It now hangs in the Shakespeare Centre, Stratford-upon-Avon.

❧ The *Sanders* portrait was painted in 1603 by a contemporary, John Sanders – an actor, according to Sanders family tradition. If genuine, it would be the only painting of Shakespeare made in his lifetime, when he was thirty-nine. It is owned by a Canadian descendant of Sanders, and was displayed in public for the first time in 2001. Controversy surrounds the painting: although its materials date from the right period, several details of the label on the back of the painting identifying 'Shakspere' suggest a later date.

Engaging with Hamlet

Richard Eyre said he always thought Hamlet *was a play about a man who learns to cope with death. Peter* [Brook] *thought it was a play about a man who learns how to kill. But to me it is about someone who comes to terms with their little existence.*

(Adrian Lester, interview in *The New York Times*, 8 April 2001)

Some leading literary contemporaries

Contemporary	Birth–Death	Age*	Profession
Beaumont, Francis	c.1584–1616	c.32	Playwright, collaborator with John Fletcher
Chapman, George	c.1560–1634	c.56	Poet and playwright
Chettle, Henry	?1560–?1607	–	Printer and writer
Daniel, Samuel	1562–1619	54	Poet and playwright
Day, John	c.1574–c.1640	c.42	Playwright, collaborator in plays for Philip Henslowe
Dekker, Thomas	c.1570–1632	c.46	Playwright and pamphleteer
Drayton, Michael	1563–1631	53	Poet and playwright
Field, Richard	1561–1624	57	Printer of Shakespeare's early poems, also from Stratford
Fletcher, John	1579–1625	37	Playwright, collaborator with Francis Beaumont, and with Shakespeare in at least *The Two Noble Kinsmen, Henry VIII*, and (lost) *Cardenio*
Ford, John	1586–c.1640	30	Playwright
Greene, Robert	1558–1592	–	Prose-writer and playwright
Henslowe, Philip	c.1550–1616	c.66	Theatre manager
Heywood, Thomas	c.1570–1641	c.46	Poet, playwright and actor
Jaggard, William	1569–1623	54	Printer of the First Folio
Jonson, Ben	1572–1637	42	Playwright, the most famous of Shakespeare's contemporaries, and a close friend; wrote dedication in First Folio
Kyd, Thomas	1558–1594	–	Playwright
Lyly, John	c.1554–1606	–	Poet and playwright
Marlowe, Christopher	1564–1593	–	Poet and playwright, leading dramatist of the Admiral's Men
Marston, John	1576–1634	40	Playwright
Massinger, Phillip	1583–1640	33	Playwright
Middleton, Thomas	c.1570–1627	c.46	Playwright, may have contributed songs to *Macbeth*
Nashe, Thomas	1567–c.1601	–	Playwright and pamphleteer
Peele, George	c.1558–c.1596	–	Poet and playwright, possible collaborator with Shakespeare in *Henry VI Part I* and *Titus Andronicus*
Rowley, William	fl. early 1600s	?	Actor and playwright
Webster, John	c.1580–c.1634	c.36?	Playwright
Wilkins, George	fl. early 1600s	?	Prose-writer and playwright collaborator

*when Shakespeare died

A 'wooden O'

The Prologue to *Henry V* describes the theatre in which the play is being performed as a 'wooden O'. This is usually assumed to be a direct reference to the Globe, whose construction was being completed in early 1599 – when *Henry V* was being written. But the reference could also have been to the similarly built Curtain theatre, where Shakespeare's company had also played.

Palladis Tamia

In 1598 the teacher and minister Francis Meres (1565–1647) compiled a book which he called *Palladis Tamia: Wit's Treasury – a comparative discourse of our English poets with the Greek, Latin, and Italian poets*. The paragraphs typically have the structure 'As [a classical author] ... so [a contemporary author].' He refers to Shakespeare no less than nine times, and mentions twelve of his plays:

> *As Plautus and Seneca are accounted the best for Comedy and Tragedy among the Latines: so Shakespeare among the English is the most excellent in both kinds for the stage; for Comedy, witnes his* Gentlemen of Verona, *his* Errors, *his* Loue labors lost, *his* Loue labours wonne, *his* Midsummers night dreame, & *his* Merchant of Venice; *for tragedy, his* Richard the 2, Richard the 3, Henry the 4, King Iohn, Titus Andronicus, *and his* Romeo and Iuliet.

> *As Epius Stolo said, that the Muses would speake with Plautus tongue, if they would speak Latin: so I say that the Muses would speake with Shakespeares fine filed phrase, if they would speake English.*

Meres also refers to Edward Earl of Oxford as a great writer of comedy – a point noted by those who have sought an alternative authorship for Shakespeare's plays.

Edmund Kean

Edmund Kean was considered the greatest Shakespearian actor of his day. His last appearance on stage was at Covent Garden, on 25 March 1833, when he played Othello to his son's Iago (Charles John Kean). Half-way through the performance (at the words 'Villain, be sure', III.3.356), he collapsed, saying to his son, 'O God, I am dying. Speak to them, Charles.' He died two months later, at Richmond.

Women's and men's voices

On the opposite page, the table shows the proportion of female to male speech in the plays. Interestingly, there are no comedies in the bottom half of the list – with the (unsurprising, given its subject-matter) exception of *The Taming of the Shrew*. Most of the English history plays are resolutely masculine. Given the 'presence' of the leading female characters in *The Taming of the Shrew*, *Troilus and Cressida* and *Hamlet*, it is surprising to find so few women's lines.

Shakespeare as witness

On 11 May 1612, Shakespeare was called to London to testify in a court case between an apprentice, Stephen Belott, and his master, Christopher Mountjoy, who lived in the Cripplegate area of London. Belott had married Mountjoy's daughter in 1604, but in 1612 brought a suit accusing Mountjoy of not providing his daughter with a promised dowry. Shakespeare was evidently staying with Mountjoy at the time, and had been asked to be a match-maker: a maidservant deposed that Mountjoy 'did send and perswade one Mr Shakespeare that lay in the house to perswade the plaintiff to the same marriadge'. Shakespeare's deposition begins:

> *William Shakespeare of Stratford vpon Aven in the Countye of Warwicke gentleman of the age of xlviij [48] yeres or thereaboutes …*

He goes on to say that he knew both parties and that he did indeed act as a match-maker. But on the crucial point, how much the dowry was to be, Shakespeare's memory proves defective:

> *To the ffourth interrogatory this deponent sayth that the defendant promissed to geue the said complainant a porcion in marriadge with Marye his daughter, but what certayne porcion he rememberethe not, nor when to be payed …*

It was, after all, eight years later, and a lot had happened in the interim – such as *King Lear*.

To swim or to drown

I think that many young actors fail to understand what Shakespeare's language has to offer them. Good verse-speaking is rather like swimming. If you surrender to the water it keeps you up, but if you fight you drown. (John Gielgud, *Stage Directions*, 1963, p. 4)

Female %	No. of lines	Male %	No. of lines	Play
39.9	1073	60.1	1618	As You Like It
35.3	992	64.7	1811	All's Well that Ends Well
32.8	917	67.2	1878	The Two Noble Kinsmen
32.2	798	67.8	1683	Twelfth Night
31.1	935	68.9	2068	Romeo and Juliet
30.5	827	69.5	1881	The Merry Wives of Windsor
29.4	757	70.6	1819	The Merchant of Venice
26.7	568	73.3	1558	A Midsummer Night's Dream
25.0	552	75.0	1656	The Two Gentlemen of Verona
24.4	727	75.6	2254	The Winter's Tale
23.9	787	76.1	2508	Cymbeline
22.6	402	77.4	1380	The Comedy of Errors
22.4	678	77.6	2348	Antony and Cleopatra
20.7	668	79.3	2564	Othello
20.7	485	79.3	1859	Pericles
20.3	547	79.7	2149	Measure for Measure
20.3	543	79.7	2128	Love's Labour's Lost
20.2	526	79.8	2084	Much Ado About Nothing
18.5	520	81.5	2289	Henry VIII
16.3	586	83.7	3016	Richard III
15.8	507	84.2	2703	King Lear
15.6	325	84.4	1758	Macbeth
14.6	374	85.4	2195	King John
14.5	446	85.5	2637	Henry VI Part II
13.3	335	86.7	2179	Titus Andronicus
12.5	361	87.5	2539	Henry VI Part III
12.4	332	87.6	2346	Henry VI Part I
11.7	390	88.3	2941	Coriolanus
11.7	302	88.3	2272	The Taming of the Shrew
11.4	385	88.6	3002	Troilus and Cressida
10.4	213	89.6	1837	The Tempest
09.9	272	90.1	2480	Richard II
09.2	300	90.8	2947	Henry IV Part II
08.6	330	91.4	3504	Hamlet
08.6	214	91.4	2279	King Edward III
04.8	155	95.2	3057	Henry V
04.8	119	95.2	2333	Julius Caesar
03.5	106	96.5	2892	Henry IV Part I
00.5	11	99.5	2323	Timon of Athens

======================= *Falling in love* =======================

The more you direct Shakespeare, the more you just fall in love.
It's not meant to be read. It's meant to be performed.

(Julie Taymor, on why make a film of *Titus Andronicus*,
in *Written By*, February 2000)

======================= *Performing* Twelfth Night =======================

The setting in which a play was originally performed can add an extra layer of interest to the interpretation of a line. 'Words are grown so false that I am loath to prove reason with them', says Feste to Viola in *Twelfth Night* (III.1.23). The point is a general one, but it would have had an extra resonance for the original audience for the play – the lawyers of Middle Temple, in the London Inns of Court, where the play was performed (some think for the first time) on 2 February 1602.

======================= *Globe remembered* =======================

In 1623, Ben Jonson wrote a long poem, 'An Execration upon Vulcan', after his personal library was burned in a fire. In it, he reflects on another fire, some years before, where Vulcan had also played a prank ...

Against the Globe, the Glory of the Bank.
Which, though it were the Fort of the whole Parish,
Flanked with a Ditch, and forced out of a Marish [marsh],
I saw with two poor Chambers [pieces of ordnance] *taken in*
And razed; were thought could urge, this might have been!
See the worlds Ruins! nothing but the piles
Left! and wit since to cover it with Tiles.

'I saw'? Jonson must have been there.

======================= *Changing names* =======================

When Shakespeare altered John Oldcastle to John Falstaff in *Henry IV Part I* (p. 42), he also altered the names of Oldcastle's companions, Harvey and Russell, to Bardolph and Peto – perhaps for the same kind of reason, to avoid offending powerful sensibilities. The family name of the Earl of Bedford was Russell, and Shakespeare would also have been well aware of the links between the family of his former patron and Sir William Harvey, who in 1598 became the third husband of the Countess of Southampton. The original names of Oldcastle, Harvey and Russell are restored in the Oxford Shakespeare edition of 1988.

Jigs

The normal way of ending a play, at least until the second decade of the seventeenth century, was with a comic song-and-dance jig performed by the company clown and other actors, typically telling a bawdy tale. One of Will Kemp's survives from 1595: *Singing Simpkin*, telling the story of 'a soldiour and a Miser and Sym the clown'. The link between jigs and bawdiness is made by Hamlet, who says of Polonius: 'He's for a jig or a tale of bawdry' (*Hamlet*, II.2.498).

Songs

The Elizabethan age was a great age of song, with many leading composers contemporaries of Shakespeare. The choristers of Windsor Chapel and St Paul's had been performing plays since the early sixteenth century, and by Shakespeare's time all boy actors would receive training in singing.

According to Ross W. Duffin's *Shakespeare's Songbook* (2004), there are 160 songs – ballads, rounds, drinking songs … – which are sung, alluded to, or quoted in Shakespeare's plays. Some are heard in more than one play: for example, Feste's song at the end of *Twelfth Night* appears again in *King Lear* (III.2.74).

The songs perform a variety of dramatic functions.

- ❧ They can be sung as a reflection of character, such as the snatches of mad Ophelia (*Hamlet*, IV.5).
- ❧ They meet a character's mood, such as the one sung to Orsino in *Twelfth Night* (II.4).
- ❧ They often mark a highly significant moment in the plot, such as Desdemona's 'Willow Song' (*Othello*, IV.3).

Most are traditional or popular songs, not composed by Shakespeare at all, and the characters know it. It is an 'old thing', says Desdemona.

Instrumental moments

Trumpets and drums were used in the plays only for military or ceremonial purposes – in fanfares, alarm calls, signals, summonses to parley and other outdoor events.* They did not form a part of the composed music which entertained people in the plays, which used such stringed instruments as the viol, bass viol, lute, hautboy (a type of oboe) and cittern. Clowns would play on a pipe and tabor (a small side-drum).

*A trumpeter on the platform at the top of the Globe announced the start of a performance.

People sing on over fifty occasions in the plays – and many other snatches of songs enter into the dialogue.

Antony and Cleopatra
    II.7.111 (Boy) Come, thou monarch of the vine
As You Like It
    II.5.1 (Amiens) Under the greenwood tree
    II.5.35 (Lords) Who doth ambition shun
    II.7.175 (Amiens) Blow, blow, thou winter wind
    IV.2.10 (Lords) What shall he have that killed the deer?
    V.3.15 (Pages) It was a lover and his lass
    V.4.138 (Hymen) Wedding is great Juno's crown
Cymbeline
    II.3.19 (Cloten) Hark, hark, the lark
    IV.2.258 (Guiderius and Arviragus) Fear no more the heat
    o'th'sun
Hamlet
    IV.5.23 (Ophelia) How should I your true-love know
    IV.5.48 (Ophelia) Tomorrow is St Valentine's Day
    IV.5.190 (Ophelia) And will 'a not come again?
    V.1.61 (First Clown) In youth, when I did love
Henry IV Part II
    V.3.17 (Silence) Do nothing but eat, and make good cheer
    V.3.32 (Silence) Be merry, be merry, my wife has all
Henry VIII
    III.1.3 (Gentlewoman) Orpheus with his lute
King Lear
    I.4.171 (Fool) Then they for sudden joy did weep
    III.2.74 (Fool) He that has and a little tiny wit
    III.6.26 (Fool) Her boat hath a leak
Love's Labour's Lost
    V.2.883 (Ver) When daisies pied
    V.2.901 (Hiems) When icicles hang by the wall
Measure for Measure
    IV.1.1 (Boy) Take, O take those lips away
The Merchant of Venice
    III.2.63 (Singer) Tell me where is fancy bred
The Merry Wives of Windsor
    III.1.16 (Evans) To shallow rivers
    V.5.93 (Mistress Quickly) Fie on sinful fantasy!

A Midsummer Night's Dream
  II.2.9 (First Fairy) You spotted snakes
  III.1.118 (Bottom) The ousel cock so black of hue
Much Ado About Nothing
  II.3.60 (Balthasar) Sigh no more, ladies
  V.2.26 (Benedick) The God of love
  V.3.12 (Balthasar) Pardon, goddess of the night
Othello
  II.3.64 (Iago) And let me the canakin clink
  II.3.84 (Iago) King Stephen was and-a worthy peer
  IV.3.38 (Desdemona) Willow, willow
Romeo and Juliet
  II.4.131 (Mercutio) An old hare hoar
The Tempest
  I.2.375 (Ariel) Come unto these yellow sands
  I.2.397 (Ariel) Full fathom five thy father lies
  II.1.305 (Ariel) While you here do snoring lie
  II.2.45 (Stephano) The master, the swabber
  II.2.176 (Caliban) No more dams I'll make for fish
  IV.1.106 (Juno) Honour, riches, marriage blessing
  V.1.88 (Ariel) Where the bee sucks
Troilus and Cressida
  III.1.112 (Pandarus) Love, love, nothing but love
Twelfth Night
  II.3.37 (Feste) O mistress mine
  II.4.50 (Feste) Come away, come away, death
  IV.2.71 (Feste) Ah Robin
  IV.2.121 (Feste) I am gone, sir
  V.1.386 (Feste) When that I was and a little tiny boy
The Two Gentlemen of Verona
  IV.2.38 (Host) Who is Silvia?
The Two Noble Kinsmen
  I.1.1 (Boy) Roses, their sharp spines being gone
  I.5.1 (Singer) Urns and odours
  III.4.19 (Daughter) For I'll cut my green coat
  III.5.60 (Daughter) The *George Alow*
The Winter's Tale
  IV.3.1 (Autolycus) When daffodils begin to peer
  IV.3.121 (Autolycus) Jog on
  IV.4.220 (Autolycus) Lawn as white as driven snow
  IV.4.295 (Autolycus) Get you hence
  IV.4.313 (Autolycus) Will you buy any tape

Richard vs Hamlet

But I love that play ... There is more pleasure in one broken-backed
Richard than in ten perfect Hamlets. I hate Hamlet.

(Terry Hands, quoted in Antony Sher,
Year of the King, 1985, p. 42)

Cousin

The kinship term, *cousin* – often familiarly abbreviated as *coz* or *cuz* – is
very much broader in its Shakespearian use than we find today. In
modern English, it is primarily used for the relationship between the
children of brothers and sisters (*first cousins*), with some extension
permitted, such as for the children of first cousins (*second cousins*, or
cousins once removed) and their children. But in Shakespeare we find it
used for virtually any relative beyond the immediate family, both for
blood relatives and relatives through marriage, and often as a term of
affection between socially equal people who are not relatives at all, such
as monarchs of different countries.

'Look where ...'

'Look where he comes' says the Duke to Escalus, of Angelo
   (*Measure for Measure*, I.1.24)
'Look where they come', says Philo to Demetrius about Antony
   and Cleopatra (*Antony and Cleopatra*, I.1.10)
'Look where she comes', says Iago to Cassio, of Bianca (*Othello*,
   IV.1.145)

There are twenty-three such cases in the plays, where one character tells
another to 'look where' someone is coming. They might seem to be
unnecessary remarks, until we remember the large dimensions of the
Elizabethan platform stage, thrusting out into a yard with spectators all
around. It would not be difficult for an audience – inattentive as they
often were – to miss an entrance from one of the doors at the very back
of the stage. Remarks like these reduce that risk.

Surfing Othello

There are times when I feel as if I am drowning ... Once you get to Act
III, Scene 3, it's like being caught up in a huge surf. You are pounded
by experiences and overwhelming feelings that oscillate violently.

(Patrick Stewart, *The Washington Post*,
12 November 1997)

Dangerous business

It is true we were there months longer than we needed to be. We had hurricanes that wiped out the set. We all got sick. Shooting shut down for a week while I had a temperature of 110. The hair and makeup person, Aldo Signoretti, who worked with Fellini, was kidnapped. The bandidos rang up and said for $US300 you can have him back – I thought: rather a bargain! So Maurizio, who is about this high, goes down clutching the money to outside the hotel, holds it up, chucks them the bag and they threw him [Signoretti] out of the car and he broke his leg. So we had adventures. It was an incredible quest.

(Baz Luhrmann, interview for omnileonardo.com
on filming *Romeo + Juliet* in Mexico, 1996)

False friends: bootless

MODERN SENSE: without boots

OBSOLETE SENSE: fruitlessly, uselessly, unsuccessfully, in vain

♣ Caesar addresses the company with 'Doth not Brutus bootless kneel?' (*Julius Caesar*, III.1.75).

♣ The Fairy inquires of Puck 'Are not you he / That ... bootless make the breathless housewife churn' (*A Midsummer Night's Dream*, II.1.37).

Verbal scenery

There was no scenery in Elizabethan theatre, and the word 'scene' did not automatically mean 'different place'. Many scenes take place without any clear indication of where the characters are. When it is important to know, it is the words which tell us. 'This is Illyria, lady', the Captain tells Viola – and the audience – at the beginning of the second scene of *Twelfth Night*. 'This is the forest of Arden', likewise, Rosalind tells Celia (*As You Like It*, II.4.12). And the Chorus opens *Romeo and Juliet* with the words 'In fair Verona, where we lay our scene'.

Tatification

Several authors have rewritten Shakespeare's tragedies to give them happy endings. The Irish author Nahum Tate (1652–1715) rewrote *King Lear* in 1681 so that Lear survives, Cordelia and Edgar marry, and the three sisters are reconciled – a version which was preferred for 150 years. The Victorians referred to this kind of interference as 'Tatification'.

Profanities

In 1606, an 'Acte to restraine Abuses of Players' was passed by Parliament, for 'the preventing and avoyding of the great Abuse of the Holy Name of God in Stageplayes Interludes Maygames Shewes and such like':

> Be it enacted ... That if at any tyme or tymes, after the end of this present Session of Parliament, any person or persons doe or shall in any Stage play Interlude Shewe Maygame or Pageant jestingly or prophanely speake or use the holy Name of God or of Christ Jesus, or of the Holy Ghoste or of the Trinitie, which are not to be spoken but with feare and reverence, shall forfeite for everie such offence by hym or them committed Tenne Pounde.

Ten pounds was a lot of money, so a great deal of expurgation took place. 'I pray God grant them a fair departure', says Portia in the Quarto (Q1) text of *The Merchant of Venice* (I.2.104). 'I wish them a fair departure', says the corresponding line in the First Folio (1623). The Act did not cover printed texts, so the First Folio contains a mixture of expurgated and unexpurgated plays, reflecting the character of their source manuscripts. Not all the texts were affected to the same extent, leaving scholars with some puzzles when they try to restore the original texts for modern readers.

Who has more lines?

Othello or Iago? (See p. 89.)

Bowdlerizing

The Family Shakespeare of 1807 presented twenty of Shakespeare's plays in an expurgated edition, with the others similarly treated in the second edition of 1818. The editors, Henrietta and Thomas Bowdler, thereby gave a new word to the language: to *bowdlerize*. Their principle was to exclude 'any word or expression ... that the first impression it excites is an impression of obscenity' and which 'cannot with propriety be read aloud in a family'. Thomas observes at one point:

> I acknowledge Shakespeare to be the world's greatest dramatic poet, but regret that no parent could place the uncorrected book in the hands of his daughter, and therefore I have prepared the Family Shakespeare.

Top ten content words

The commonest words in the language are the grammatical words, such as *the*, *I*, and *and*, along with words of very general meaning, such as *make* and *then*. If we ignore these, what words of specific meaning does Shakespeare use most often? The totals below, from the *Shakespeare's Words* database, include all grammatical uses of each word (as a noun, verb, etc.) and all variant forms (*know*, *knows*, *knew*, etc.):

good	3995	know	2252
lord	3164	give	2114
man	3091	think/thought	1911
love	3047	king	1680
sir	2548	speak	1626

Missing genres

Shakespeare didn't explore every genre of literary creation. Unlike several of his contemporaries

♣ he wrote no large-scale pastoral romances or court masques – though elements are incorporated into such plays as *The Tempest* and *The Winter's Tale*;

♣ he made no translations or biblical adaptations, nor did he produce works of prose fiction.

We find no examples of city comedy or domestic tragedy in his plays, genres which were both exploited by his contemporaries (and popular still today, as seen in many a television soap). The nearest we get are *The Merry Wives of Windsor* (for the former) and *Othello* (for the latter), but the one is rural rather than urban, and the domesticity of the other is several removes away from what we normally understand by the term.

Laughter and pain

What would you expect to find in a comedy? Clowns, perhaps. Songs? A case of mistaken identity? We do find these features in Shakespeare's comedies. But how about the attempted rape of a best friend's fiancée? Blackmail and betrayal? Banishment and bereavement? We get these too. Darker themes run through the comedies, and have made some of the plays – such as *The Two Noble Kinsmen* – difficult to classify. Betrayal is also a strong theme in the Sonnets. *The Merry Wives of Windsor* seems to be the merriest, with only a spot of mild (attempted) betrayal. As David Richman says in his *Laughter, Pain, and Wonder* (1990, p. 21):

Most of Shakespeare's comic characters are victims of scornful laughter, and the derision often approaches or becomes violence.

Malapropisms

Mrs Malaprop, in Sheridan's play *The Rivals* (1775), used long words in a ludicrous way – comical errors which came to be called 'malaprops'; later, 'malapropisms'. But malaproprian behaviour long predates Sheridan.

❧ Mistress Quickly (*The Merry Wives of Windsor*, II.2.112): 'Her husband has a marvellous infection to the little page' [affection]

❧ Launcelot Gobbo (*The Merchant of Venice*, II.2.126): 'the suit is impertinent to myself' [pertinent]

❧ Dogberry (*Much Ado About Nothing*, III.5.43): 'our watch ... have indeed comprehended two aspicious persons' [apprehended ... suspicious]

❧ Elbow (*Measure for Measure*, II.1.49): 'I ... do bring in here before your good honour two notorious benefactors' [malefactors]

❧ Dull (*Love's Labour's Lost*, I.1.181): 'I myself reprehend his own person' [represent]

❧ Nurse (*Romeo and Juliet*, II.4.124): 'I desire some confidence with you' [conference]

❧ Launce (*The Two Gentlemen of Verona*, II.3.3): 'like the prodigious son' [prodigal]

❧ Costard (*Love's Labour's Lost*, I.1.187): 'the contempts thereof are as touching me' [contents]

❧ Slender (*The Merry Wives of Windsor*, I.1.234): 'I am freely dissolved, and dissolutely' [resolved ... resolutely]

❧ Sir Andrew (*Twelfth Night*, V.1.178): 'he's the very devil incardinate' [incarnate]

❧ Bottom (*A Midsummer Night's Dream*, III.1.35): 'saying thus, or to the same defect' [effect]

Visiting the Globe

The Swiss traveller Thomas Platter visited the newly built Globe theatre on 21 September 1599 (translated from the German by Ernest Schanzer):

After dinner, at about two o'clock, I went with my party across the water; in the straw-thatched house we saw the tragedy of the first Emperor Julius Caesar, very pleasingly performed, with approximately fifteen characters; at the end of the play they danced together admirably and exceedingly gracefully, according to their custom, two in each group dressed in men's and two in women's apparel.

This was probably *Julius Caesar* – and the first recorded performance at the Globe.

The OSC

The Original Shakespeare Company was founded in 1992 by Patrick Tucker and Christine Ozanne. Its aim was to explore the ways in which Shakespeare's company would have produced, rehearsed and performed his plays. Tucker, in his *Secrets of Acting Shakespeare* (2002), describes their method. The actors:

- ♣ used only the First Folio texts
- ♣ were given their parts as *cue scripts* (the character's speeches, their entrance and exit points and the three words spoken before their speech, to cue them)
- ♣ were asked not to read the entire play (Shakespeare's actors wouldn't have been able to)
- ♣ did not rehearse; they had only 'Burbadge' time, which was time spent with the director pointing out various intricacies of the text the actors may not have noticed
- ♣ provided their own costumes and props
- ♣ practised any fights or dances the morning before the performance
- ♣ had no idea who was performing opposite them, and only a vague idea of the entire play.

A *platt* was nailed backstage, detailing the comings and goings of the actors on and off stage, a brief outline of the scene and who would play the minor parts.

A *book-keeper* sat on-stage with a full copy of the play, prompting the actors whenever a line was dropped, and ringing a bell to signify the beginning and end of each act and scene. (*Book* in this context at the time meant 'script': see p. 26.)

Demonstrations were presented in 1992, but the OSC's first full production was in 1993, in Germany, with *A Midsommer Nights Dreame*. In 1993–2000 they produced up to three shows a year, and performed three shows at Shakespeare's Globe: *As You Like It* (1997), *King John* (1998) and *Cymbeline* (1999).

Getting it

It's interesting because you can do something from Shakespeare and think that you're feeling it or whatever you're doing, you love it, and you think you're communicating it and the person you just said it to has not understood a word you said, *and you can't believe they didn't get it.*　　　　　(Al Pacino, *Looking for Richard*, 1996)

Foul play

My third Shakespeare for the RSC was Macbeth, *which opened in the middle of a thunderstorm. So foul and fair a day I have not seen. It was beautifully done on the cheap in The Other Place, the old tin hut along from the main theatre. John Napier's entire set cost £200 and the costumes were a ragbag of second-hand clothes. My uniform jacket had buttons embossed with 'Birmingham Fire Service'; my long, leather coat didn't fit, nor did Banquo's so we had to wear them slung over the shoulder; Judi Dench, as Lady Macbeth, wore a dyed tea-towel on her head. Somehow it was magic: and black magic, too. A priest used to sit on the front row, whenever he could scrounge a ticket, holding out his crucifix to protect the cast from the evil we were raising.* (Ian McKellen, official website)

Kinship terms

Most Shakespearian kinship terms – *father*, *mother*, *sister* … – look the same as their modern counterparts. The chief exceptions are the terms for grandparents, *grandam* (as in *King John*, II.1.159) and *grandsire* (as in *The Merry Wives of Windsor*, I.1.54) alongside *grandmother* and *grandfather*, and *stepdame* (as in *Cymbeline*, I.7.1) alongside *stepmother*. *Sire* and *dam* are also used as a contemptuous way of referring to a father and mother, as in Queen Margaret's insult to Richard, 'thou art neither like thy sire nor dam' (*Henry VI Part III*, II.2.135).

False friends: fact

MODERN SENSE: actuality, datum of experience
OBSOLETE SENSE: evil deed, wicked deed, crime*
❧ Warwick cannot think of a 'fouler fact' than Somerset's treason (*Henry VI Part II*, I.3.171).
❧ The rape of Lucrece is described as a 'fact' to be abhorred (*The Rape of Lucrece*, 349).

*The Shakespearian sense hasn't entirely disappeared; it will still be encountered in a few legal phrases, such as 'confess the fact'.

False friends: blasted

MODERN SENSE: expression of general dislike; intoxicated, high
OBSOLETE SENSE: blighted, withered
❧ Macbeth meets the witches on a 'blasted heath' (*Macbeth*, I.3.76).
❧ Richard calls his arm a 'blasted sapling' (*Richard III*, III.4.69).

What is truth?

I think it's too simple to say: the truth. What do we mean by truth? Truth of reality. Truth of poetry, which is a little bit of super-reality. And truth of character. It's the fusion of poetry, truth and character that is required in Shakespeare.

(Peggy Ashcroft, on the most important thing to go for in playing
Shakespeare, in John Barton, *Playing Shakespeare*, 1984, p. 208)

Failed grave-digger

The leading nineteenth-century exponent of the Baconian theory of authorship was an American writer, Delia Bacon, who published *The Philosophy of the Plays of Shakespeare Unfolded* in 1857. In 1856 she spent a night in Holy Trinity church with the intention of opening Shakespeare's grave, where she believed documents with the key to the mystery had been buried; but she was overwhelmed by the physical scale of the task as well as growing doubts about its outcome, and she left the church the next morning with the tomb untouched. She explained why in a letter to the American writer Nathaniel Hawthorne, who later wrote about the episode in 'Recollections of a Gifted Woman' (1863):

I had a dark lantern like Guy Fawkes, and some other articles which might have been considered suspicious if the police had come upon us ... I was alone there till ten o'clock ... all the long drawn aisle was in utter darkness. I heard a creaking in it, a cautious step, repeatedly, and I knew that the clerk was there and watching me ... I had made a promise to the clerk that I would not do the least thing for which he could be called in question, and though I went far enough to see that the examination I had proposed to make, could be made, leaving all exactly as I found it, it could not be made in that time, nor under those conditions. I did not feel at liberty to make it, for fear I might violate the trust this man had reposed in me, and if I were not wholly and immediately successful I should have run the risk of losing any chance of continuing my research.

Giving theatre up for Lent

According to the law, plays were not allowed during the six weeks of Lent – the pre-Easter period of penitence in the Christian calendar. In 1579, the Privy Council issued a directive that 'there be no plaiers suffered to plaie during this tyme of Lent, until it be after the Ester weke'. The directive was often ignored.

Knowing Shakespeare

Shakespeare is the only biographer of Shakespeare; and even he can tell nothing, except to the Shakespeare in us; that is, to our most apprehensive and sympathetic hour ... So far from Shakespeare's being the least known, he is the one person, in all modern history, known to us. What point of morals, of manners, of economy, of philosophy, of religion, of taste, of the conduct of life, has he not settled? What mystery has he not signified his knowledge of? What office, or function, or district of man's work, has he not remembered? What king has he not taught state, as Talma taught Napoleon? What maiden has not found him finer than her delicacy? What lover has he not outloved? What sage has he not outseen? What gentleman has he not instructed in the rudeness of his behavior?

(Ralph Waldo Emerson, *Shakespeare; or, the Poet*, 1904)

Pilgrimage

The cultural pilgrimage to Stratford that people from all over the world make to see the work as they have imagined it makes Shakespeare almost impossible to stage. It imposes the burden that you are intoning a liturgy.

(Cicely Berry, remark to Paul Maier, who added,
'of course she wasn't being entirely serious',
The Daily Telegiraffe, 30 October 1995)

Baconians

The case for Francis Bacon, 1st Baron Verulam and Viscount St Albans (1561–1626), as the author of Shakespeare's plays (p. 166) gathered strength during the second half of the nineteenth-century, especially in the USA, based on the view that Bacon's social position and profound learning made him a more plausible candidate as author of the content in the plays than the son of a Stratford glover. Several studies claimed to find cryptograms in the language of the plays, such as an anagram in the word *honorificabilitudinitatibus* in *Love's Labour's Lost*: 'hi ludi F. Baconis nati tuiti orbi' = 'these plays F. Bacon's offspring preserved for the world'. The debunking of the cryptographic studies, along with the demonstration of notable stylistic differences between the writers, reduced the appeal of the approach in the twentieth century, but it is still espoused.

In *The Great Cryptogram* (1888), Ignatius Donnelly devoted two large volumes to (as his sub-title asserts) *Francis Bacon's Cipher in the So-called Shakespeare Plays*. Devising a complex system of recurring numbers, roots and arithmetical operations, he demonstrated to his own satisfaction (but to few others at the time or since) the existence of hidden messages in his facsimile of the First Folio which gave clues to the 'real' author.

Here are two examples which illustrate the way Donnelly's method works:

> On p. 53 of the Histories he finds the line 'I have a gammon of Bacon and two razes of ginger'. He calculates that *Bacon* is the 371st word on the page, divides this by the page number and gets 7. This then becomes the cypher number for Bacon.

> On p. 67, *St Albans* is the 402nd word on the page. Divide 402 by 67 and you get 6, which is the corresponding number for St Albans.

He then applied this method to many thousands of words, and was able to find such messages hidden within the text as:

> *Francis Bacon Nicholas Bacon's Son.*

He works out a single root-number, 327, to obtain the message:

> *More low* [Marlowe] *or Shak'st spur never writ a word of them.*

It was an amazing feat of misdirected energy, but it involved hundreds of arbitrary and inconsistent decisions (such as whether a hyphenated word would count as one word or two). Nor is it difficult to turn such a method against its author – and indeed, in the same year, someone used Donnelly's exact procedure to show the following message hidden within the plays:

> *Master Will i a Jack Spur writ this play*
> *and was engaged at the Curtain.*

Shakespeare, it seems, was the author after all.

===== *Hate mail* =====

There has been the usual run-up to WS's birthday of hate letters and facetious articles suggesting he never existed. Tell that to the shades of Ben Jonson, Kit Marlowe and all.

(Alec Guinness, *My Name Escapes Me*, 1996, p. 162)

Oxfordians

The case for Edward de Vere, the 17th Earl of Oxford (1550–1604) as the author of Shakespeare's plays (p. 166) continues to attract support. As a poet and playwright, he had the right kind of learned and aristocratic qualifications to write the plays, but – the argument goes – as a noble he could not allow his name to be publicly associated with such a low-rated profession as dramatist, nor could he safely write about English political history without protecting his identity. He therefore stopped writing under his own name in 1593, and began to use the name of Shakespeare. His death in 1604 poses a difficulty, given that so many plays appear after that date. Supporters argue that they could have been written earlier, and kept hidden, or that the dates of publication are wrong, but there are many problems, such as the dating evidence found in the later plays. *The Tempest*, for example, has been shown to make extensive use of narratives describing the wreck and survival of the crew of the *Sea-Venture* in Bermuda in 1609.

The Geneva Bible annotations

There is a copy of the Geneva Bible in the Folger Shakespeare Library in Washington which apparently belonged to the Earl of Oxford. It contains handwritten annotations which, according to Oxfordians, correspond closely to the biblical allusions in the works of Shakespeare. The annotator has marked about a thousand verses, and there are several words or phrases (e.g. 'giue vnto the poore') written in the margin. About 200 of the verses (especially those in Deuteronomy, Isaiah and Revelation) have been argued to have parallels in the plays or poems. This total, however, is only 20 per cent of the 2000 or so biblical allusions thought to be present in the texts. Correspondingly, only about 10 per cent of Shakespeare's biblical allusions are marked by the annotator in this Bible: for example, there are very few markings in the text of the four Gospels, which Shakespeare alludes to extensively. The 'De Vere Bible' nonetheless continues to be cited as supporting evidence for Oxford's authorship of the plays.

Respect

Should we respect the text? I think there is a healthy double attitude, with respect on the one hand and disrespect on the other. And the dialectic between the two is what it's all about. If you go solely one or the other way, you lose the possibility of capturing the truth.

(Peter Brook, *The Shifting Point*, 1987, p. 95)

Marlovians

The case for Christopher Marlowe (1564–93) as the author of Shakespeare's plays (p. 166) continues to attract supporters. Marlowe, known to have been a spy in Elizabeth I's employ, is said not to have died in Deptford in 1593. Rather, he faked his death and fled from England to escape charges of atheism. While in Italy, he wrote the plays, which were then sent back to his patron, Sir Thomas Walsingham, where they were released under the name of the actor William Shakespeare. Supporters of the theory arranged for the Walsingham tomb in Kent to be opened in 1984, where they expected to find evidence of play manuscripts, but they found nothing. Difficulties include Ben Jonson's reference in the First Folio to the way Shakespeare 'didst … outshine' other authors – Marlowe being named in his list.

False friends: awful

MODERN SENSE: exceedingly bad, terrible; (American English) incredibly good
OBSOLETE SENSE: awe-inspiring, worthy of respect

✤ In *Pericles*, Gower describes Pericles as a 'benign lord / That will prove awful both in deed and word' (II.Chorus.4).
✤ One of the outlaws in *The Two Gentlemen of Verona* tells Valentine that they have been 'Thrust from the company of awful men' (IV.1.46).

Turning in his grave

'Do you know how they are going to decide the Shakespeare–Bacon dispute?' asked W. S. Gilbert (of Gilbert and Sullivan fame). 'They are going to dig up Shakespeare and dig up Bacon; they are going to set their coffins side by side, and they are going to get [Herbert Beerbohm Tree] to recite Hamlet to them. And the one who turns in his coffin will be the author of the play.'

Age fifty-three

Shakespeare's monument records his death at the age of fifty-three – which, given his birth in 1564, must mean 'in his fifty-third year'. This is a strong piece of evidence in favour of his birthday occurring on or before 23 April 1564. He would still have been in his fifty-second year if his birthday had been on or after 24 April.

The staff

This list of the men involved in the Chamberlain's or King's men during Shakespeare's lifetime is based on the Appendix compiled by Andrew Gurr in *The Shakespeare Company 1594–1642* (2004).

Name	Role	Dates
Robert Armin*	Sharer**	1599–1601
Richard Balls	Musician	1608–22
Christopher Beeston	Boy player or hired man	1598–9
Robert Benfield*	Hired man and sharer	1615–42
George Bryan*	Sharer	1594–7
Cuthbert Burbage	Housekeeper*** and company manager	1594–1636
Richard Burbage*	Sharer	1594–1619
Henry Condell*	Housekeeper and sharer	c.1598–1627
Richard Cowley*	Hired man	c.1594–1619
Alexander Cook*	Boy player, hired man, sharer	?–1614
Samuel Cross*	Player	?
John Duke	Hired man	c.1598
William Eccleston*	Hired man	1609–11, 1613–25
Nathan Field*	Housekeeper and sharer	1615–19
Lawrence Fletcher	Player in Scotland	1595–1601
Samuel Gilbourne*	Player	early 1600s
Robert Gough*	Hired man	early 1600s
John Heminges*	Sharer	1594–1630
John Holland	Hired man	1594
Humfrey Jeffes	Hired man?	1594–7
Will Kemp*	Sharer	1594–7
John Lowin*	Hired man and sharer	1603–42
William Ostler*	Sharer	1609–14
Augustine Phillips*	Sharer	1594–1605
Thomas Pollard	Hired man and sharer	1613–42
Thomas Pope*	Sharer	1594–1603
John Rice*	Boy player and hired man	1607–10, 1614–25
Richard Robinson*	Boy player and sharer	1611–42
James Sands	Boy player	early 1600s
Will Shakespeare*	Sharer and housekeeper	1594–1614
John Shanks*	Sharer	1613–36
John Sincler	Hired man	1594–c.1606
Will Sly*	Sharer	c.1594–1608
Joseph Taylor*	Sharer and housekeeper	1619–42
Nicholas Tooley*	Boy player and hired man	c.1600–23
John Underwood*	Sharer	1608–24
John Wilson	Musician	c.1611–?

* In the First Folio cast list
** Sharer: someone with a financial share in the acting company, and who took one of the leading parts (as opposed to the minor parts taken by the hired men)
*** Housekeeper: someone with a financial share in the playhouse

Which play has the fewest scenes?

Three plays have only nine scenes each:
The Tempest, *A Midsummer Night's Dream* and *Love's Labour's Lost*.

Dialect words

People often look for dialect words in Shakespeare, perhaps hoping to see something of the man behind the language. But so little information is available about English regional dialects in the sixteenth century that it is difficult to be sure whether a word has a dialect origin or not. Well over a hundred of his words are shown to be dialectal in Joseph Wright's *English Dialect Dictionary*, published at the end of the nineteenth century; but we can only speculate about the extent to which they were regionally restricted in Elizabethan England.

♣ Several words seem to have been common in Warwickshire, but many of them are found as far north as Lancashire and Yorkshire. They include:

blench 'glance, shy at', *blowze* 'wench', *bots* 'maggots', *chaps* 'cracks', *fardel* 'bundle', *honey-stalks* 'clover', *inkle* 'kind of tape', *malkin* 'female servant', *pash* 'strike', *pick-thank* 'flatterer', *quat* 'pimple', *raddock* 'robin', *squinny* 'squint-eyed', *urchin* 'hedgehog'

♣ Several words are found predominantly in the north. They include:

brabble 'quarrel', *brach* 'dog', *cogging* 'cheating', *coistrel* 'knave', *dint* 'blow', *eysel* 'vinegar', *fadge* 'fit', *fleer* 'sneer', *foison* 'harvest', *geck* 'fool', *gleek* 'scoff', *kam* 'wrong', *ken* 'know', *margent* 'edge', *mated* 'confused', *nuncle* 'uncle', *swart* 'dark', *yare* 'ready'

Meeting Richard?

Some writers have speculated that William met his future associate Richard Burbage during one of the visits of the Earl of Leicester's Men to Stratford (see p. 21). James Burbage was a member of that company and might have brought his young son with him. Unless both were extremely precocious, however, such a meeting would not have meant much in 1569, when Shakespeare was five and Richard about two.

The Latin eulogy

The Latin motto on Shakespeare's Stratford monument (see p. 9) compares him to some of the greatest figures of the past:

Iudicio Pylium, Genio Socratem, Arte Maronem:
Terra tegit, populus maeret, Olympus habet.

'In judgement a Nestor, in genius a Socrates, in art a Virgil:
The earth covers him, the people mourn him, Olympus has him.'

Alternative Shakespeares

Several people have been proposed as alternative candidates for the authorship of Shakespeare's plays (p. 166). They include the Earls of Derby, Essex, Rutland and Oxford, Christopher Marlowe, Francis Bacon and Queen Elizabeth herself. The three who have been most widely supported are Francis Bacon ('Baconians', p.158), Christopher Marlowe ('Marlovians', p.161) and Edward de Vere, the Earl of Oxford ('Oxfordians', p.160). The cases for Marlowe and Oxford both suffer from the difficulty that they died before many of the plays were written – which has fuelled the creation of complex conspiracy theories. Authorship controversies began only in the eighteenth century. There are no contemporary Jacobean references suggesting other writers for the plays.

Directors of the RSC

1960–8	Peter Hall (Managing Director)
1968–78	Trevor Nunn (Artistic Director)
1978–86	Trevor Nunn and Terry Hands (Joint Artistic Directors)
1986–91	Terry Hands (Artistic Director)
1991–2000	Adrian Noble (Artistic Director)
2003–	Michael Boyd (Artistic Director)

The first picture of a play

The first drawing of a Shakespeare play is found in the Longleat manuscript – a single leaf in the Portland papers of the Marquess of Bath at Longleat. It is a transcription of lines from *Titus Andronicus* headed by a drawing of seven characters in the opening scene under the heading 'Tamora pleadinge for her sonnes going to execution'. Three Roman characters on the left face the three Goths on the right, with Aaron alongside them, shown as a black man. The page is signed by Henry Peacham, a teacher and artist, and is dated *c.*1595.

Poetry or prose

Three plays have no prose lines at all – *Richard II*, *King John* and *King Edward III* – and two more have hardly any. Conversely, *The Merry Wives of Windsor* is notable for being predominantly in prose.

Poetry %	No. of lines	Prose %	No. of lines	Play
100	2752	0	0	Richard II
100	2569	0	0	King John
100	2493	0	0	King Edward III
99.7	2892	0.3	8	Henry VI Part III
99.5	2664	0.5	14	Henry VI Part I
98.6	2479	1.4	35	Titus Andronicus
97.6	3517	2.4	85	Richard III
97.4	2735	2.6	74	Henry VIII
94.5	2641	5.5	154	The Two Noble Kinsmen
93.5	1948	6.5	135	Macbeth
90.1	2208	9.9	244	Julius Caesar
89.8	2718	10.2	308	Antony and Cleopatra
86.9	2610	13.1	393	Romeo and Juliet
86.6	1543	13.4	239	The Comedy of Errors
85.2	2808	14.5	487	Cymbeline
83.7	2580	16.3	503	Henry VI Part II
81.2	1903	18.8	441	Pericles
80.6	2076	19.4	498	The Taming of the Shrew
80.6	1713	19.4	413	A Midsummer Night's Dream
80.4	2599	19.6	633	Othello
78.6	2025	21.4	551	The Merchant of Venice
77.2	2571	22.8	760	Coriolanus
76.5	1569	23.5	481	The Tempest
73.2	2181	26.8	800	The Winter's Tale
73.1	2345	26.9	865	King Lear
73.1	1707	26.9	627	Timon of Athens
73.1	1613	26.9	595	The Two Gentlemen of Verona
71.5	2742	28.5	1092	Hamlet
66.4	2250	33.6	1137	Troilus and Cressida
64.2	1716	35.8	955	Love's Labour's Lost
60.6	1634	39.4	1062	Measure for Measure
60.5	1943	39.5	1269	Henry V
55.6	1666	44.4	1332	Henry IV Part I
51.6	1447	48.4	1356	All's Well that Ends Well
47.6	1547	52.4	1700	Henry IV Part II
47.4	1276	52.6	1415	As You Like It
38.2	949	61.8	1532	Twelfth Night
28.3	739	71.7	1871	Much Ado About Nothing
12.5	338	87.5	2370	The Merry Wives of Windsor

Did Shakespeare write his plays?

'Anti-Stratfordians' say no. 'Stratfordians' say yes.

Against The son of a glover, with only a grammar-school education, could never have written such profound works; there isn't even a record of his attending grammar school.

For The curriculum of an Elizabethan school had a strong classical, historical and literary bias; as the son of the leading Stratford citizen, he would have been entitled to free education. There are no records of *any* of the pupils at Stratford grammar school until a century later.

Against Only someone with a university education could have written about law, astronomy and the sciences, alluded so often to the Classics or the Bible, or used Latin and French so extensively.

For Stratford school would have given him a solid grounding in Latin; and Elizabethan London was a multilingual city, where French especially was widespread. It is a commonplace that considerable learning can be acquired from books and conversation, as well as at university, and a profound biblical awareness is by no means restricted to academics. Shakespeare's Classical awareness is not especially sophisticated, compared with other poets of the time. Ben Jonson did not attend university either, yet he went on to be renowned for his learning. Many of the university playwrights, by contrast, wrote inferior plays.

Against There are no extant manuscripts or letters by Shakespeare about himself or his activities.

For Biographical details are missing for most Elizabethan writers. We know more about Shakespeare than about most of his fellow-dramatists. (*continues*)

False friends: umpire

MODERN SENSE: arbitrator in certain games and contests
OBSOLETE SENSE: arbitrator, mediator (a dispute of any kind, not necessarily for sports)

- ♣ Mortimer refers to death as a 'kind umpire of men's miseries' (*Henry VI Part I*, II.5.29).
- ♣ King Henry asks: 'Let me be umpire in this doubtful strife' (*Henry VI Part I*, IV.1.151).
- ♣ Juliet is not thinking of a game when she tells the Friar, 'this bloody knife / Shall play the umpire' (*Romeo and Juliet*, IV.1.63), for her thought is of suicide.

Against He was not acknowledged in his lifetime as a great writer.

For Shakespeare's name is on several Quarto plays of the period. Indeed, his reputation was such that his name was illicitly attached to plays he never wrote. Several contemporaries refer to him as a notable writer, and Francis Meres in 1598 lauds him repeatedly (p. 143).

Against The plays show intimate awareness of court life and politics, which would have been beyond his experience.

For As a member of the company that played regularly in court, and later as one of the King's Men, and a liveried Groom of the Chamber, he would have had many opportunities to see courtly life. But in fact the picture of the court in the plays does not accurately show how a noble household was ordered. A real Lord Capulet would never have involved himself with domestic wedding details in the way Juliet's father does.

Against The plays show an awareness of foreign countries, especially Italy, yet there is no record of his ever travelling abroad.

For He may well have travelled during the 'lost years'; but there is a more important counter-argument. Several errors in his geographical locations suggest that he obtained his information from conversation or library sources. He locates Delphi on an island and gives Bohemia a shore (in *The Winter's Tale*), suggests that Milan is near the sea (in *The Tempest*), and puts Padua in Lombardy (in *The Taming of the Shrew*). Seasoned university travellers, such as the Earl of Oxford (who actually visited Padua in 1575), would not have made such errors.

Against His textual vocabulary of around 20,000 words was too large for someone with a rural background.

For A vocabulary of that size was not especially large, then or now (see pp. 41, 169).   (*continues*)

False friends: fabulous

MODERN SENSE: marvellous, terrific; astonishing, incredible
OBSOLETE SENSE: mythical, fabricated, invented

♣ In *Henry VI Part I*, the Countess looks at the English general Talbot, thinks that his appearance does not live up to his reputation, and says, 'I see report is fabulous and false' (II.3.17).

♣ In *Henry VIII*, Norfolk describes to Buckingham the meeting of the kings of England and France, comparing the event to a 'former fabulous story' (I.1.36).

These are the only uses of *fabulous* in the entire canon.

(*continued from p. 167*)

Against How could Shakespeare afford his expensive source books?

For Anyone who could afford to pay £60 for a house in 1597 would have been able to afford to buy a few books. But apart from this, there were many possible ways. From his London friends. From the Earl of Southampton's library (p. 128). But above all, from his Stratford contemporary Richard Field, who not only printed *Venus and Adonis* and *The Rape of Lucrece* but also Holinshed's *Chronicles* and North's English translation of Plutarch's *Lives*, the two most common sources for the plays. Field was also the leading publisher of language-teaching books in Elizabethan London.

Against Shakespeare must have had a large library, but there is no mention of any books in his will.

For Books, even whole libraries, are usually not mentioned in Elizabethan wills. The theologian Richard Hooker's library (known from a surviving inventory) was worth half of his estate, but was not mentioned in his will. Nor are books mentioned in Francis Bacon's will. Shakespeare's will is typical of a man intent to see his property properly disposed. If there was an inventory, it has been lost, as were most such inventories of the time. However, in 1637 there is a law-court reference to 'divers bookes' still housed at New Place.

Against Shakespeare mentions none of his play manuscripts in his will, and none have survived.

For They were not his to leave: his scripts belonged to the King's Men. In any case, hardly any manuscript evidence of the successful plays of the period has survived. Manuscript paper was evidently recyclable: in Beaumont and Fletcher's *A King and No King*, one of the characters says that he makes a profit by selling manuscripts of the challenges he receives to the grocers for packaging. (*continues*)

=========== *False friends: sensible* ===========

MODERN SENSE: * endowed with good sense, intelligent

OBSOLETE SENSE: capable of receiving sensation, responsive, sensitive

❧ Constance describes herself as 'not mad, but sensible of grief' (*King John*, III.4.53)

OBSOLETE SENSE: perceptible by the senses, evident

❧ Macbeth addresses an imaginary dagger: 'Art thou not, fatal vision, sensible / To feeling as to sight?' (*Macbeth*, II.1.36).

*The modern meaning was beginning to come into the language in Shakespeare's day: Ford describes Pistol as 'a good sensible fellow' (*The Merry Wives of Windsor*, II.1.137).

Against There is no hint of his literary background in his will.

For The will names John Heminge, Richard Burbage and Henry Condell as his 'ffellowes' – the only three members of the original Chamberlain's Men still alive in 1616. Two are the editors of the First Folio in 1623, which they compiled, they say, 'onely to keepe the memory of so worthy a Friend, & Fellow aliue, as was our Shakespeare'. They include several verses dedicated to his memory, including the famous memorial by Jonson – poet laureate, no less – in which he calls Shakespeare the 'Sweet Swan of Avon'.

Against His death received no public acknowledgement or eulogy, which would surely have happened if he had been so famous.

For Only the most prominent personalities, such as nobles and church-men, were the subject of printed eulogies on their death. For poets and playwrights, the eulogies came much later. The first eulogy for Francis Beaumont, who also died in 1616, did not appear until 1629. In fact, Shakespeare was eulogized more than any of his fellow play-wrights except Jonson (who died much later). William Basse wrote a poem 'On Mr. Wm. Shakespeare, he died in April 1616', suggesting that he should have been buried in Westminster Abbey. And it is difficult to think of more expressive eulogies than those in the First Folio and on the monument in Holy Trinity Church, Stratford (p. 9).

False friends: wink

MODERN SENSE: * close and open one eye, to communicate amusement or a secret message

OBSOLETE SENSE: shut the eyes, ignore

☙ York advises his friends to 'wink at the Duke of Suffolk's inso-lence' (*Henry VI Part II*, II.2.70).

☙ Othello castigates Desdemona by saying 'Heaven stops the nose at it, and the moon winks' (*Othello*, IV.2.76). We must avoid the modern implication that the matter is not serious.

*The modern usage also existed in Shakespeare's day: 'I will wink on her to consent', says Burgundy to Henry, of Princess Katherine, in *Henry V*, V.2.301.

How large is your lexicon?

The vocabulary attributed to Shakespeare approaches 20,000 words (p. 41) – but how large is that? You can make a quick comparison with present-day usage by measuring your own active vocabulary. Choose a 1% sample of pages from a dictionary and tick the words you think you use; then multiply the answer by 100. These days, an average adult active vocabulary is 30–40,000 words.

Stage fright

I've never been frightened of anything, much. I've never had stage fright, unlike Larry [Laurence Olivier]. *Larry was so nervous on his first night of* Richard III *in 1943 that he asked John Mills and his wife, Mary Hayley Bell, to go and hold his hand in the dressing room. He felt that he had the make-up ready but not the performance. The Millses sat with him while he applied his long plasticine nose, his dank, straggly black wig, his great hump. He then shortened one leg. He backed on to the audience for his first soliloquy, then turned, and the house fell about: they screamed with laughter at the sight of this absurd grotesque. And that gave him the spur to play it for comedy; until that moment, when they laughed, he did not know how he would play it. I have never done that, that is, been so unsure of myself that I did not know how to play a part before I went on the stage.*

(Robert Stephens, *Knight Errant*, 1996, p. 179)

Definitive performances

Has Olivier done the part definitively? Surely not. Surely the greatness of the play is lessened if such a feat is possible? Surely contemporaries thought the same about Irving, Kean, even Burbage? The trouble is, Olivier put it on film.

(Antony Sher, on playing Richard III, *Year of the King*, 1985, p. 28)

Hall *on* Hamlet

Peter Hall, on the opening night of his 1975 production of *Hamlet* at the Royal National Theatre:

I have discovered a great deal about Shakespeare which I have always known in my head: the way scene must follow scene; the way lines are written for coming on and going off; the way every scene has a thematic line five or six lines in, to catch the audience's attention so that they know what the scene is about.

(*Peter Hall's Diaries*, 10 December 1975)

Mentioning the Bible

Though there are many biblical allusions in the plays, Shakespeare mentions the Bible, as such, only once. This is in *The Merry Wives of Windsor*, when the comic Frenchman Dr Caius says he is glad that Sir Hugh Evans has not come to fight him: 'He has pray his Pible well that he is no come' (II.3.7).

Challenging prose

Why, you may ask, should we worry about [prose] *at all? Surely it's much easier to manage than verse? Doesn't it look after itself? Well, in Shakespeare it very often doesn't. His prose has very strong rhythms and if an actor does not get in touch with them there will be a loss of definition and energy and clarity. There's also an awful lot of it. It's worth quoting a statistic: just over twenty-eight per cent*of the text of Shakespeare's plays is in prose, over a quarter. So it's not a minor question, it's a major challenge.*

(John Barton, *Playing Shakespeare*, 1984, p. 69)

*Using the concordance to the *Shakespeare's Words* database, the proportion is actually 24.2 per cent. It is still a lot.

Conversions

A distinctive feature of English, since the loss of most word-endings in the early Middle Ages, is the formation of new words by changing their word class, or part of speech – a process known as *word-class conversion*. It is a major stylistic feature of Shakespeare's use of English. The commonest form is when a noun is used as a verb, as in 'I eared her language' (*The Two Noble Kinsmen*, III.1.29). One of the creative reasons for conversion is to find more vivid ways of expressing everyday notions, as when Iago's 'lip a wanton' (*Othello*, IV.1.71) replaces the mundane 'kiss', or Coriolanus's 'godded me' (*Coriolanus*, V.3.11) replaces 'treated me as a god'.

Expressing all

If we try to pull at a rich text to make sense of it too quickly we will simply end up with shreds. We have to be aware that Hamlet is more intellectual than the greatest intellectual, more in love than the greatest lover before or since, more angry than the most violent man there has ever been, and the most important thing is that Hamlet gives expression to it all.   (Peter Brook, quoted by Adrian Lester,
The Independent, 20 August 2001)

Old fool

'Bother Shakespeare,' said Jane, impetuously, '– old fool that expects credit for saying things that everybody knows!'

(George Bernard Shaw,
Unsocial Socialist, 1883, Chapter 3)

A comment from D. H. Lawrence

When I read Shakespeare I am struck with wonder
That such trivial people should muse and thunder
In such lovely language.

(D. H. Lawrence,
'When I Read Shakespeare', 1929)

Elision

As in modern English, Shakespearian words often appear in a reduced or *elided* form, with the omitted element shown by an apostrophe, such as *'tis* (it is), *th'art* (thou art), *i'th'* (in the), and *to't* (to it). The reason for the elision varies: in some cases it enables a word to fit the metrical character of a line or focuses the emphasis within a sentence more sharply; in others it helps to capture the colloquial character of conversational speech or identifies a character's idiosyncratic way of talking.

False friends: inhabitable

MODERN SENSE: capable of being lived in
OBSOLETE SENSE: *not* capable of being lived in, uninhabitable
♣ This is the sense you need when you hear Mowbray say to King Richard that he would fight Henry Bolingbroke even if he were 'tied to run afoot / Even to the frozen ridges of the Alps, / Or any other ground inhabitable' (*Richard II*, I.1.65).
Shakespeare uses the word only once in the whole canon.

Zwaggered

This is a rare example of a regional dialect representation in the plays. It appears in *King Lear* (IV.6.230) when Edgar, in the guise of a mad country beggar, defends his blinded father against the approach of Goneril's steward Oswald. Normally, Edgar speaks in a colloquial but non-regional way, though in an accent that prevents his father recognizing him. But when he confronts Oswald, he switches into a regional persona, and uses such mock west-country forms as *vortnight* for *fortnight*, *zwaggered* for *swaggered* ('bullied'), and *chill* for *I'll*.

Upsetting actors

No one can convince me Shakespeare didn't make up words just to upset the actors. (Jack Lemmon, on trying to learn his lines for his part in Kenneth Branagh's film of *Hamlet*, 1996)

False friends: bully

MODERN SENSE: tyrannical coward who terrorizes the weak
OBSOLETE SENSE: dear friend; sweetheart; fine fellow

There is something of the 'Hail fellow, well met' tone about it, for it is used

♣ by a drunken Stephano to Caliban: 'Coragio, bully-monster' (*The Tempest*, V.I.258)

♣ by the braggart Pistol about the King: 'I love the lovely bully' (*Henry V*, IV.I.48)

♣ by the rustics to the overpowering Bottom: 'Bully Bottom' (*A Midsummer Night's Dream*, III.I.7).

Originally used to people of either sex, it was later restricted to men. Shakespeare usually uses it as a kind of honorific prefix to a man's name.

Hollywood

People say Hollywood is in love with Shakespeare. That's not true. Some of the mini's are financing Shakespeare but no major is doing a Shakespeare as far as I can recall. I thought Kenny Branagh did a terrific job with Much Ado About Nothing *and I particularly liked his* Henry V, *but the grosses for those films are $20 million domestic. They're tiny. Why do you think majors don't bother — they're not worth the biscuits.*

(Baz Luhrmann,
interview for omnileonardo.com, 1996)

Visiting Queens

Although the film *Shakespeare in Love*, and a great deal of popular wishful thinking, have Queen Elizabeth going to see a Shakespeare play at the theatre, this would never have happened. No monarch went to such smelly, rough places, and it was not until the time of Charles II that conditions and fashion changed sufficiently for royal visits to be made. For a play to be seen by the Queen, it would have to have been performed at Court. The only Shakespeare play we know to have been definitely performed before her was *Love's Labour's Lost* (but see p. 7). The title-page of *The Merry Wives of Windsor* claims that it was acted before the Queen, but there is no official record. The story that it was written at the express command of Elizabeth to show Falstaff in love, whatever its truth, is a tale which did not arise until the eighteenth-century (see p. 63). More wishful thinking, possibly.

Shakespeare's collaborators

At least ten of Shakespeare's plays are thought to be collaborations.

Date	Collaborator	Play	Type of collaboration
1590–1	George Peele	Titus Andronicus	Co-author or revisor
1591–2	George Peele	Henry VI Part I	A team of writers?
1590–94	?unknown	King Edward III	A team of writers?
1604	?Thomas Middleton	Measure for Measure	Possible revisor
1604–7	?Thomas Middleton	Timon of Athens	Possible co-author
1606	?Thomas Middleton	Macbeth	Possible revisor
1608–9	?George Wilkins	Pericles	Co-author or revisor
1613	John Fletcher	Henry VIII	Co-author
1613-15	John Fletcher	The Two Noble Kinsmen	Co-author?
1613	John Fletcher	Cardenio	A lost play

Keeping fit

Let's be absolutely clear.
* ♣ *To speak Shakespeare you have to be fit*
* ♣ *Not just physically fit, but throughout the body, breath, voice and speech muscles*
* ♣ *You have to be fit intellectually and emotionally and awake in your spirit*
* ♣ *You have to be passionate, political and curious*
* ♣ *You have to keep up with a writer who operates through his words and forms on every human level*

To put it another way, in order to act Shakespeare, you have to be a complete human athlete – not just a footballer or a philosopher, but both. His plays are the most thorough work-out an actor can have, and they should be central to any actor's training. They challenge physically, intellectually and emotionally, and require access through the imagination to what it is to be human.

(Patsy Rodenburg, *Speaking Shakespeare*, 2002, p. 13)

On Shakespeare Street

There is a remarkable paucity of places named after Shakespeare. No town in the UK has been named for him. However, in Kolkata (Calcutta) there is a Shakespeare Sarani (Street), a name which was retained even when many other locations in India had their British names replaced by indigenous forms. And on Shakespeare Street several shops proudly display the name – including the enticingly named 'Shakespeare Parlour'.

Collaboration

Collaboration was normal practice in Elizabethan England. Theatre manager Philip Henslowe's diary (kept from 1592 to 1603) records 282 plays written by more than one author. In some cases as many as five writers were involved. Literary historian Gerald Eades Bentley has estimated that half the plays written by professional dramatists between 1590 and 1642 were collaborations. The extent of the practice is often obscured by the title pages, which often do not list all the writers.

Which acts have just one scene?

Fifteen acts consist of a single scene:

The Comedy of Errors, V.1   *A Midsummer Night's Dream*, V.1
King Edward III, V.1   *Richard II*, IV.1
King John, I.1 and II.1   *The Taming of the Shrew*, II.1
Love's Labour's Lost, II.1 and III.1   *The Tempest*, IV.1 and V.1
Measure for Measure, V.1   *Titus Andronicus*, I.1
The Merchant of Venice, V.1   *Twelfth Night*, V.1

Three Globes

The first Globe theatre burned down in 1613 during a performance of *Henry VIII*, when a spark from a cannon set fire to the roof thatch.

The second Globe was rebuilt in 1614 with a tile roof. It was closed by the Puritans in 1642, along with all other theatres, and was demolished in 1644 to be replaced by public dwellings.

The third Globe opened in 1997, a hundred metres from the original site (modern apartments now cover most of the old site). It was the first thatch-roofed building allowed to be built in London since the Great Fire of 1666.

An absolutely perfect play

I think that Shakespeare's plays are not all written with the same degree of finish. Some plays are looser and some plays are tighter. In A Midsummer Night's Dream *I didn't have the least wish to cut a word, to cut or transpose anything, for the simple and very personal reason that it seemed to me an absolutely perfect play ... It helps to have the absolute conviction that each word is there because it has to be; by total belief in a text you find its rightness.* (Peter Brook, *The Shifting Point*, 1987, p. 95)

Bubbling

If you do Macbeth *and you don't believe in witches,
then, you know, why do the play?*
(Mark Rylance, interview, June 1994)

The Scottish Play

It is held to be incredibly bad luck to mention the name 'Macbeth', outside of rehearsal rooms or while the play is being performed. Many people in the profession refuse to call it by its chosen name, preferring 'The Scottish Play'. As English Shakespearian actor Michael Pennington once said: 'Macbeth is an unholy riddle we still hesitate to name for the fear of retribution.'

The Curse of Macbeth

'Macbeth is to the theatrical world what King Tut's tomb is to archaeologists,' said writer Norrie Epstein. But why does an atmosphere of bad luck surround Shakespeare's Scottish play of deceit, manipulation and assassination?

Many productions have suffered from their actors dying or being injured. King James banned the play for five years after seeing it, perhaps because (as he was an author of a work on witchcraft) the witches' incantations were too real for comfort.

But there are more down-to-earth reasons.

* ♣ There is a great deal of violent action in it.
* ♣ It often takes place in the dark, which makes it more likely that accidents will happen.
* ♣ It is the shortest tragedy Shakespeare wrote, making it cheaper to put on – which has led to the theory that companies having a difficult financial time would mount a production to make money fast, and perhaps cut corners when it came to rehearsals and safety.

And, of course, it is now a self-fulfilling prophecy: actors expect something to go wrong and, unwittingly, make it happen.

Discovering witchcraft

Reginald Scot (1538–99) wrote his *Discoverie of Witchcraft* in 1584. In it, he demystifies many of the standing superstitions of the time concerning witches and witchcraft. There is a tradition that Shakespeare read and greatly admired the book. It is believed to be a secondary source for *Macbeth*, and the source for *A Midsummer Night's Dream*'s Puck and aspects of Bottom's transformation.

Macready and Forrest

In the mid-1800s, England's most revered actor, William Charles Macready, and America's leading Shakespearean actor, Edwin Forrest, were bitter rivals. Forrest toured England in 1846 and received ill-favoured reviews from the critics, who preferred Macready's acting. In revenge, Forrest hissed Macready during a performance of *Hamlet*, in Edinburgh. Later, in 1848, Macready toured America, and Forrest tried to ruin the tour by performing the same plays at nearby theatres. They both performed in *Macbeth* on the same night in New York, and Macready, at the Astor Place Opera House, had to contend with his theatre full of Forrest fans throwing things at him. When a chair landed at his feet and smashed, he bowed to the audience, and left the stage. On 10 May, three nights later, he was persuaded to perform again, but despite police protection several Forrest supporters formed part of the audience, disturbed the show, and a riot began outside the theatre. Over twenty people died.

Superstitious?

Some productions of *Macbeth* that have felt the curse:

* During the play's first performance, Hal Berridge, the boy playing Lady Macbeth, died backstage, and (tradition says) Shakespeare had to play the part.

* In a production in Amsterdam, in 1672, the actor playing Macbeth used a real dagger, and killed the actor playing Duncan in front of the audience.

* During rival performances of the play in New York, in 1849, a riot broke out and over twenty people died.

* In John Gielgud's 1942 production, three actors died – Duncan and two of the witches – and the set designer committed suicide.

* Two fires and seven robberies happened during David Leary's 1971 production.

* Cambridge Shakespeare Company, 2001: Macduff injured his back, Lady Macbeth hit her head, Ross broke his toe and two cedar trees crashed to the ground, destroying the set.

* Royal Shakespeare Company, 2004: the cast were given a questionnaire on the first day of rehearsals, asking them all how superstitious they were.

Exorcism

On 3 September 2001, a white witch tried to exorcise the curse of Macbeth. He attempted to raise the spirit of King Macbeth, on the site of Inverness Castle. The present Lady Cawdor was asked if her castle could be used, but she refused. The attempt was nearly cancelled because the cameraman fell ill during the filming of the ritual, and several witches cancelled the trip due to mysterious happenings.

Polanski curse

The director Roman Polanski made a film of *Macbeth* in 1971 starring Jon Finch and Francesca Annis as the Macbeths, co-writing the screenplay with the theatre critic Kenneth Tynan. The 'curse' of the play seems to have affected their production too. A cameraman was nearly killed on the first day on location in Snowdonia National Park when a fierce wind blew him into a crevasse. The murder of his wife, the actress Sharon Tate, by Charles Manson has also been related to the curse – as Tynan wrote in his diary on 11 February 1971:

> *Roman directing the murder of Lady Macduff's little daughters. He explains that they must pretend to be dead – it's a game – while he puts funny paint (i.e. blood) on their faces. He arranges the smaller girl sprawled in a cradle. As he sprinkles the blood, he says, 'And what's your name?' 'Sharon,' she says.*

Cure

If someone does say 'Macbeth' outside of performance or rehearsal, there are a number of cures to the curse. Here are two:

♣ Leave the room or space you are in, close the door behind you. Turn around three times, swear, knock on the door, and ask to be let back in.

♣ If there is no time for all of that, quoting Hamlet's 'Angels and ministers of grace defend us!' (1.4.39) will do it.

Mackers

We're calling it Macbeth ... *Not* Mackers, *not* The Scottish Play, *none of the euphemisms.* Macbeth, Macbeth, Macbeth – *there, I've said it and haven't been struck down. There's supposed to be a curse on this play. Bollocks! The only curse is that it's so hard to do.*

(Gregory Doran, on the first day of rehearsals for his 1999 production of *Macbeth* at the Royal Shakespeare Company)

False friends: penthouse

MODERN SENSE: a (usually luxurious) apartment situated at the top of a tall building

OBSOLETE SENSE: a covered way of some kind, usually a sloping porch or overhanging roof

♣ 'Stand thee close ... under this pent-house', says Borachio to Conrade (*Much Ado About Nothing*, III.3.101).

OBSOLETE SENSE (metaphorical): emphasizing the vertical dimension

♣ Mote describes Armado's hat as resting 'penthouse-like o'er the shop of your eyes' (*Love's Labour's Lost*, III.1.16).

♣ The First Witch uses it in cursing a sailor: 'Sleep shall neither night nor day/Hang upon his penthouse lid' (*Macbeth*, I.3.20).

False fire

References to weapons pervade Shakespeare's plays, especially the histories and tragedies – but the allusions are not always obvious, to a modern audience. When Claudius rushes away from the 'play within a play' in *Hamlet*, Hamlet calls after him, 'What, frighted with false fire?' (III.2.275). The meaning of the phrase is to discharge a gun using blank cartridges. It is an unusual reference today, but it would have had real point for any soldiers in the Elizabethan audience, who would have been trained in firearms, but not, it seems, to a very high level of proficiency. Charles Edelman, in his book *Shakespeare's Military Language* (2000), reports Sir Francis Walsingham's complaint that soldiers usually shut their eyes while firing, or pulled their head away from the gun, 'wherby they take no perfect levell, but shoote at random'! Cartridges were expensive, so it became routine to use blanks during training. The Lord Lieutenant of Northamptonshire told his muster masters in 1586 that 'the first training bee made with false fyer'. Hamlet's usage is apposite, for Claudius has seen only a story, not the real thing.

Something that doesn't bear thinking about

Because the Globe burned down during a performance, it proved possible to save a great deal of the company's assets – which presumably included the scripts for those of Shakespeare's plays that had not yet been published (half the total). No such fortune attended the Fortune theatre, which also burned down (in 1621) – but at midnight, when nobody was there to help, and everything was destroyed. If the Globe had burned at midnight ...

Learning foreign matters

Plays seem to have provided the Elizabethan audience with a great deal of their knowledge about foreign countries. The Swiss tourist Thomas Platter commented in his diary in 1599 about how the English pass their time 'learning at the play what is happening abroad'. He adds: 'indeed men and womenfolk visit such places without scruple, since the English for the most part do not travel much, but prefer to learn foreign matters and take their pleasures at home.'

Multilingual Shakespeare

Shakespeare is performed in a number of foreign languages magnificently. I know I would be the poorer if I had not seen Shakespeare in Japanese and indeed in Russian or, as we did a long time ago at the National, in Swedish when Bergman came, and the plays are no less accessible than they are in our own language.

(Thelma Holt, National Theatre interview, March 2003)

Garbled tongues

Some of the characters who speak a foreign language are actually speaking no language known to mankind.

- ♣ There is mock Latin when Feste says *bonos dies* (*Twelfth Night*, IV.2.12) and Costard says *ad dunghill* (*Love's Labour's Lost*, V.1.72).

- ♣ There is mock French when Pistol (*Henry V*, II.1.68) says *couple a gorge* (= *couper la gorge*, 'cut the throat'), Parolles (*All's Well that Ends Well*, II.3.43) utters the pseudo-oath *mor du vinager*, and Jack Cade (*Henry VI Part II*, IV.7.25) says *Basimecu* (= *baise mon cul*, 'kiss my arse').

- ♣ The motto described by Thaisa in *Pericles* (II.2.27) is said to be Spanish, but it is actually much closer to Italian: *pue per doleera kee per forsa* ('more by gentleness than by force').

- ♣ Pistol's utterances (*Henry IV Part II*, II.4.176, V.5.99) are also a garbled mixture of Italian and Spanish: *Si fortuna me tormente sperato me contento* and *Si fortuna me tormenta, spero me contenta* ('if fortune torments me, hope contents me'). His *calen o custure me* (*Henry V*, IV.4.4) is completely nonsensical.

- ♣ Christopher Sly also seems to be attempting Spanish when he says *paucas pallabris* ('few words') in *The Taming of the Shrew* (Induction I.5). Dogberry, of all people, gets the second word right: *palabras* (*Much Ado About Nothing*, III.5.15).

Eskimo?

*Autolycus's speeches – like all Shakespeare's clowns – are virtually
incomprehensible; it's like reading a joke book in Eskimo.*

(Antony Sher, *Beside Myself*, 2001, p. 313)

Performing for James I

Under James I, Shakespeare's company received a licence to perform at
Court, and became known as The King's Men. It was a prestigious position: they were Grooms of the Outer Chamber, and entitled to wear the
king's livery (p. 140). In the ten years that Shakespeare was royal playwright, his company performed at Court 138 times – either at Whitehall
or at Hampton Court (where the Great Hall is still used as a theatre when
the companies of Shakespeare's Globe perform there). The conditions
were not ideal. Plays began at ten in the evening, after much feasting, in
stuffy, cramped surroundings. In Alvin Kernan's *Shakespeare, the King's
Playwright* (1995) we read of James falling asleep on such occasions.
Apparently the only Shakespeare play he asked to see again was *The
Merchant of Venice* – but it is a moot point whether this was because he
found it fascinating or because he had missed the ending the first time.

To pry or not to pry

'Should we be prying into the family life of a great man?' asks Russell in
James Joyce's *Ulysses* (Bodley Head edition, p. 177). And he is given a
firm reply by Stephen Dedalus:

*Interesting only to the parish clerk. I mean, we have the plays.
I mean when we read the poetry of King Lear what is it to us
how the poet lived? As for living, our servants can do that for us,
Villiers de l'Isle has said. Peeping and prying into greenroom
gossip of the day, the poet's drinking, the poet's debts. We have
King Lear: and that is immortal.*

Gielgud and Olivier – Mercutio and Romeo

In 1935 John Gielgud directed *Romeo and Juliet* at the New Theatre, with
Laurence Olivier as Romeo, Peggy Ashcroft as Juliet, and himself as
Mercutio. Olivier and Gielgud, however, alternated their parts. Critic
Herbert Farjeon summarized the event:

*As Romeo, Mr Olivier was twenty times as much in love with
Peggy Ashcroft's Juliet as Mr Gielgud was. But Mr Gielgud
spoke most of the poetry far better than Mr Olivier.*

Italics

Italics are far more often used in Elizabethan Quarto and Folio texts than we find today. They are most commonly used in the following contexts (examples from the First Folio):

❧ Stage directions: *Enter Duke and Friar Peter.*

❧ Names, usually abbreviated, which precede speeches: *Val.*, *Launce.*, *Mist.*, *Page.*

❧ Proper names in a text, as when Mistress Ford addresses Falstaff in *The Merry Wives of Windsor*: Go, go, sweet *Sir John*: *Mistriis Page* and I will looke some linnen for your head

❧ Songs, as when Ariel sings in *The Tempest*: *Ariell* Song. *Full fadom fiue thy Father lies,* ...

❧ Letters, as when Malvolio starts to read Olivia's letter in *Twelfth Night*: *Mal. To the unknowne belou'd, this, and my good Wishes*: Her very Phrases ...

A letter to Shakespeare

The only surviving letter addressed to Shakespeare was written by his fellow Stratfordian Richard Quiney on 25 October 1598. Tradition says that it was written at the Bell Inn, Carter Lane, in London, and a plaque today marks the site. The letter is addressed:

To my Loveinge good ffrend & contreymann m^r w^m Shackespeare

It asks for a loan of £30 'in helpeing me out of all the debettes I owe in London'. In fact, Shakespeare never got the letter, for Quiney took it back to Stratford with him, where it was discovered in his papers. Why did he not send it? Presumably, as some biographers have suggested, because he was able to meet Shakespeare in London and the letter became redundant.

Banned!

In 1574 the puritan-influenced City of London, acting against what they perceived to be great disorder and immorality in places where plays were performed, issued an Act of Common Council:

henceforthe no playe, Commodye, Tragidye, enterlude, nor publycke shewe shalbe openlye played or shewed within the liberties of the Cittie ...

As a result all theatres within the City moved outside the City boundaries, and the first theatres appeared on the South Bank of the Thames.

During the past century, there have been a number of notable perform-ances of some or all of the cycle of history plays (though without *King Edward III*, since that play has only recently received a degree of recog-nition as part of the canon, and its status is controversial). Here are some of them.

Date	Company / Project Title (where applicable)	Productions
1906	The Benson Company, Shakespeare Memorial Theatre, Stratford-upon-Avon	All plays from *Richard III*, but excluding *Henry IV Part I*, played in historical order over one week Thought to be the first performance of all three parts of *Henry VI* since Shakespeare's time
1923	Old Vic, London	*Henry IV* to *Richard III* presented in sequence
1935	Pasadena Community Playhouse, California, USA	*Richard II* to *Richard III*, presented in sequence, but with each play performed on several successive days
1951	Shakespeare Memorial Theatre, Stratford-upon-Avon	*Richard II* to *Henry V* One set design used for all the plays
1961	BBC Television, 'The Age of Kings'	*Richard II* to *Richard III*
1963–4	Royal Shakespeare Company 'The Wars of the Roses and History Cycle'	*Richard II* to *Richard III*, with the three *Henry VI* plays amalgamated into two by John Barton
1975–81	Royal Shakespeare Company 'The Wars of the Roses and History Cycle'	1975–6 *Henry IV* and *Henry V* 1977–8 *Henry V* and the three *Henry VI* plays 1980–81 *Richard II* and *Richard III*
1986–9	English Shakespeare Company, 'The Wars of the Roses'	*Richard II* to *Richard III*, with the three *Henry VI* plays amalgamated into two
1988–9	Royal Shakespeare Company, 'The Plantagenets'	The three parts of *Henry VI* and *Richard III* amalgamated into three plays
2000–2001	Royal Shakespeare Company, 'This England'	*Richard II* to *Richard III* performed in sequence in Stratford and London *King Edward III* also performed in 2002 in Stratford and London

MODERN SENSE: * devoid of sense, foolish

OBSOLETE SENSE: (of objects) lacking human sensation, incapable of feeling

♣ In *Cymbeline*, Innogen describes Posthumus' handkerchief as 'senseless linen' (I.4.7) and later in the same play Pisanio calls a letter a 'senseless bauble' (III.2.20).

OBSOLETE SENSE: (of people) insensible, oblivious

♣ Timon's steward bemoans the way his master spends money 'senseless of expense' (*Timon of Athens*, II.2.1).

♣ Innogen says to Cymbeline, 'I am senseless of your wrath' (*Cymbeline*, I.2.66).

*This meaning was coming into the language in Shakespeare's day. Petruchio describes Grumio as 'a senseless villain' (*The Taming of the Shrew*, I.2.36).

===================== *Humbling roles* =====================

Shakespeare's great parts are humiliating to play, or at least, humbling. You get to meet his genius face to face.

(Antony Sher, *Year of the King*, 1985, p. 247)

===================== *South Bank theatres* =====================

The first theatre south of the river, Newington Butts, dates from around 1575, but it did not prove to be a popular venue because of its distance out of town, and it seems to have fallen out of use during the 1590s. The Rose, near the river in Southwark, was opened in 1592, and was an immediate success; performances continued until 1603. The Swan, further west along the river, was opened probably in 1596. It certainly impressed the Dutch traveller, Johannes de Witt, who visited it at around that time and made a famous sketch of its interior:

> *There are four amphitheatres in London of notable beauty, which from their diverse signs bear diverse names. In each of them a different play is daily exhibited to the populace. The two more magnificent of these are situated to the southward beyond the Thames, and from the signs suspended before them are called the Rose and Swan ... Of all the theatres, however, the largest and the most magnificent is ... the Swan Theatre; for it accommodates in its seats three thousand persons, and is built of a mass of flint stones ... and supported by wooden columns painted in such excellent imitation of marble that it is able to deceive even the most cunning.*

Print-runs

In the 1580s, the Stationers' Company introduced a restriction on the print-run of a book, usually to 1000 copies. The aim of the regulation was to keep typesetters in work. Printing type was in limited supply, so the type used to set a book was broken up after the typesetting was completed – and, in the case of long books, such as the First Folio, often after a short section of the book (a 'quire' of six leaves) was completed. If, then, there was a demand for a book to be reprinted, it had to be set all over again.

Three roles

Shakespeare had three roles in the Chamberlain's Men. He was an actor, the company's in-house playwright, and one of the company's shareholders. No other personality of the period held such a multi-faceted position.

Congratulations

Not everyone was devastated when the Shakespeare Memorial Theatre burned down in 1926. George Bernard Shaw saw it as a blessing in disguise (quoted in M. C. Day and J. C. Trewin, *The Shakespeare Memorial Theatre*, p. 184):

> *I am extremely glad to hear the news. Stratford-upon-Avon is to be congratulated on the fire. Mr Bridges-Adams* [the director of the Stratford Festival Company] *will be delighted. The Memorial was one of those shockingly bad theatres put up in the nineteenth century, and it will be a tremendous advantage to have a proper modern building. There are a few other theatres I should like to see burned down. Meantime, I suppose, they will play Shakespeare in a tent. I don't see why not.*

He was close. They played in a cinema for the next five years (see p. 20).

First playhouses

The first London playhouses were built in the suburbs to the north of the city. The Theatre was built in 1576 by James Burbage on land at Bishopsgate. The Curtain followed, in 1577 – named after its location in nearby Curtain Close, and not because it used curtains (which were not an Elizabethan practice). The Chamberlain's Men probably performed there regularly between 1597 and 1599. John Marston, in *The Scourge of Villainy*, refers to *Romeo and Juliet* receiving 'Curtain plaudities'.

There were ten main provisions in Shakespeare's will, drawn up in January 1616, and revised on 25 March. The extracts below represent less than a half of the detail contained in the will, which in total is over 1400 words. Deleted text is not shown.

❧ *In the name of god Amen I William Shackspeare, of Stratford upon Avon in the countrie of War.*[Warwickshire], gent., *in perfect health and memorie, God be praysed, doe make and ordayne this my last will and testament in manner and forme followeing …*

❧ *I gyve and bequeath unto my daughter Judyth one hundred and fyftie poundes of lawfull English money …*

❧ *I gyve and bequeath unto my saied daughter Judith one hundred and fyftie poundes more, if shee or anie issue of her bodie by lyvinge att thend of three yeares next ensueing the daie of the date of this my will …*

❧ *I gyve and bequeath unto my saied sister Jone xx.li.* [£30] *and all my wearing apparrell, to be paied and delivered within one yeare after my deceas; and I doe will and devise unto her the house with thappurtenaunces in Stratford, wherein she dwelleth, for her naturall lief, under the yearlie rent of xij.*^{d} [12 pence].

❧ *I gyve and bequeath unto her three sonnes, William Harte,* [the name of Thomas is missing] *Hart, and Michaell Harte, fyve pounds a peece, to be paied within one yeare after my deceas.*

❧ *I gyve and bequeath unto the saied Elizabeth Hall, all my plate, except my brod silver and gilt bole* [bowl], *that I now have att the date of this my will.*

❧ *I gyve and bequeath unto the poore of Stratford aforesaied tenn poundes; to Mr. Thomas Combe my sword; to Thomas Russell esquier fyve poundes; and to Frauncis Collins, of the borough of Warr.* [Warwick] *in the countie of Warr. gentleman, thirteene poundes, sixe shillinges, and eight pence, to be paied within one yeare after my deceas.*

❧ *I gyve and bequeath to Hamlett Sadler xxvj.*^{8} *viij.*^{d} [26 shillings 8 pence] *to buy him a ringe; to William Raynoldes gent., xxvj.*^{8} *viij.*^{d} *to buy him a ringe; to my godson William Walker xx*^{8} [20 shillings] *in gold; to Anthonye Nashe gent. xxvj.*^{8} *viij.*^{d}*; and to my fellowes John Hemynges, Richard Brubage, and Henry Cundell, xxvj.*^{8} *viij.*^{d} *a peece to buy them ringes,*

✤ *I gyve, will, bequeath, and devise, unto my daughter Susanna Hall, for better enabling of her to performe this my will, and towards the performans thereof, all that capitall messuage or tenemente with thappurtenaunces, in Stratford aforesaid, called the New Place, wherein I nowe dwell, and two messuages or tenementes with thappurtenaunces, scituat [situated], lyeing, and being in Henley streete, within the borough of Stratford aforesaied; and all my barnes, stables, orchardes, gardens, landes, tenementes, and hereditamentes, whatsoever, scituat, lyeing, and being, or to be had, receyved, perceyved, or taken, within the townes, hamletes, villages, fieldes, and groundes, of Stratford upon Avon, Oldstratford, Bushopton, and Welcombe, or in anie of them in the saied countie of Warr. And alsoe all that messuage or tenemente with thappurtenaunces, wherein one John Robinson dwelleth, scituat, lyeing and being, in the Blackfriers in London, nere the Wardrobe; and all my other landes, tenementes, and hereditamentes whatsoever,*

✤ *I gyve unto my wief my second best bed with the furniture**

✤ *I gyve and bequeath to my saied daughter Judith my broad silver gilt bole.*

✤ *All the rest of my goodes, chattel, leases, plate, jewels, and household stuffe whatsoever, after my dettes and legasies paied, and my funerall expenses dischardged, I give, devise, and bequeath to my sonne in lawe, John Hall gent., and my daughter Susanna, his wief, whom I ordaine and make executours of this my last will and testament*

---

*This is the most famous sentence in the will. It is written as an insert above the main lines of writing – almost as an afterthought.

Many have interpreted the bequest in a negative light, as if to suggest a distance between Shakespeare and his wife. Others have interpreted it as a special endearment, because this was the bed the couple would have regularly used (the best bed being reserved for visitors).

Of the two views, the latter is more likely: the phrase 'second-best bed' has been found elsewhere in an Elizabethan will where the context is undeniably affable. And, in cold factual terms, there was no strict necessity to mention Anne at all. She would have had a legal right as a widow to continue living at New Place and to receive a third of her husband's estate.

That Shakespeare did not express any affectionate tone about his spouse is – compared with many other wills of the period – unusual; but the absence of endearments anywhere in his will suggests that it is a legal style of writing rather than a personal memorandum.

People do not seem to have begun lecturing on Shakespeare until the mid-eighteenth century. The first known public lecture series was given in 1754 by the eccentric actor Charles Macklin, as part of his proposed 'British Institution'. The lectures took place in the evenings, in a Covent Garden tavern.

Hamlet here

All the great writers root their characters in true human behaviour — that is why Hamlet is a great role, because Hamlet is probably sitting in this auditorium now. It's a true, real person.

(Ben Kingsley, interview at the National Film Theatre,
17 September 2003)

Poems certain and uncertain

Several poems have been firmly attributed to Shakespeare:

> *Venus and Adonis* (1593)
> *The Rape of Lucrece* (1594)
> *The Phoenix and Turtle* (1601)
> The Sonnets (1609)
> *A Lover's Complaint* (1609, printed with the Sonnets)

The sequence of twenty poems called 'The Passionate Pilgrim' was published in 1599 by William Jaggard, who ascribed it to Shakespeare. It includes corrupt versions of Sonnets 138 and 144 and three extracts from *Love's Labour's Lost*, but some of the other poems are known to be by other writers, and eleven have unknown authorship (see p. 129).

Several other poems are ascribed to Shakespeare in various seventeenth-century manuscripts:

> A posy 'Upon a pair of gloves' – 3 lines
> 'Shall I die?' – 9 stanzas of 10 lines each
> Epitaph on Elias James – 6 lines
> Part-epitaph for Ben Jonson – 2 lines
> Two epitaphs on John Combe – 4 lines and 6 lines
> Verses on the Stanley tomb in Tong, Shropshire –
> two 6-line verses
> On King James (1616) – 4 lines
> Shakespeare's own epitaph (p. 91) – 4 lines

All these poems are collected in the Oxford Edition edited by Stanley Wells and Gary Taylor.

Burial

The burial of 'Will Shakspeare gent' is recorded in the Stratford parish register on 25 April 1616.

Farewell?

The Tempest is one of the last plays that Shakespeare wrote alone. Prospero's epilogue, beginning 'Now my charms are all o'erthrown', has often been thought of as the author's farewell to the stage and to playwriting.

Who was that again?

After a lengthy discussion about Shakespeare in James Joyce's *Ulysses* (Bodley Head edition, p. 186), the participants turn to Buck Mulligan and ask for his opinion:

> *Buck Mulligan thought, puzzled:*
> *— Shakespeare? he said. I seem to know the name.*
> *A flying sunny smile rayed in his loose features.*
> *— To be sure, he said, remembering brightly. The chap that*
> *   writes like Synge.*

Hope for us all

In September 2004, a Stockport housewife received a letter out of the blue from her solicitor informing her that she had inherited a copy of the First Folio from a distant relative who had left no will. It was assumed to be a facsimile, but turned out to be genuine. It is missing forty leaves, including most of *The Tempest* and the Droeshout engraving. One of only six copies in private hands, it was auctioned the following month, and sold for £176,750.

The authors of the present book await in hope the arrival of just such a letter from their solicitors.

TIMELINE

	Life	Politics	Culture
1564	• 23 April, birth of William Shakespeare, third child of John and Mary Shakespeare • 26 April, William Shakespeare baptized	• Robert Dudley, Earl of Leicester, made chancellor of Oxford University • David Rizzio becomes French secretary of Mary, Queen of Scots	• Death of sculptor Michelangelo • Death of Protestant reformer John Calvin • Birth of astronomer Galileo
1565		• Mary, Queen of Scots, marries Lord Henry Darnley • Death of Pope Pius IV	• Giambattista Giraldi publishes *Ecatommiti*, which inspired *Measure for Measure* and *Othello* • Tintoretto paints his 'Crucifixion'
1566	• Gilbert Shakespeare baptized, John and Mary Shakespeare's fourth child • John Shakespeare elected Alderman	• David Rizzio murdered • Birth of future James VI of Scotland and I of England (1603–25) • Election of Michele Ghislieri as Pope Pius V • Birth of Robert Devereux, 2nd Earl of Essex, soldier and courtier	• Death of Nostradamus • Building of London's Royal Exchange begins
1567		• Lord Henry Darnley killed in an explosion • Mary, Queen of Scots, abdicates in favour of her son, James VI of Scotland, following her marriage to Bothwell • James VI crowned King of Scotland • Second War of Religion begins in France	• Birth of composer Claudio Monteverdi
1568	• John Shakespeare made High Bailiff of Stratford	• Mary, Queen of Scots, arrested in England by Elizabeth I • Second War of Religion ends and Third War begins in France	• Completion of London's Royal Exchange

	Shakespeare family	British & political events	Papal & European events	Arts & science
1569	• Joan Shakespeare baptized, John and Mary Shakespeare's fifth child	• First state lottery held in England • Mary, Queen of Scots, applies to the pope for a divorce from Bothwell	• Birth of Pope Urban VIII	• Death of Flemish painter Pieter Brueghel the Elder • Mercator introduces map projections to aid navigation
1570		• James Stewart, 1st Earl of Moray, regent of Scotland, assassinated • Pope Pius V excommunicates Elizabeth I • Birth of Guy Fawkes, conspirator against Parliament		• Titian produces two paintings, 'The Fall of Man' and 'Christ Crowned with Thorns' • Birth around now of optician Hans Lippershey, possible inventor of the telescope
1571	• John Shakespeare elected High Alderman • Anne Shakespeare baptized, John and Mary Shakespeare's sixth child			
1572		• Thousands of Huguenots slaughtered in the St Bartholomew's Day massacre, Paris • Death of Pope Pius V • Election of Ugo Buoncompagni as Pope Gregory XIII		• Michel Montaigne begins publishing his *Essais* (1572–80, 1588), quoted by Shakespeare • Birth of poet John Donne around now
1573				• Birth of architect Inigo Jones • Birth of Henry Wriothesey, 3rd Earl of Southampton
1574	• Richard Shakespeare baptized, John and Mary Shakespeare's seventh child	• Birth of Princess Anne of Denmark, future wife of James VI of Scotland		
1575				• Composers William Boyd and Thomas Tallis granted a monopoly by Elizabeth I to print music and music paper

	• Italian painter Federigo Zuccari paints portraits of Elizabeth I, and Robert Dudley, Earl of Leicester • Death of Titian, Venetian painter • Tycho Brahe builds the Uraniborg observatory on an island east of Copenhagen
1576	• Failure of John Shakespeare's wool business around now • Application for a coat of arms
	• Raphael Holinshed, English chronicler, publishes *The Chronicles of England, Scotland, and Ireland*, a major source for many of Shakespeare's plays • Birth of Rubens, Flemish artist
1577	• Francis Drake begins his circumnavigation of the Globe, leaving Plymouth in *The Golden Hind*
	• Birth of William Harvey, physician who described the circulation of blood
1578	• Death of James, 4th Earl of Bothwell, previously husband to Mary, Queen of Scots • Sir Edward Coke called to the Bar
	• Thomas North publishes his translation of Plutarch's *Lives*, which inspired Shakespeare's history plays • Death of Sir Thomas Gresham, who built the Royal Exchange
1579	• Francis Drake lands on the west coast of North America (present-day California), and claims it for Queen Elizabeth I, calling it New Albion
	• Death around now of Raphael Holinshed
1580	• Edmund Shakespeare baptized, John and Mary Shakespeare's eighth child
1581	• Francis Drake completes his circumnavigation of the world, and is knighted by Elizabeth I

1582	• Marriage of William Shakespeare to Anne Hathaway	• Introduction of the present-day Gregorian calendar by Pope Gregory XIII
1583	• Baptism of Susanna, Shakespeare's first child	
1584	• Assassination of William of Orange • Philip Sidney knighted	
1585	• Baptism of Hamnet and Judith, Shakespeare's twins • Beginning of the 'lost years'	• Death of Thomas Tallis, English musician and composer • First colony established on Roanoke Island, near Carolina, by Walter Raleigh • Sir Francis Drake sails with twenty-five ships against the Spanish Indies • Death of Pope Gregory XIII • Election of Felice Peretti as Pope Sixtus V, responsible for building St Peter's Dome in Rome
1586	• Anthony Babington executed for his part in the Babington Plot to free Mary, Queen of Scots	• Death of Sir Philip Sidney, poet and courtier • First potatoes brought to England from Colombia by scientist Thomas Harriot • Artist El Greco begins his 'Burial of Count Orgaz'
1587	• Shakespeare leaves Stratford for London about now	• Execution of Mary, Queen of Scots, for treason • Spanish fleet sunk in Cadiz harbour by Sir Francis Drake • Virginia, USA, named by Sir Walter Raleigh in honour of Queen Elizabeth I • Founding of the Banco di Rialto, Venice

1588	• Spanish Armada sent by Philip II of Spain to invade Britain, ending in failure	• Antonio da Ponte begins building the Rialto Bridge over the Grand Canal, Venice • Publication of Robert Greene's *Pandosto*, inspiration for *The Winter's Tale*
1589	• Deaths of Catherine de Medici and Henry III of France • Henry IV crowned King of France • James VI of Scotland marries Anne of Denmark	
1590	• Shakespeare writes his first plays about now	• Playwright and poet Thomas Lodge publishes *Rosalynde*, inspiration for *As You Like It*
1591	• Death of Pope Sixtus V • Election of Giambattista Castagna as Pope Urban VII, followed by his death nearly two weeks later • Election of Niccolo Sfondrati as Pope Gregory XIV • Death of Pope Gregory XIV • Election of Gian Antonio Facchinetti as Pope Innocent IX, followed by his death a few months later	• Rome hit badly with the plague • Translator Thomas North knighted
1592	• Election of Ippolito Aldobrandini as Pope Clement VIII	• Plague hits London, many theatres closed • Trinity College founded in Dublin • Completion of the Rialto Bridge, Venice • Death of Thomas Watson, lyric poet • Death of Michel Montaigne, essayist and courtier
1593	• Robert Greene writes the first public reference to Shakespeare, calling him an 'upstart crow' • Over the next two years Shakespeare writes *Venus and Adonis*, and *The Rape of Lucrece* • Sir Edward Coke becomes Speaker of the House of Commons	• Death of humanist Jacques Amyot, who translated *Parallel Lives of Plutarch*

1594	• Robert Devereux, 2nd Earl of Essex, made privy councillor • Henry IV of France returns to the Catholic faith • Sir Edward Coke becomes Attorney General • Death of Venetian painter Tintoretto • Death of composer Palestrina • Death of mathematician and map-maker Mercator
1595	• Shakespeare first officially recorded as belonging to the Chamberlain's Men • Publication of Mercator's atlas • Posthumous publication of Sir Philip Sidney's *Defence of Poesie* • Founding of the Bodleian library, Oxford, by Sir Thomas Bodley • Birth of Pocahontas, American Indian princess
1596	• Death of Shakespeare's son, Hamnet • Coat of arms granted to John Shakespeare • Death of Sir Francis Drake, seaman and explorer • Birth of René Descartes, French philosopher • Sir John Harington, courtier and writer, writes *The Metamorphosis of Ajax*, with the earliest known design for a water closet • Li Shih-chen, father of Chinese herbal medicine, publishes his *Great Pharmacopoeia*
1597	• Shakespeare buys New Place • William Shakespeare, of Bishopsgate, fails to pay the local tax due in 1596 • Robert Devereux, 2nd Earl of Essex, made earl marshal • Death of William Barents, Dutch navigator and explorer
1598	• William Shakespeare, of Surrey and Sussex, fails to pay a tax • Henry IV of France issues the Edict of Nantes, giving civil and religious freedom to his Huguenot subjects • Poet and playwright George Chapman begins his translation of the *Iliad*

1599	• Shakespeare's plays begin to appear in print • First written record of a performance – probably *Julius Caesar* – at The Globe, 21 September	• First Poor Law Act formulated, setting up workhouses for the poor in urban areas • Birth of Oliver Cromwell, soldier and statesman • Robert Devereux, 2nd Earl of Essex, briefly made Lord Lieutenant of Ireland	• Poet John Donne becomes secretary to Thomas Egerton, keeper of the Great Seal • Birth of Sir Anthony van Dyck, master of portraiture • Death of poet Edmund Spenser, author of *The Faerie Queen* • Astronomer Tycho Brahe appointed Imperial Mathematician to the Holy Roman Emperor
1600	• Tax records show that William Shakespeare is living south of the Thames	• Birth of Charles I of England • British East India Company established • James VI establishes bishops in Scotland	• Death of Sir Thomas Lucy, who may have prosecuted Shakespeare for stealing deer
1601	• Death of John Shakespeare, William's father • Shakespeare writes *Hamlet* about now	• Execution of Robert Devereux, 2nd Earl of Essex, for his revolt against Elizabeth I • Houses of correction for vagabonds have to be established in all shires	• Death of Tycho Brahe, Danish astronomer • Death of translator Sir Thomas North
1602	• On 2 February *Twelfth Night* performed at Middle Temple, London • In May Shakespeare buys 127 acres of land in Old Stratford • In September Shakespeare buys a cottage and garden opposite New Place		• Opening of the Bodleian library, Oxford • Founding of the Dutch East India Company
1603	• On 2 February the Chamberlain's Men play before Queen Elizabeth I • On 19 May the Chamberlain's Men become known as the King's Men • All performances of plays banned in Stratford-upon-Avon	• Death of Elizabeth I • James VI of Scotland becomes James I of England • Sir Walter Raleigh imprisoned in the Tower of London for treason	• German astronomer Johann Bayer produces his star atlas

1604	• Shakespeare sues a neighbour for moneys owing to him	• Coronation of James I of England • End of the war with Spain • Tobacco tax increased, and tobacco itself condemned by James I	• Death of architect Giacomo della Porto, best known for the cupola of St Peter's, Rome
1605	• Shakespeare writes *King Lear* about now • Shakespeare buys interest in tithes in some places in the locality of Stratford-upon-Avon	• Failure of the Gunpowder Plot to blow up the Houses of Parliament • Death of Pope Clement VIII • Election of Camillo Borghese as Pope Paul V	• Publication in Spain of the first part of Cervantes' *Don Quixote*
1606	• Shakespeare writes *Macbeth* about now	• Execution of Guy Fawkes and his fellow conspirators in the Gunpowder Plot • Union flag (the Union Jack) created • Sir Edward Coke becomes Chief Justice of the Common Pleas	
1607	• Marriage of Susanna to John Hall • Death of Shakespeare's brother Edmund	• Act of Union unites the parliaments of Scotland and England • First permanent colony established in the Americas, in Jamestown, Virginia	• River Thames freezes over, and the first Frost Fair is held on the ice • Halley's Comet appears • Publication of Monteverdi's *Orfeo*, his first opera
1608	• Death of Mary Shakespeare, William's mother • Baptism of Shakespeare's granddaughter, Elizabeth • Shakespeare sues another neighbour for moneys owing to him • The King's Men lease Blackfriars Theatre		• First refracting telescope given to the Netherlands government by Dutch optician Hans Lippershey
1609			• Kepler announces his first, second and third laws of planetary motion

1610	Shakespeare writes *The Tempest* about now	• Discovery of Jupiter's four satellites by Galileo • Galileo's observations show that the Milky Way is full of stars • Monteverdi produces his *Vespers of the Blessed Virgin*
1611		• First publication of the King James Bible, the Authorized version
1612	• Death of Shakespeare's brother Gilbert • Shakespeare returns to Stratford about now	• Cervantes' *Don Quixote* published in London
1613	• Death of Shakespeare's brother Richard • Shakespeare buys a house near Blackfriars, London • Globe Theatre burns down during a performance of *Henry VIII*	• Sir Edward Coke becomes Chief Justice of the King's Bench	• Death of Sir Thomas Bodley, whose wealth founded the Bodleian library • Founding of Trinity Hospital, Greenwich, London
1614	• Shakespeare completes his final play *The Two Noble Kinsmen* about now • Building of the new Globe Theatre completed	• Formation and dissolution of the Addled Parliament	• Death of artist El Greco • Pocahontas, American Indian princess, marries English colonist John Rolfe
1615			• Inigo Jones made King's surveyor-general of the Royal buildings • Publication of the second part of Cervantes' *Don Quixote*
1616	• Marriage of Judith to Thomas Quiney • 23 April, death of Shakespeare • Baptism of Judith's son, Shakespeare Quiney	• Release of Sir Walter Raleigh from the Tower of London	• Death of Cervantes • Death of theatre manager Philip Henslowe, whose diary contains much information about theatre during this period

Sources and
Further Reading

The sources of many of our extracts are given on earlier pages. Here we list some of the more general works which have informed our thinking when compiling this book.

Jonathan Bate, *The Genius of Shakespeare*. Picador, 1997.

David Crystal and Ben Crystal, *Shakespeare's Words*. Penguin, 2002.

R.W. Duffin, *Shakespeare's Songbook*. Norton, 2004.

Charles Edelman, *Shakespeare's Military Language*. Athlone, 2000.

Stuart Gillespie, *Shakespeare's Books: A Dictionary of Shakespeare Sources*. Athlone, 2001.

Andrew Gurr, *The Shakespearian Playing Companies*. Clarendon Press, 1996.

Andrew Gurr, *The Shakespeare Company 1594–1642*. Cambridge University Press, 2004.

Jonathan Hope, *The Authorship of Shakespeare's Plays*. Cambridge University Press, 1994.

Frank Kermode, *The Age of Shakespeare*. Weidenfeld & Nicolson, 2004.

Alvin Kernan, *Shakespeare, the King's Playwright: Theatre in the Stuart Court*. Yale, 1995.

Nicholas Robins (ed.), issues of *Around the Globe*. London: Shakespeare's Globe.

Kenneth Rothwell, *A History of Shakespeare on Screen*. Cambridge University Press, 1999.

S. Schoenbaum, *William Shakespeare: A Documentary Life*. Clarendon Press, 1975.

S. Schoenbaum, *Shakespeare's Lives*. Clarendon Press, 2nd edn, 1991.

B. J. and M. Sokol, *Shakespeare's Legal Language*. Athlone, 2000.

John Sutherland and Cedric Watts, *Henry V, War Criminal? and Other Shakespeare Puzzles*. Oxford University Press, 2000.

Gary Taylor, *Reinventing Shakespeare*. Hogarth, 1990.

Stanley Wells, *A Dictionary of Shakespeare*. Oxford University Press, 1998).

Stanley Wells, *Shakespeare: For All Time*. Macmillan, 2002.

Stanley Wells and Lena Cowen Orlin (eds.), *Shakespeare: an Oxford Guide*. Oxford University Press, 2003.

Websites

www.shakespeareswords.com (for glossary and concordance data, and on-line texts)

www.findout.tv (for timeline data)

www.ShakespeareAuthorship.com

Shakespeare Birthplace Trust at www.shakespeare.org.uk

Royal Shakespeare Company at www.rsc.org.uk

Shakespeare quotations throughout are from the First Folio or the New Penguin Shakespeare series, and the edition of *King Edward III* used for *Shakespeare's Words*.

INDEX